IMMIGRATION AND AMERICAN UNIONISM

Immigration *and* American Unionism

VERNON M. BRIGGS JR.

ILR Press
an imprint of
Cornell University Press | ITHACA AND LONDON

Cornell Studies in Industrial and Labor Relations No. 33
Copyright © 2001 by Cornell University

First published 2001 by Cornell University Press
First printing, Cornell Paperbacks, 2001

Printed in the United States of America

Library of Congress Cataloging-in-Publication Data

Briggs, Vernon M.
   Immigration and American unionism / Vernon M. Briggs, Jr.
      p. cm.
Includes bibliographical references and index.
   ISBN 0-8014-3870-5 (cloth)—ISBN 0-8014-8710-2 (pbk.)
   1. Alien labor—United States. 2. United States—Emigration and immigration. 3. Labor
unions—United States. I. Title.
   ✓ HD8081.A5 B75 2001
   331.88'0973—dc21

                                                                00-011871

Cornell University Press strives to use environmentally responsible suppliers and materials to
the fullest extent possible in the publishing of its books. Such materials include vegetable-
based, low-VOC inks and acid-free papers that are either recycled, totally chlorine-free, or
partly composed of nonwood fibers. Books that bear the logo of the FSC (Forest Stewardship
Council) use paper taken from forests that have been inspected and certified as meeting the
highest standards for environmental and social responsibility. For further information, visit
our website at www.cornellpress.cornell.edu.

Cloth printing   10 9 8 7 6 5 4 3 2 1

Paperback printing   10 9 8 7 6 5 4 3 2 1

Contents

Immigration is, in its fundamental aspects, a labor problem.

Samuel Gompers
President of the American Federation of Labor
(1886–1893, 1895–1924)

Acknowledgments

In the preparation of this book I have greatly benefited from the use of the resources of the Catherwood Library of the School of Industrial and Labor Relations at Cornell University in Ithaca, New York. The depth and breadth of its collections are a constant source of amazement and gratitude. I am also indebted to the library's excellent staff. Stuart Basefsky, reference librarian, was of particular assistance. His competence in his work and his dedication to providing service with good cheer were always both helpful and encouraging.

I also acknowledge the time and insights provided by several officials of the American Federation of Labor and the Congress of Industrial Organizations (AFL-CIO) in Washington, D.C. I have acceded to their request that our conversations be regarded as off the record; nonetheless, the information and perspective they provided were important to my understanding of the organization's evolving position on immigration. Any interpretations of this information given here are, of course, my responsibility alone.

Finally, but most important, I wish to express my most sincere gratitude to Norah Burch for her work on the preparation of the manuscript. There were many drafts and many revisions. Her professionalism and patience are deeply appreciated.

V.M.B.

Ithaca, N.Y.

IMMIGRATION AND AMERICAN UNIONISM

Introduction

Few issues have caused the American labor movement more agony than immigration. During periods of mass immigration, unions have struggled to find an appropriate response. It is ironic that this has been the case, for many if not most adult immigrants directly enter the labor force; so eventually do most of their family members. But because immigration can affect the scale, distribution, and composition of the labor force, it can affect labor market conditions; hence, organized labor can never ignore it. Immigration has in the past and continues to this day to affect the developmental course of American trade unionism, and labor's responses, in turn, have influenced the policies that have shaped the nature and scope of immigrant entries.

The interrelationship of immigration and unionism began with the founding of the nation. Prior to the Revolutionary War, most of the colonial settlers who arrived from abroad were not immigrants as the term is understood today. The legal theory under which English colonization was initiated held that the land belonged to the Crown, which made grants of land either to commercial companies or to individual proprietors. When these companies or individuals received their royal charter to establish a colony, they acquired the right to own and govern the land. In turn, they could transfer land titles to the actual settlers. Thus, most of the white settlers were English citizens, still subject to the rule of the Crown. They were not seeking admission to a new nation or abandoning their original citizenship. In fact, they believed that they were entitled to exactly the same rights and privileges as their fellow countrymen who remained behind in England.

Africans, the other principal "settlers" of the colonial era, first arrived in Virginia in 1619 on a Dutch slave ship. They were initially treated as indentured servants (as were many white settlers), working to buy their own freedom. At some point between 1640 and 1660 this system came to an end, and blacks were no longer indentured servants but slaves.[1] Racism cannot explain the origins of slavery in the English colonies, but it soon became the explanation for its continuance. The arrival of black Africans to the colonies, however, is not analogous to the subsequent arrival of other racial or ethnic groups. African slaves were "involuntary" immigrants. Not until the adoption of the Civil Rights Act of 1866 and the Fourteenth Amendment to the Constitution that same year were blacks granted the right to be citizens.

As for unions, no freestanding organizations of workers seeking to negotiate with employers on a continuing basis survived the country's transition from colonial status to self-governing nation. American unionism began from scratch.

Since the United States became an independent nation, however, the evolution of the country's immigration policies and its union movement have experienced a contentious relationship. The young republic had to confront both issues: the admission of workers and their families from foreign nations, and the inclination of some of its workers to form organizations to represent their collective interests within the emerging business sector. From the outset, these two forces came into conflict and have remained at odds ever since. Immigration was traditionally perceived by most workers' organizations as a menace to the development of American unionism. Unions have tended to focus on economic issues that impinge on the well-being of workers. Hence, they have usually viewed immigrants as a short-run threat to their efforts even though most immigrants, over the long run, enlarge the ranks of working people. Hence, immigration has always represented a dilemma for organized labor. Should the labor movement actively seek to restrict immigration in order to protect and to advance the well-being of its present membership (both native-born and foreign-born)? Or should it actively support the special interests both of immigrants whom are explicitly permitted to enter and those who enter illegally, because they too are here? And what policy position should unions take on the size of the annual flow of immigrants into the nation and its labor market? More? Fewer? None?

If organized labor seeks restrictions on the scale of immigration as well as the active enforcement of prevailing laws, it risks alienating the immigrants who do come and making it difficult (if not impossible) to organize those who enter the workforce. Yet if labor welcomes immigrants, endorses liberal admission policies, and favors lax enforcement against violators, the labor supply is inflated, and market pressures make it more difficult for unions to win economic gains for their membership—the main reason after all, that many workers join unions. Organized labor's support for immigrants would be adverse as well to the interests of American workers who are not in unions because of increased competition for jobs as well as the wage suppression pressures they exert. Immigration, then, has always been a no-win situation for American unions. It presents a classic dilemma. But a choice must be made, and the alternatives are mutually exclusive.

My purpose is to review the confrontation of these two opposite forces and how it has played out. The broad lessons of the historical encounter quickly emerge. Unions thrive (membership grows) when immigration is low or levels are contracting; unions falter (membership declines) during periods when immigration is high or levels are increasing. Understanding the past can help explain the state of contemporary unionism and its prospects for the future under immigration scenarios that public policy can influence.

To be sure, any analysis of union membership trends is a complicated process in which many factors aside from immigration may be momentarily influential and, for the sake of establishing proper context, need to be mentioned. Hence, each of the following chapters discusses the broad historical events that were at work as the nation's economy evolved in a given period ("the setting"); the shifting labor supply and labor demand trends over time ("the labor force and employment patterns"); the ebbs and flows of immigration trends and policies ("immigration"); the state of unionism as manifested by its internal leadership and policy objectives and as affected by government and business in each era ("unionism"); and, finally, the interactive effects of these forces on union membership in each period ("consequences"). Thus, though I grant that multiple factors affect the fluctuations of union membership over time, the skein of insight that consistently runs from the past to the present is that the state of American unions (i.e., the percentage of the labor force that is unionized) is inversely related to prevailing immigration trends. For most of their history, American unions and their leaders intuitively believed this to be the case and acted accordingly. Subsequent research has consistently justified labor's restrictive posture.

At every juncture prior to the 1980s, the union movement either directly instigated or strongly supported every legislative initiative enacted by Congress to restrict immigration and to enforce its policy terms. But in the late 1980s the leadership of organized labor began to waffle on the issue. By the 1990s the labor movement was hesitant to support comprehensive reform, even though the nation was in the midst of the largest wave of immigration it had ever known and the percentage of the labor force in unions was falling. Finally, in February 2000, the executive council of the American Federation of Labor-Congress of Industrial Organizations (AFL-CIO) announced that it was changing its historic position: it would now support immigration and the special needs of immigrants.[2] If it actually follows through with its new policy position, which has been roundly criticized, it will be a historic turnabout. The question is, why? Were its actions wrong in the past? Are they right for the future? What is the broader implication of this change in position by organized labor for the majority of American workers, who do not belong to unions?

The nation's labor movement has traditionally focused its concern on the quantitative scale of immigration because of its effect on the size of the available supply of labor. But there is also a qualitative issue. At present, as throughout most of the past, a disproportionately high number of immigrants are poor, unskilled, and minimally educated. Typically, they are more than willing to fill low-skilled jobs—jobs that often have low pay and bad working conditions, judged by American standards, but to many immigrants are considerably better than conditions were in their homelands. Furthermore, because of the extensive presence of illegal immigrants, many such workers are more docile and more dependent on satisfying employers than are native-born workers and are therefore often preferred by employers for such jobs even when native-born workers are available. That fact, combined with immigrant networking arrangements, can affect employer hiring practices and preferences as well as the size of local labor pools. Can unions organize such workers?

Immigration Is a Discretionary Policy

Of all the factors that influence the American labor force, immigration is the one directly determined by public policy. In most instances where public policy intervenes in the labor market, it is in direct response to factors that are causing changes (e.g., technology, demography, social attitudes toward the status of minorities and women, economic depressions, or external threats such as wars). Immigration policy is the clear exception, for some form of it is always in existence. No citizens of a foreign country have a right to visit, reside, work, or seek refuge in the United

States simply because they desire to do so. They may legally enter only with the express permission of the federal government. Accompanying such exclusive power to regulate is government's implied duty to design a policy that conforms to the best interests of the United States at any time and under varying circumstances.

Given the prominent role that immigration played in the early history of the nation, it may seem surprising that the subject is not mentioned anywhere in the U.S. Constitution. But as its significance to the national well-being was gradually recognized, the federal government—in the late nineteenth century—laid claim to the exclusive authority to regulate all aspects of it.[3] Thus, immigration policy must be viewed for what it is: a purely discretionary duty of the U.S. government to set annual admission levels, to establish admission categories, to specify entry requirements, to order entry priorities, and to enforce the restrictions it imposes.

Because immigration involves the movement of people rather than of products, it is labor market consequences that are ultimately at the heart of any effort to assess the congruence of immigration policy with the national interest.[4] The issue here is the effect of immigration upon one of the nation's most venerable institutions: the organized labor movement.

Unionism: Is Its Fate of Consequence?

Aside from the self-interest of union leaders and current members, should American society in general be concerned over the fate of its union movement? The answer, of course, depends on whether or not unions perform a valuable function. If their usefulness is perceived to have been limited to serving in earlier times as a transitional mechanism when the country shifted from its agrarian roots to an industrialized, durable goods–oriented economy, then their fate is sealed: unions are a relic of the past.

The U.S. economy at the beginning of the twenty-first century is entering an entirely new phase of development. It is becoming an information-based, service-oriented economy that functions in a global marketplace. Management, as it has always contended, claims it must be more flexible in this environment. Consolidation of business enterprises in the 1990s has exceeded in scale and scope that of the last such era of merger mania: the 1890s and early 1900s. Increasingly, these new conglomerates have resulted in the creation of multinational corporations unprecedented in the magnitude of their market domination. Yet at the same time a plethora of small enterprises have been created that rely on the use of internet technology and e-commerce opportunities, which seek, at least in the short run, to establish specific niches in this marketplace.

Meanwhile, workers are it is said, becoming more individualistic. Dual workers in families have become commonplace; in addition, new types of household units have been formed that no longer resemble the traditional household structures of the past. Telecommuting means, for many workers, that their homes are their workplaces. For some of these workers, unions may not be relevant. But what of the many others?

The appropriate question for workers in this setting is whether unions, and their system of collective bargaining to resolve workplace disputes, transcend these changes? If so, then there is a vital reason to worry about adverse influences—such as immigration trends—that affect the labor movement's size and vitality in this new environment.

Aside from media images that focus largely on strikes, picket-line violence, or the personal failures of officials, the societal function of unions is quite mundane. American unions provide workers a participatory role in determining the conditions of their employment. Overwhelmingly, the issues unions address have focused on economic matters such as wages, hours, working conditions, and job security. "Job conscious unionism" has been recognized as "the key to understanding American unionism."[5] Past appeals to American workers were based on utopian goals, political reform, and radical change, but none elicited a sustainable following. Since the later part of the nineteenth century, American workers have proved most receptive to job-conscious unionism.

A key philosophical position of anticapitalist writers and critics has always been the contention that capitalism is divisive, putting workers at the mercy of employers. But that criticism overlooks the conflict inherent in all forms of societal organization: the quest for freedom by the individual versus the requirement for order by society. The workplace simply reflects this broader social conflict. Management must be reasonably free to perform its function of running the enterprise in an efficient manner. But experience has shown that giving management a completely free hand does not work well. The reason is simple. Workers in a free society object to arbitrary decision-making—especially when the decisions affect the vital determinants of their own and their families' well-being. Wages, hours, and working conditions also affect job security and job satisfaction. Indeed, there is a tendency throughout free societies to resist arbitrary exercises of power in all aspects of life—be it by parents, police, teachers, administrators, union officers, or employers. Most employers are not devils—they usually do not purposely inflict harm on their employees by acting in capricious or evil ways—but hard-working, conscientious, and decent persons. But neither are they saints. They do make mistakes, sometimes with deliberate malice but more often as the result of honest errors of judgment, or at worse, indifference to the concerns of those who are dependent on their decisions.

The function of unions, therefore, is to establish a form of workplace government, sometimes referred to as a system of industrial jurisprudence. They seek to assure that the workplace is governed by written rules, mutually agreed-upon, rather than run by arbitrary whim. They seek to set these rules only after reasoned study and discussion. Ideally, they are widely publicized, known by all, and applied impartially. The emphasis is on settlements by the parties who must live with the consequences of their actions: the employer and the employees.

It is for this reason that American unions focus so much attention on the written contract that is signed by both labor and management. The collective bargaining agreement embodies all the components of the American system of government, but on a smaller scale. The legislative function is analogous to the negotiation sessions of labor and management, during which the binding written rules are made; the executive function involves the enforcement of the written terms (as well as of unwritten past practices and customs) that are carried out both by management's supervisory personnel and by the union's business agent or shop steward; the judicial function is performed by the administration of whatever grievance and arbitration provisions are specified in the contract.

Thus, when compared with the only other two ways possible to resolve the inevitable conflicts that arise at the workplace in industrial societies— unilateral determination by management or by government which both labor and management abhor in the United States—collective bargaining has proved to be the form of self-government that is most consistent with the American principle of government by consent.

As long as work means that some people have authority over others, there will be differences of opinion over crucial decisions involving compensation, performance, promotions, dismissals, training opportunities, and discipline. Such issues are omnipresent. Collective bargaining is sometimes called "the least lousy way" to resolve these mutual concerns. The same has been said about democracy as a system of governance for the nation: it may not always be the most efficient way to do things, but it is the fairest of the available options.

It is not readily apparent that the changing character of the nation's production system as it enters the twenty-first century—as dramatic as that is—has done anything to reduce the basic premises that gave rise to the nation's collective bargaining system in the past. Yet employers' power to dominate outcomes seems to have been greatly enhanced by these developments. In their wake, union membership has plummeted, immigration levels have soared, and income disparity among families within the U.S. population has been greatly polarized. Is this the way it should be?

The Base Line (1788–1800)

The Setting

As the eighteenth century came to its close, the United States had won independence and—with the ratification of the U.S. Constitution in 1788—had become a unified nation. It existed as a political entity but had yet to establish its economic viability. The country was an agrarian society and would remain so well into the next century. Despite the intense efforts of some of its most influential founders—such as Alexander Hamilton and the Federalist Party—to steer a course toward manufacturing and industrial diversity, their ideas were strongly resisted. Thomas Jefferson and his supporters, in contrast, deplored the prospect of a nation of cities and factories with a congregated urban workforce dependent on wages for their survival. The Jeffersonian view, that it would be "far better to send over materials to Europe for manufacture than to bring workmen to these virgin shores," advocated the maintenance of the status quo.[1] After all, most of the new nation's vast land area was still pristine wilderness. As of 1800, 90 percent of a population of 5.3 million people lived along the Atlantic slope of the Appalachian Highlands, with fully two-thirds residing within fifty miles of the Atlantic tidewater.

Britain also sought to keep the former colonies tied to their agricultural heritage by forbidding the emigration of skilled workers and the exportation of machinery to the new republic. In so doing, the British hoped to assure that the economy of the United States would continue to be based on the export of food and fiber resources and dependent on the import of manufactured goods that Britain produced. They were not entirely successful; the prohibition on the departure of skilled craftsmen from Britain was frequently evaded during these years by the recruitment efforts of U.S. employers. The ban itself, however, was not formally repealed until 1824.[2]

The Labor Force and Industrial Employment

In 1800—the first year that a semblance of relevant data began to be available—the labor force totaled about 1.9 million workers, 80 percent employed in agriculture. Those in the nonagricultural sector were essentially involved in handicrafts. Indicative of the nature of the labor market is the telling fact that 90 percent of the nation's labor force in 1800 were *not* employees as the term is generally understood today. Either they were self-employed persons—farmers, mechanics, craftsmen, or small tradesmen—or they were slaves.[3]

The Indians of the East Coast numbered about 76,000 at the time of independence, but there was little interest in their incorporation into the emerging labor force or its institutions. Many had already begun their retreat to the interior of the country, or to Canada, or to Florida (which belonged to Spain until 1819). Exclusion and conflict, not assimilation and peace, were the rule. As in the colonial era, the continuing spread of agriculture meant an increasing encroachment by settlers on the hunting and fishing grounds of the Indians. Hostility, often violently expressed, was the frequent consequence. Indian culture had no sense of private property which, of course, was a fundamental tenet of the capitalist economic system inherited by the new nation from its colonial ties with Britain.[4] Further, with the notable exception of the Cherokees of northern Georgia and the western Carolinas, eastern Indians manifested little interest in being assimilated or in joining the nation-building process. And the Cherokees, despite their efforts to adapt, were forcibly removed later (1835–38) to the Oklahoma territory.

As always, there were only two ways for the nation to build its labor force: biological reproduction within the existing population and immigration from foreign countries. Both means were used by the United States in its early years. As had been the case during colonial times, the primary method was reliance on high birth-rates—especially among the massive farm population. In 1800 the nation's birthrate was a staggering 5.5 percent a year (i.e., 55.0 births per 1,000 persons in the population). This is about as close as any human population can come to the physiological maximum (since about half the population is male, and many women are either too young, too old, or otherwise unable to bear children at any given time). The U.S. birthrate has never been that high again; (in 1994, for example, it was 1.5 percent).

Immigration

In the early decades the United States had no statutory law pertaining to immigration. Even if it had adopted a formal admission policy, the country was hardly in a position to enforce its terms. Consequently, immigration continued to follow the colonial era patterns—with one major exception: one of the earliest resolutions of the first Continental Congress in 1788 was to recommend that the newly formed states adopt laws to ban the practice of accepting convicts from foreign nations for use as workers, and they soon did so.[5] Otherwise, immigrants fell into two groups: free (or soon to be) persons, and slaves.

There are no official data on immigrants until 1820, but historical studies estimate that some 250,000 immigrants entered the United States from 1776 to 1820—for an annual average of about 7,300.[6] The annual flows were uneven, however; moreover, as table 1.1 shows, the foreign-born proportion of the population declined from 12.8 percent in 1790 to 11.3 percent in 1800.[7] In fact, it continued to fall for the next forty years.

England never ceased to be a source of immigrants in this era of nation-building (despite its ban on the emigration of skilled workers), but the preponderance of early arrivals came from other parts of the British Isles—Ireland and Scotland in particular—and from the European continent, especially Germany.

Despite the lack of a formal national policy, immigration, especially of skilled workers, was encouraged by all the new states. As labor historian Philip Taft concluded, "Work skills had to be imported before they were 'grown' at home, and a number of craftsmen were brought here in the first part of the nineteenth century on contract."[8]

The immigration of free labor, though primarily the product of individual decisions, was also affected by the enticements of recruitment agents. It was often the case that immigrants had to borrow the passage money from these agents, for whom they were then bound to work for a period of time to pay off the advance. The beckoning frontier and the open social order in most localities, however, made enforcing the full terms of such contracts difficult in the extreme.[9]

The overwhelming majority of the free immigrants of this beginning

Table 1.1. The Foreign-Born Population, 1790–1800

Year	Foreign-Born Population (millions)	Percentage of Total Population
1790	0.5	12.8
1800	0.6	11.3

Source: Elizabeth W. Gilboy and Edgar M. Hoover, "Population and Immigration," in *American Economic History,* ed. Seymour E. Harris (New York: McGraw-Hill, 1961), table 6. Copyright © 1961 by McGraw-Hill, Inc. Reprinted with permission of the publisher.

era settled in the states of the Northeast, since the South was disproportionately tied to an agriculture-based economy, and it continued to rely on slavery as the primary source of labor. Slaves, of course, were involuntary immigrants, and their heavy concentration in the South significantly affected the settlement pattern of free immigrant workers for years to come: since free labor could not compete with slave labor, few free immigrants settled in the southern states even when mass immigration began in the 1830s. At the outbreak of the Civil War in 1860, only 13 percent of the nation's entire foreign-born population resided in the South.[10]

Black workers constituted almost 28 percent of the nation's labor force in 1800. Most were slaves, and about 95 percent of them were in the South, though slaves could be found in every state and territory. North of Maryland, however, slaves served chiefly as servants for wealthy families and were never an integral part of the northern economy. In the plantation regions along the southern coast, it was entirely another story: slaves outnumbered the free white workers, in many areas, and legal codes adopted during the colonial era were still used to keep blacks in a state of subjection.

Following independence from Britain, the slave population of the South continued to be enlarged by importation, because the slave trade itself was permitted under article 1, section 9, of the U.S. Constitution until the year 1808. This provision was the price of securing the union of the original thirteen colonies: Georgia and South Carolina had made it clear they would not join the union if the practice were prohibited. Under the compromise adopted by the drafters of the Constitution, the importation of slaves could continue without interference for twenty years, after which time Congress could vote on the issue. (It is of significance to subsequent discussions that this mention of "the migration or importation of such persons" is the *only* reference in the U.S. Constitution to the topic of immigration.)

On 2 December, 1806, President Thomas Jefferson recommended to Congress that the practice be prohibited at the earliest date possible under the Constitution, and a vote in late 1807 did outlaw the importation of slaves as of 1 January 1808. The trade did not end with its legal prohibition in 1808, however. Since laws do not enforce themselves, the practice continued until slavery itself was outlawed decades later with the adoption of the Thirteenth Amendment to the Constitution in 1865. It is estimated that at least 270,000 slaves were illegally smuggled into the country between 1808 and 1860.[11]

Unionism

As the nineteenth century began, there was no labor movement as such. The first union of workers who joined together to improve wages had been established by shoemakers in Philadelphia in 1792 (it disbanded within a year but was reconstituted in 1794). As long as most of the free labor force was self-employed and most of the nonagricultural production sector relied on handicraft workers, however, there was little place for unions. Tradesmen were often both employee and employer. Many mechanics and artisans plied their crafts in shops, alone or with the assistance of an apprentice and maybe a journeyman or two. Others traveled from place to place, or from farm to farm, carrying their tools as they went. These skilled workers typically followed customs and practices of their crafts which dated back to medieval times in Europe. Standards of work and product prices were their primary concerns when disputes arose.

Consequences

During the initial phase of the nation's economic development, its industrial structure, labor force, and labor market institutions remained essentially the same as they had been during the lengthy colonial era. Neither immigration or unionism were of any particular consequence. But with the advent of the nineteenth century, all this was soon to change. The United States economy would never again resemble its original character.

CHAPTER TWO

Mass Immigration Begins; Unionism Sparks but Sputters (1800–1860)

The Setting

The Napoleonic wars in Europe during the first thirteen years of the nineteenth century, as well as the ensnarement of the United States into another war with the British (1812–14), broke the spell of support for a Jeffersonian-style society. The United States could not have remained an agrarian-based economy even if it wanted to, for Britain's naval blockades and domination of the sea-lanes meant that the young republic could no longer depend on imports of manufactured goods. The incipient manufacturing sector, led by the rise of the textile industry in New England, needed urgently to expand and diversify. And it did.

When the War of 1812 ended, the manufacturers pressed the federal government for tariffs to protect their wartime investments and their newly acquired market shares from the renewal of foreign competition. In 1816, Congress responded by adopting the first tariffs designed for purely protective reasons. More manufacturing growth ensued, and although its scale of development fluctuated with the whims of the business cycle, in principle the disciples of Jefferson had by 1820 yielded to the expanded lobbying influences of the Hamiltonians. Industrial diversification, growth-oriented development, urban population clusters, and wage-dependent workers would be the nation's future. These actual manifestations of economic change did not occur at once. The transition had begun, but it would be decades before the consequences were obvious.

Throughout the Northeast, where most of the new industrialism was taking place, labor remained in short supply. The availability of urban factory workers was still affected by the lure of the vast western lands for the native-born population. Some did move to the Midwest and beyond. For others the West represented mere wishful thinking, and they stayed where they were. Some who were raised in rural northeastern communities, however, chose migration to the urban areas where new factories were being built and jobs were being created.

By the late 1820s, manufacturing enterprises were themselves spreading slowly westward. Milling and meatpacking led the industrial migration of jobs to the Midwest and were soon followed by the manufacture of farm machinery. The discovery of coal deposits in the prairie country and iron ore around the Great Lakes spurred the development of both mining and heavy industry in these regions.

The westward drift of the population was accentuated by the enormous land expansion that occurred during the first half of the century. The Louisiana Purchase from France in 1803 enlarged the nation by 828 thousand square miles of land; a treaty with Britain in 1846 which added the Oregon Territory and set the 49th parallel as the northwestern border with Canada brought 250 thousand square miles; the 1848 treaty with Mexico ending a two-year war, 1 million square miles and a subsequent (1853) land purchase from Mexico, which set the remainder of the nation's southern border from Texas to California, 45 thousand square miles. Thus the western portion of the continental United States was established, and in the process new frontiers were created for both settlement and economic development.

As had previously occurred in the eastern half of the nation, it was the native-born—led by farmers—who largely pioneered the population of the new territories prior to the outbreak of the Civil War in 1861. Of course, the people already living in these western lands as they were acquired by the United States who also became part of the nation's growing population. Most numerous were Indians of the myriad tribes that inhabited the area; they numbered perhaps as many as a million people (including the many thousands who were forcibly displaced from their former homelands in the East). In addition, there were persons of European heritage groups, the population remnants of earlier traders and trappers from the French, Spanish, and English days of domination in the Mississippi Valley and the Northwest. Also there were about 75,000 persons of Spanish heritage in the Southwest as the consequence of earlier Spanish (and later, Mexican) exploration, missionary, and trading activities. There were black slaves as well in parts of these regions.

None of these groups can be considered immigrants as the term is usually defined. In fact, most of the Indian and the Spanish-heritage populations at that time "were annexed by conquest."[1] Under the terms of the Treaty of Guadalupe Hidalgo in 1848, all former citizens of Mexico in the ceded lands were given one year to leave the territory. Only about 2,000 persons chose to do so, and a few thousand others subsequently took advantage of formal naturalization procedures to become U.S. citizens; the remainder became citizens "by default."[2] As for the Indians, not until 1887 did Congress approve the Dawes-Severalty Act, which awarded citizenship to those Indians who formally renounced their tribal allegiances, and not until 1924 did the Burke Act grant all Indians citizenship. Nonetheless, these incorporated people did become part of the labor force development process of the West.

The Labor Force and Industrial Employment

Table 2.1 shows the labor force and industrial employment patterns that characterized the pre–Civil War decades from 1800 to 1860. Over this time span the size of the labor force expanded by almost six times. Both free labor and slave labor increased significantly, but free labor accounted for 80 percent of the total growth. By 1860, slave labor—still significant in total size—had fallen from 28 percent of the nation's labor force in 1800 to 21 percent.

Although trade and services were increasing, it was the four goods-producing industries—agriculture, manufacturing, mining, and construction—that dominated job growth. Agriculture remained the major employment sector—as late as 1860, it accounted for 55 percent of total employment in the nation although there was considerable regional variation—but by the 1840s and 1850s a more diversified industrial structure was well under way. Agricultural employment fell in the northern and western states from 68 percent of the labor force in 1800 to 40 percent in 1860; in the South, however, the percentage actually rose slightly, from 82 to 84 percent, over the same time span.[3]

By 1850, manufacturing had begun to take a firm hold in the Northeast and, to some extent, in the Great Lakes region of the Midwest. Mining and construction were also sustaining rapid growth. By 1860 these four goods-producing industries collectively accounted for 74 percent of the nation's total employment. The vast preponderance of these jobs, of course, were blue-collar work that relied extensively on the manual abilities of workers. Education and skills were not sought—nor for that matter was such human capital available among either the native-born or the foreign-born

Table 2.1. The Labor Force and Industrial Employment, 1800–1860 (in thousands)

Year	Labor Force (10 years and up)			Employment[a]							
	Total	Free	Slave	Agriculture	Fishing	Mining	Construction	Manufacturing	Trade	Transport	Service
1800	1,900	1,370	530	1,400	5	10	n.a.	2	n/a	40	45
1810	2,330	1,590	740	1,950	6	11	n/a	90	n/a	60	82
1820	3,135	2,185	950	2,470	14	13	n/a	17	n/a	50	130
1830	4,200	3,020	1,180	2,965	15	22	n/a	75	n/a	70	190
1840	5,660	4,180	1,480	3,570	24	32	290	596	350	102	285
1850	8,250	6,280	1,970	4,520	30	102	410	1,327	530	145	430
1860	11,110	8,770	2,340	5,880	31	176	520	1,695	890	225	715

Source: Stanley Lebergott, *Manpower in Economic Growth: The American Record since 1800* (New York: McGraw-Hill, 1964), table A-1. Copyright © 1964 by McGraw-Hill Inc. Reprinted by permission of the publisher.

Note: Because labor market data were not collected in a consistent manner during the nineteenth century, the figures for separate industries do not add up to the Labor Force total. Separate sources were used to compile data. Nonetheless, these are the best historical estimates available.

[a]"Persons Engaged," the classification used during early census counts, included employees, the self-employed, and unpaid family workers.

labor force. Indicative of this situation is the fact that the new factories in the Northeast initially sought to find a way to avoid the need to provide higher wages to attract unskilled men to staff their plants. Instead, they turned to recruiting what were considered "non-competing groups": namely, children and young women, whom they regularly paid less than men to do the same work.[4]

In the South, the perpetuation of the slave system contributed to the continuing regional domination of agriculture. It was in the 1820s that cotton became "king" and output soared, leading to the ancillary birth of regional cotton textile manufacturing. But the slaves were primarily employed in agricultural production. The slave population and labor force grew rapidly over the first sixty years of the nineteenth century (see Table 2.1). Natural reproduction was the primary explanation for the growth, but as noted earlier, the illegal importation of slaves after 1808 continued to flourish. It was also the case that the nation's slave population increased as a result of the land expansion that also took place in this era. The Louisiana Purchase added some 40,000 slaves to the U.S. population, and 60,000 more (mostly in east Texas) were acquired as a result of the vast land acquisition in the Southwest following the war with Mexico.[5]

Whatever the changes occurring in the nation's overall industrial structure, however, it was the case that by the middle of the nineteenth century 70 percent of its labor force were *not* employees.[6] They were still mostly self-employed persons—farmers, mechanics, small tradesmen—or slaves.

Immigration

It was in this context of employment flux that mass immigration commenced. In 1820, the first year for which there are official data, 8,385 immigrants entered the United States. Then, as shown in Table 2.2, the number soared to 143,439 immigrants over the ensuing decade, with more than half of these having arrived during its last three years. More important, from 1830 through the 1850s the total numbered 5 million— constituting the first wave of mass immigration. Table 2.3 shows the effect on the population: the percentage of foreign-born, which declined for the first fifty years of the nation's history, suddenly reversed course during the 1840s.

Most of immigrants in this period came from Germany, Ireland, and the French-speaking region of eastern Canada. French Canadian emigration to the United States, involving tens of thousands of persons, began in

Table 2.2. Immigration to the United States, 1820–1860

1820	8,385
1821–1830	**143,439**
1821	9,127
1822	6,911
1823	6,354
1824	7,912
1825	10,199
1826	10,837
1827	18,875
1828	27,382
1829	22,520
1830	23,322
1831–1840	**599,125**
1831	22,633
1832	60,482
1833	58,640
1834	65,365
1835	45,374
1836	76,242
1837	79,340
1838	38,914
1839	68,069
1840	84,066
1841–1850	**1,713,251**
1841	80,298
1842	104,565
1843	52,496
1844	78,615
1845	114,371
1846	154,416
1847	234,968
1848	226,527
1849	297,024
1850	369,980
1851–1860	**2,598,214**
1851	379,466
1852	371,603
1853	368,645
1854	427,833
1855	200,877
1856	299,436
1857	251,306
1858	123,126
1859	121,282
1860	153,640

Source: U.S. Immigration and Naturalization Service.

Table 2.3. The Foreign-Born Population, 1790–1860

Year	Foreign-Born Population (millions)	Percentage of Total Population
1790	0.5	12.8
1800	0.6	11.3
1810	0.8	11.1
1820	1.0	10.4
1830	1.2	9.3
1840	1.4	8.2
1850	2.2	9.7
1860	4.1	13.2

Sources: 1790–1840: Elizabeth W. Gilboy and Edgar M. Hoover, "Population and Immigration," in *American Economic History* (New York: McGraw-Hill, 1961), table 6. Copyright © 1961 by McGraw-Hill, Inc. Reprinted with permission of the publisher. 1850 and 1860: Bureau of the Census, *Historical Census Statistics on the Foreign-Born Population of the United States* (Washington, D.C.: U.S. Department of Commerce, 1999), table 2.

the wake of a failed rebellion against British rule in 1837, which was followed by a prolonged depression in the timber industry in eastern Canada in the 1840s. Irish emigration in the 1840s was prodded by a potato blight which, following years of inadequate agricultural practices, destroyed crop production. In the famine and unemployment that ensued—thousands died, and many more lived at bare subsistence levels—almost a quarter-million persons elected to leave Ireland for the United States. German emigration was the consequence of a wave of political unrest, attempted reforms, and violent reaction from the late 1840s through the mid-1850s. In the aftermath, more than a million Germans fled to the United States.

Most of these Canadian, Irish, and German immigrants were unskilled, but some skilled workers, mostly from England, came during these years as well. Attracted by the prospect of higher real wages, writes David Montgomery, they were craft workers "whose skills were being undermined by the industrial revolution in England but still in demand in the more backward American economy."[7]

The ensuing settlement pattern of the North and Midwest can be likened to a relay race. Pioneering was primarily the task of native-born farmers: rural populations tended to migrate westward from more developed to less developed regions of the nation. Few European immigrants of this era moved directly to the western frontiers; they tended to settle in the easterly cities or other interior areas where earlier immigrants of the same ethnic background had clustered. Any westward migration on their part was a gradual process that usually followed a period of adaptation in the eastern cities—and even when they moved west, they tended to stay in the towns and the cities.

There were exceptions, of course; some immigrants did go directly into farming: Germans in Pennsylvania, Germans and Scandinavians in the territories that would become Wisconsin and Minnesota. But Stanley Lebergott best stated the paradox that: "somewhat surprisingly, the greatest beneficiary of the flow of immigrant labor was never agriculture, though farming was our primary industry for a century or more."[8] Rather, before the Civil War it was work in construction (especially the building of infrastructure such as canals, roads, and railroads) in the 1820s and 1830s, followed by mining, services, and factory work in the 1840s and 1850s, which attracted most of the new immigrants. The result, according to Lebergott, was that immigration generated a "supply of labor to a specific group of industries."[9] This pattern of occupational clustering of immigrant workers—rather than of industrial dispersal—has been an employment characteristic of all the subsequent waves of mass immigration.

There was one new group of immigrants who, beginning in the late 1840s and at an accelerating rate throughout the 1850s, entered the United States along its West Coast and sought employment mainly in California. These were the Chinese, many fleeing the terror and disorder of a violent peasant rebellion that broke out in seventeen provinces of southern China in 1850 and lasted until 1864.[10] California had been formally acquired by the United States from Mexico on 2 February, 1848; gold had been discovered just nine days earlier on an estate owned by a German immigrant named Johann Sutter; and soon the population was expanding rapidly. By the end of 1849, California had 90,000 people, and it was admitted as a state in 1850.

The Chinese immigrants were overwhelmingly male. About 41,000 arrived during the decade of the 1850s, settling chiefly in California. Despite the fact that most of the Chinese immigrants were from agricultural backgrounds, few were employed in agriculture in California or elsewhere in the West. Initially, many sought work as miners; others gained employment in a myriad of unskilled jobs in service industries, domestic work, and small factories.

The immediate reaction of U.S. workers to Chinese workers in California was bitter disapproval, for they were perceived as persons who would work under the worst circumstances and for the lowest pay, yet seldom complain. Consequently, the state enacted a host of anti-Chinese laws in response to citizen protests. A state tax was placed on all Chinese miners in 1852; a head tax on Chinese immigrants was imposed in 1855; and a reconfirming resolution to enforce these statutes was adopted in 1862.

All these laws were subsequently struck down by both the California Supreme Court and the U.S. Supreme Court; nonetheless, they served as a statement of popular ill will.

With respect to broader issues, Table 2.2 shows that by the late 1850s the first wave of mass immigration was coming to an end. As the abolition of slavery became the major domestic issue, the prospect that its resolution would be accomplished only by war reduced the number of would-be entrants.

Unionism

At the beginning of the nineteenth century, the slow spread of factory production led some craft workers to form unions, primarily as a defensive reaction. Their membership was strictly limited to persons who actually practiced the craft, and they were wholly local in character; as a consequence, their individual memberships were small. Their original objectives were to secure economic gains in improved wages, hours, and working conditions. In some instances, efforts to discuss these issues collectively with local employers led to the nation's first strikes.

From the outset, unionism was bitterly resented by employers, who initially resorted to the legal system to assist in their opposition. In 1806, when a shoemakers' union in Philadelphia struck for wage increases, the employers took them to court. They charged that the union represented an illegal combination designed to raise incomes for some (workers) and to injure others (employers). The court found the union leaders guilty on both counts and equated the formation of unions for economic purposes with criminal conspiracy. The remnants of the local unions that remained following the enunciation of the conspiracy doctrine all perished in the depression of 1819.

When prosperity returned in the 1820s (thanks largely to improvements in transportation), union activity revived. Because the relative scarcity of labor in urban areas initially provided a strong bargaining position for craft workers, local craft unions again sprang up. They were not hindered by the courts as long as they simply urged shorter work hours and were not forceful in their efforts. In 1827, a carpenters' strike in Philadelphia led to the formation of the Mechanics' Union of Trade Associations, an effort to organize the various local crafts in the city into a citywide federation. The unifying theme was the quest to obtain a ten-hour workday (reflecting the nation's agricultural heritage, the typical workday at the time in all industries was from sunup to sundown). The organization stressed that it did not see itself as being anti-employer; rather, it emphasized the idea that the enhancement of the welfare of skilled workers would promote the interests of the entire community. Similar citywide associations sprang up in other major cities of the Northeast.

Unable to take direct economic action, the Mechanics' Union turned to political action as a way to improve conditions for workers. Out of its activities arose the Working Men's Party, which quickly spread from Philadelphia to other cities. It was the world's first labor party. As universal white male suffrage had been granted in most states by this time, the party offered slates of candidates for city and state office who supported a platform of political reforms. Its agenda included such issues as the abolition of imprisonment for debt and of the compulsory militia system; support for workers rights to secure liens on property to assure payment of wages; restrictions on child labor; the ten-hour workday; the creation of public schools; and bans on the use of convict labor to compete with free labor.[11] The party generally failed to achieve these objectives, but it did serve to publicize workers' grievances. Indeed, many of those issues were soon taken up by the major political parties and later adopted by various state legislatures. By the early 1830s, however, the Working Men's Party had collapsed.

Against this backdrop, the local unions of craft workers continued to flourish, and in 1834 a number of city federations—called city centrals—met in New York City to organize the National Trades Union. This first effort by American workers to create a national federation of trade associations, however, came to a quick end with the onset of the depression of 1837, which lasted into the early 1840s.

In the 1840s, as the pace of mechanization quickened, production workers were buffeted by the rapidity of the changes in occupational structure and working conditions. This was also the decade in which the first wave of mass immigration brought large numbers of additional job seekers and bewilderment among workers about what was happening and how they should respond. In this period of uncertainty, intellectuals—looking for a power base of mass support for various utopian schemes to reform society—descended upon workers groups wherever they assembled. They advocated various forms of collective association—"back to the earth movements," cooperative movements, agrarianism communalism, consumer unions—all representing forms of attempted escapism from the onset of industrialism. Most of the schemes failed, in part because of employer opposition, and in their wake, efforts by workers to establish unions were largely shunted aside. The enactment by Congress of the Homestead Act of 1862 did reflect the input of the agrarian move-

ment of the 1840s, but workers were for the most part worse off as a result
of distractions that did not address the twin issues that were actually affecting worker welfare: industrialization and mass immigration.[12]

Meanwhile, the question of the legitimacy of unions once more came
before the courts. In 1842 the Massachusetts Supreme Court struck down
the criminal conspiracy doctrine, holding that unions established for economic purposes *were* legal: if the means used remained peaceful, the end
objective of establishing a union was justified. A union of bootmakers in
Boston had agreed among themselves not to work for any employer who
hired a worker who was not one of their members. (They were seeking a
closed-shop hiring system.) Although heralded as a labor victory, the
court's decision did not immediately alter the legal difficulties confronting union organizational efforts. But unions seeking economic advancement were no longer considered to be illegal per se.

In the 1850s the growing significance of the national market made it
necessary for local unions to combine on a national basis in order to prevent nonunion conditions in any one locality from undermining prevailing standards in another.[13] National unions also facilitated the movement
of craft workers from place to place in search of employment. Many of
these consolidation attempts failed, but in 1852 the typographical workers (printers) founded the first national union that proved to be sustainable. Soon afterward in the same decade the locomotive engineers, hat
finishers, iron molders, blacksmiths, and machinists followed suit. Thus
roots of a continuous union movement were planted (no union can be
taken seriously by workers or employers if its life is like that of a fruitfly—
here today, gone tomorrow). With the organizational continuity provided
by these national unions came the realistic prospect of a viable labor
movement.

Consequences

Whatever presence the fledgling labor movement achieved before the Civil War was largely in the Northeast; there was virtually no organization of labor in the South or in the West. Unionism essentially reflected the efforts and the interests of craft workers. The mushrooming
ranks of unskilled workers were unprotected and left to confront the vagaries of the marketplace on their own; efforts to organize them were almost always unsuccessful, for the plentiful supply of eager immigrant job
seekers allowed employers to use them directly as strikebreakers or indi-
rectly as an alternative pool of workers from which to draw employees.[14]

In the burgeoning textile industry, for instance, employers by the 1840s had turned to the recruitment of immigrant workers where they had previously relied upon native-born young women and children to fill their job rosters. But high turnover made housing and supervising such workers costly and as competition increased, wrote labor historian Foster Rhea Dulles, "the benevolent paternalism of the mill owners gave way to stricter controls which had nothing to do with well-being of the workers."[15] Wages were cut, hours lengthened, the "speed-up" was introduced into the production process. Irish immigrants, mostly young single men, were initially employed to replace the women and children. They, in turn, were displaced by French Canadian immigrants, who were hired on a whole-family basis—husband, wife, and children—because employers believed they were more willing "to accept conditions as they found them." The preference for French Canadians was reinforced in the 1850s when a group of Irish workers became involved in a series of unsuccessful efforts to establish unions for textile workers. Many employers never forgave them. So, by the eve of the Civil War, French Canadians had become the dominant immigrant group employed in many New England textile mills.[16]

In summarizing employment conditions in the 1840s and 1850s, Dulles pointed out that immigrants "were available for all kinds of work, more often unskilled than skilled, at wages greatly reduced from anything which native artisans and mechanics considered essential for decent conditions." Moreover, labor supply conditions were significantly altered: immigration, Dulles concluded, was providing for the first time "a labor surplus which counteracted the cheap land and the frontier drawing workers off from the eastern states."[17]

That "labor surplus," however, not only depressed wages and stifled union organizing efforts but adversely affected the living conditions of virtually all urban workers. Historians who have studied social unrest in U.S. cities have noted that the harsh living and working conditions during this period triggered "the greatest urban violence that America has ever experienced."

The pattern of the urban immigrant slum as a source of poverty, vice, crime, and violence was set by Five Points in Lower Manhattan before the Civil War. Ulcerating slums along the lines of Five Points and severe ethnic and religious strife stemming from the confrontation between burgeoning immigrant groups and the native American element made the 1830s, 1840s, and 1850s a period of sustained urban rioting, particularly in the great cities of the Northeast.[18]

Over this time span there were at least thirty-five major riots in the four principal cities of the Northeast—Baltimore (12), Philadelphia (11), New York (8), and Boston (4)—and antiimmigrant sentiments were frequently the explicit or implicit cause of these civil outbursts. As Dulles concluded in his summary of the actions of native-born workers at that time, "The workers themselves began to protest against immigration as creating a numerous poor and dependent population."[19]

Xenophobia was no doubt also involved in the reaction against first-wave immigrants. The late 1840s and the 1850s were the period of the Know-Nothing movement, so named because the password "I know nothing about it" was used by members of secret lodges when asked about their knowledge of their clandestine organization called the Order of the Star Spangled Banner. It had been founded in New York state in 1849, and was a manifestation of nativist reaction against non-Anglo-Saxon and Catholic immigrants. This short-lived political movement reached its zenith in the mid-1850s with the creation of the Native American Party (which, of course, had nothing to do with Indians).[20] For a time, the Know-Nothings "attracted considerable support": in 1854 their party elected six state governors and seventy-five members of the U.S. Congress.[21] In 1856 the party actually fielded a candidate for the presidency: former president of the United States, Millard Fillmore of New York. He carried only one state, Maryland (which, ironically was the one colony originally founded by Catholic settlers, though it had since come firmly under the control of Protestant influences). Still, only the growing concern over slavery, which split the party, was able to quell its mounting nativist influence.

Nonetheless, the presence of xenophobia should not be used to mask the fact that unregulated mass immigration *was* exacting a human toll on the economic well-being of most urban workers and, in the process, suppressing union organizing efforts. Unfortunately, the paucity of reliable data on union membership prior to the Civil War makes impossible a precise relation of trends in unionism with trends in immigration. Absent official figures, it has fallen upon labor historians to construct estimates. The figure most often cited is that unionism hit its high point in 1836 at 300,000 members, the estimate of famed labor economist John R. Commons in 1910.[22] Since he offered no documentation, however, this number has been strongly criticized by an equally eminent labor historian, Maurice Neufeld. After careful scrutiny, Neufield concluded that Common's total figure "lacks not only the foundation of an informed source with minimal details, but also the plausibility of a membership total that occupies an explicable position on the curve of an historical trend."

Neufeld constructed a far more "modest" figure for 1836 of 44,000 union members, which translates to 2.5 percent of the nonagricultural labor force—a percentage which he considered "more consonant" with subsequent estimates of the proportion of workers who were union members during the latter half of the nineteenth century.[23]

Despite controversy over actual union membership, what is undeniable is that its high point for this period was reached in the mid-1830s, *just as the first wave of immigration commenced in earnest.* For the remaining years until 1860, unionism floundered and membership declined, while immigration soared and the foreign-born population grew substantially as a percentage of the total population (see Table 2.3). It was the beginning of a continuing inverse pattern: a rise in immigration paralleled by a decline in union membership—and vice versa.

CHAPTER THREE

The "Second Wave" of Mass Immigration: Unionism Struggles but Takes Root (1861–1890)

The Setting

The outbreak of the Civil War in the spring of 1861, followed by four years of incessant fighting before the North was victorious, did more than resolve the slavery issue; it accelerated the industrialization process. As a consequence, the war era represents what historian Vernon Parrington has called the economic "break point" between "agricultural America" and "industrial America." The prospect of a "static, decentralized, and idealistic" nation gave way to a vision of its future as "dynamic, centralized, and opportunistic."[1]

Although the war wreaked havoc and devastation on the economy of the South (from which the region would take another century to recover), it spawned enormous economic gains in the North, where many businessmen seized the opportunity to gain financial wealth. As government expenditures to provision and execute the war soared, industrialists scrambled to use the newly available machine technologies to meet the massive demand for their output, and bankers acquired control over vast amounts of liquid wealth. In the process, a new class of financiers and manufacturers was created. The wealth of this *nouveau riche* class greatly exceeded that of the older patrician aristocracy who had accumulated their riches, gradually largely through commerce, over the previous generations. It was this new class, with no tradition to guide itself in the use of its wealth, that captured control of the nation's political system for the remainder of the nineteenth century. Corruption in both business and government became rampant.

The war also enabled industrialists and political advocates of economic expansion to acquire positions from which they could shape the course of federal government policy, during both the war years and the decades that immediately followed. Parrington described the era as the age of "the great barbecue," with the state providing the "beef" in the form of tariffs, land grants, subsidies, and opportunities for graft.[2]

Just days before the inauguration of President Abraham Lincoln, the outgoing president, James Buchanan, signed into law the Morrill Tariff Act of 1861. Subsequent increases during the war raised the *ad valorum* duty on imports to 47 percent—the highest in U.S. history up to that time. The initial pretext for this action was the need to raise revenue to finance the war, but the law also served to shield the nation's manufacturers from foreign competition. When the war ended in 1865, the high tariffs remained in place, and protectionism became the rationale for their continuance.

The collective body of legislation adopted during the Civil War era laid the foundation for the economic expansion that occurred during the remainder of the nineteenth century.

In 1862 the construction of a transcontinental railroad was authorized. The proposal had been debated for years in Congress but it had been bogged down in regional disagreements over whether such a railroad should follow a northern or a southern route. The 1853 purchase of a strip of land from Mexico (along the present-day southern border of New Mexico and Arizona) had been primarily to facilitate the construction of the southern route to California, but the secession of the southern states in 1861 dashed those plans. Accordingly, in 1862 President Abraham Lincoln signed the Pacific Railroad Act, which authorized construction to commence along a route that extended from Omaha, Nebraska, to Sacramento, California. Lincoln pressed for this ambitious undertaking as a way to assure the allegiance of the people of the West—especially those in California—to the Union during these years of domestic turmoil. The legislation provided that 21 million acres of public land be given to the Union Pacific Railroad (working from east to west) and the Central Pacific Railroad (working from west to east) to build the railroad as well as the proceeds of government loan bonds that were raised to cover the actual construction costs.

The two rails were joined in Utah in 1869, and over the course of the remainder of the century three other transcontinental railroad routes (two of which also involved generous land grants) were completed. As these opened new territories to settlers, the railroad companies sent their own representatives to Europe to lure immigrants to the American West. The completed railroads also made it possible for other industries to tap into the vast natural resources of the western lands, which significantly contributed to the nation's rapid industrial development.

It was in 1862 as well that the Homestead Act was enacted. Earlier efforts to distribute public land for settlement and farming had been opposed by factory owners in the East (who were more interested in building urban surpluses of labor in order to keep wage costs low) and by southern slaveholders (who feared that western homesteaders would oppose slavery). With the withdrawal of the South from the Union, Lincoln was able to secure passage of this historic legislation that gave 160-acre allotments of public land to individual settlers who agreed to live there continuously for five years. By 1870, 14 million acres of land had been taken up by homesteaders, and by the end of the century 80 million acres of land had been settled under its auspices.

Also adopted in the war years was the National Bank Act of 1863, which sought to provide the nation with a stable paper currency. The new money system was far from perfect, but it did ultimately succeed in replacing the numerous notes in use at the time which had been issued by state-chartered banks. As the government bonds used to back the new "greenbacks" were redeemed over the years following the war, however, the quantity of notes in circulation decreased. As a consequence, shortages of cash caused severe hardship to debtor groups (i.e., working people in general and western farmers in particular). Available money tended to be concentrated in the financial centers of the Northeast. The nation's currency system for the remainder of the century was not sufficient to meet the needs of an expanding economy. But the banking system was not overhauled again until the Federal Reserve System, with its twelve regional depository banks, was established in 1913.

The Labor Force and Industrial Employment Patterns

Over the thirty-year time span 1861–90, the labor force of the United States doubled in size. As shown in Table 3.1, its growth was slow while the nation was at war with itself and in the years immediately following. Not only had some 600,000 persons—mostly men of working age—been killed and many more maimed, but immigration had declined

Table 3.1. The Labor Force and Industrial Employment, 1860–1890 (in thousands)

Year	Labor Force (10 years and up)	Employment[a]							
		Agriculture	Fishing	Mining	Construction	Manufacturing	Trade	Transport	Service
1860	11,110[b]	5,880	31	176	520	1,695	890	225	715
1870	12,930	6,790	28	180	780	2,683	1,310	295	1,170
1880	17,390	8,920	41	900	900	3,595	1,930	541	1,360
1890	23,320	9,960	60	440	1,510	4,701	2,960	870	1,930

Source: Stanley Lebergott, *Manpower in Economic Growth: The American Record since 1800* (New York: McGraw-Hill, 1964), table A-1. Copyright © 1964 by McGraw-Hill Inc. Reprinted by permission of the publisher.

Note: Because labor market data were not collected in a consistent manner during the nineteenth century, the figures for separate industries do not add up to the Labor Force total. Separate sources were used to compile data. Nonetheless, these are the best historical estimates available.

a"Persons Engaged," the classification used during the census counts, includes employees, the self-employed, and unpaid family workers.

bIncludes 2,340,000 slaves.

sharply prior to the outbreak of the fighting and throughout the first few years of the war. But in the 1870s the labor force was again growing, thanks to the pressure of rapid industrialization and westward land expansion—and as well, the renewal of mass immigration.

The four years of the Civil War accelerated business development in the states of the Northeast and the Midwest. Government contracts for immense quantities of weapons, munitions, clothes, tents, cannons, ships, and food supplies to support the war effort were an immediate stimulant to production. As labor was made scarce by the mandatory military conscription of the working class (wealthier families could buy out participation of their male members for $300 a person), the heightened level of production demand could be met only by the rapid introduction of machinery. The consequent spread of mechanization and of mass production techniques hastened the transition of the economy from its earlier handicraft orientation. In this environment of increasing economic scale, large enterprises had significant advantages over small ones. New factories sprang up in all other regions than the South; mining, transportation, and construction activity also expanded. Industrial employment patterns became more diversified. Despite severe fluctuations in the postwar demand for labor (the economy was in recession 1866–68, 1873–79, and 1884–89), the labor force sustained significant growth over this thirty-year time span.

Agriculture continued to be the nation's largest employment sector, and agricultural employment increased in absolute size, but its *relative* importance began to slip in the 1880s. As Table 3.1 indicates, its percentage of total employment was virtually constant—at about 50 percent—from 1860 until 1880. But during the decade of the 1880s there was a rapid introduction of laborsaving agricultural technologies. The steel plow, reaper, and thresher had been invented before the Civil War but came into widespread use only after the war. The Homestead Act and the spread of railroading following the war provided new opportunities in the West for rapid settlement and expanded farming. The relative treelessness and the vast scale of the flat prairie extending from the Mississippi Valley to the foothills of the Rocky Mountains invited the use of machinery and the development of a one-crop farming system. In short order, the combination of a rapid influx of people and the utilization of machine technology brought food production soaring to levels never experienced or imagined before in either the United States or the rest of the world. Not only was the nation able to feed even its own surging population, but it also produced a substantial surplus—especially of wheat—for export to the industrial countries of western Europe.[3]

Not all the new prairie settlers could adjust to the rigors and loneliness of pioneer rural life, but a sufficient number did remain to contribute to the rapid rise of population in the Plains states. Despite jockeying in Congress, most of the western territories were admitted to statehood by 1890. The three still excluded were so treated not for lack of people but for political reasons: in Utah, opposition to the marriage practices of the Mormons; in New Mexico and Arizona, concern over the ethnic composition of the dominant populations; Oklahoma, previously "Indian Territory," had just been opened to white settlement, ostensibly because Indian leaders had been "disloyal" to the nation by siding with the South during the Civil War.

Immigration

Between 1860 and 1890, 10.3 million immigrants entered the United States (see Table 3.2), twice the number that had entered in the thirty-year period prior to 1860. By 1890 the foreign-born accounted for 14.8 percent of the population—the highest percentage that the nation has ever experienced (see Table 3.3). This "second wave" of mass immigration however, was not a steady flow. Indeed, immigration levels had declined prior to the outbreak of the Civil War and continued to fall as the fighting commenced. But as labor shortages developed, not even the widespread adoption of machine technology was sufficient to meet the demand for output. As a consequence, it was not long before the business interests in the North turned to immigration as a means of enlarging the supply of labor. In December 1863 Lincoln sent a message to Congress proposing a law to foster immigration. Congress responded in 1864 by passing the Act to Encourage Immigration, which Lincoln quickly signed. It was the nation's first statutory law pertaining to the level of immigration admissions.

The act had unique procedural characteristics. Business and government were not interested at the time in attracting immigrants as settlers; they wanted immigrants who would immediately become urban workers. Nor did they want workers with families, who might be tempted to move westward and settle in the newly opened territories. Hence, this new law allowed private employers to go abroad, recruit would-be immigrants in their homelands, and pay their transportation expenses; their enlisted workers, in turn, were required to sign binding contracts whereby they pledged their wages to the employer for up to twelve months to repay their transportation costs. (Typically, the workers were also induced to

Table 3.2. Immigration to the United States, 1861–1890

1861–1870	**2,314,824**
1861	91,918
1862	91,985
1863	176,282
1864	193,418
1865	248,120
1866	318,568
1867	315,722
1868	138,840
1869	352,768
1870	387,203
1871–1880	**2,812,191**
1871	321,350
1872	404,806
1873	459,803
1874	313,339
1875	227,498
1876	169,986
1877	141,857
1878	138,469
1879	177,826
1880	457,257
1881–1890	**5,246,613**
1881	669,431
1882	788,992
1883	603,322
1884	518,592
1885	395,346
1886	334,203
1887	490,109
1888	546,889
1889	444,427
1890	455,302

Source: U.S. Immigration and Naturalization Service.

sign contracts for additional periods of work to defray the costs of their meals and housing.) For this reason, the law was also known as the Contract Labor Act. Because these provisions essentially required indentured servitude, the law encountered the immediate wrath of the labor leaders, who sensed unfair competition and human exploitation.

Meanwhile, contract labor was being used in the West to recruit and employ some 5,000 workers from China for the construction of the west-to-east portion of the newly authorized transcontinental railroad. The Chinese immigrants too were overwhelmingly males (approximating nine for every female). When the last spike was driven in 1869, signaling the completion of the railroad, most of these Chinese immigrants sought employment in California and other western areas primarily as unskilled

Table 3.3. The Foreign-Born Population, 1860–1890

Year	Foreign-Born Population (millions)	Percentage of Total Population
1860	4.1	13.2
1870	5.6	14.4
1880	6.7	13.3
1890	9.2	14.8

Source: U.S. Bureau of the Census, Historical Census Statistics on the Foreign-Born Population of the United States, 1850–1990, Population Division, Working Paper no. 29 (Washington D.C.: U.S. Department of Commerce, 1999), table 1.

workers in mining, service enterprises, and small manufacturing firms. By 1870, Chinese workers were the largest single component of the foreign-born workforce in California. By the mid-1870s, adult Chinese males constituted about one-third of the adult male population of the state and approximately the same percentage of the state's labor force. Soon, competition for available jobs became acute as the opening of the transcontinental rail connection enabled thousands of workers in the East to move to California.

The preponderance of second-wave immigrants, however, arrived along the East Coast. Like those of the pre–Civil War era, most were from Germany, Britain, Ireland, and Canada. There was, however, a notable increase in the number from northern Europe. These Scandinavians proved to be the exception to the general immigrant work patterns of the period: they tended to pursue agricultural work, often in the upper Midwest. Most other new immigrants to the East continued the earlier pattern of seeking work in the manufacturing, mining, construction, and service sectors. As a consequence, only 10 percent of the nation's agricultural workers were foreign-born in 1870; by 1900, only 13 percent.[4] This was so despite the fact that agriculture was still the nation's largest employment sector and that annual immigration was at historic heights throughout most of this period.

Unionism

As with all other segments of American life at the close of the 1850s, the slavery issue began to impinge on the fate of the infant union movement. Labor had not given much support to the abolitionist movement because many felt that the status of white wage earners in the industrial centers of the Northeast and Midwest was just as degrading as slavery was to blacks in the South. Real wages were too low to provide much in the way of disposable income; spells of unemployment often caused income to be irregular; hours of work were long; and employers manifested little or no concern for the health and safety of employees at the workplace. Hence, many workers and their organizations felt that if the abolitionists in the North were truly concerned about the welfare of people, there was ample need to start their reforms at home.

Furthermore, when the war actually commenced, workers resented the discriminatory fact that the rich could buy their sons out of military service. They also feared that pro-abolitionist businessmen were planning to transport freed black slaves to the North to use as strikebreakers and as a source of cheap labor. Although union leaders tried to quell these concerns, in 1863 antidraft and antiblack riots broke out across the Northeast (the worst being a three-day riot in New York City in July 1863) and the Midwest that were led by workingmen.[5]

As would be expected under these circumstances, labor was bearing a heavy burden of the consequences of the war. Men of the industrial working class as well as those from farms made up most of the two million soldiers who served in the Union army. Those workers who remained behind found their purchasing power reduced by wartime inflation and, after mid-1864, by wage competition with the reviving immigration flow, this time of contract workers.

The National Labor Union

When the war ended in 1865, organized labor sought to go on the offensive with efforts to mold a national organization that would unify the actions of the existing national craft unions. In 1866 the National Labor Union (NLU) was founded in Baltimore. It was a federation comprising various city assemblies of local craft unions as well as some of the existing national craft unions. It had no real organizational structure, but from its ranks emerged the first nationally recognized labor leader, William Sylvis.

Active from the organization's beginning, Sylvis became president of the NLU in 1868. Formerly an iron molder in Philadelphia, he had had little formal education, but recuperating from an industrial accident earlier in his life had provided him with the time and opportunity to study economics and history. He could not understand how the low wages, long hours, and the dire working conditions confronting workers on a daily basis could be reconciled with adherence to the *laissez-faire* principles espoused by classical economic writers. As a consequence, he concluded that "the whole tribe" of professional economists were little more than "theoretical apologists for capitalism." He therefore vowed to devote himself to improving the conditions of workers, who, he believed, had just as much right to seek a better life as did employers.[6]

The NLU began its activities by proposing a practical program for the improvement of the conditions of employment. But with reduced government spending on war-related goods and services following the war, the economy slipped into recession. The NLU contended that part of the explanation for the surge in unemployment was the continuing entry of immigrant contract workers. Workers had bitterly resented the 1864 legislation that fostered the practice, viewing its labor recruitment features as an artificial effort to stimulate immigration. Also, of course, they believed that the terms of competition were simply unfair. How could native workers, dependent on wages for their livelihood, compete with contract workers who were not receiving wages and who could not quit their jobs, regardless of treatment? That contract workers were often used as strikebreakers contributed further to labor's ire. The NLU, therefore, made the repeal of the Act to Encourage Immigration a primary legislative goal.[7] Thanks to their efforts, the law was repealed in 1868, but the victory proved to be largely symbolic: though the legislative endorsement for such labor recruitment was ended, the practice itself had not been banned. Hence, many employers continued to recruit contract labor, albeit now as a purely private hiring system.

Although Sylvis strongly believed that the interests of working people transcended national borders, he viewed contract workers and unregulated immigration as a threat to the standards of living of American workers which he perceived as already too low.[8] Therefore, he sought to make contacts with labor leaders in Europe to see if there were not ways to control the scale of the flow of immigrant workers to the United States. Likewise, the NLU responded to the mounting concern of workers on the West Coast that the immigration of Chinese workers was leading to the imposition of "coolie" labor market conditions for the whole region.[9] To this end, the NLU adopted a resolution in 1868 that called for the rigid enforcement of a California statute prohibiting the importation of "coolie" labor (which meant unskilled workers obligated to work under contractual terms).[10]

Initially, however, the NLU did approve of *voluntary* Chinese immigration to the United States, sanctioned in 1868 by the signing of the Burlingame Treaty with China. It recognized the right of Chinese persons to emigrate to the United States on the same terms as Europeans—except that the Chinese were denied the prospect of becoming naturalized citizens. The primary intention of the treaty was to open the Chinese domestic market to American trade. But as Chinese immigration soared in California, as local protests by white workers became more vehement, and after Chinese strikebreakers were imported by a shoe factory in North Adams, Massachusetts, in 1869 and hired for one-third the wages previously paid to white workers, the NLU changed its mind. By 1870, it was openly advocating the abrogation of the Burlingame Treaty.[11]

Not only did the NLU leaders believe that a successful labor movement depended upon the existence of strong trade unions; they also backed a broad political platform of societal reform. These goals led the leaders to seek a coalition in the early 1870s with western farmers in a vain attempt to overhaul the nation's monetary system and thereby make credit more available. In the process, the organization lost the support of many rank-and-file workers. After becoming involved in the presidential campaign in 1872 in which it tried to transform itself into a national political party, the NLU collapsed and disappeared from the scene.

The Knights of Labor

The most significant effort to organize workers in the immediate postwar era followed the establishment of the Knights of Labor in Philadelphia in 1869. Originally a secret society founded by a group of garmentworkers led by Uriah Stephens, it sought both to glorify the role of workers and to improve their economic status by means of political reforms. In 1878 the Knights abandoned their secrecy—at the insistence of the Catholic Church and to mitigate the fears of others that it was a radical organization—and adopted a new platform designed "to make industrial and moral worth, not wealth, the true standard of industrial and national greatness."[12] In 1879, Stephens was replaced as leader of the organization by Terrence V. Powderly, a machinist by trade. Under his guidance the Knights sought to form a single heterogeneous union of all workers—except lawyers, bankers, and bartenders, who were considered to be "economic parasites."

Otherwise, their membership goal was to include both skilled and unskilled workers, regardless of race or gender or national origin. They hoped to unite those skilled workers who had already established independent and separate craft unions with the vast number of unskilled workers for whom there had never been a union option. For the most part, the skilled workers remained aloof, although some did belong to both the Knights and their own craft union.

Powderly strongly opposed militant activity, including the use of strikes. He favored arbitration of differences—which meant peaceful settlements—with employers, but very few employers at the time were willing to comply with such requests. Ironically, the growth of the Knights—from about 9,000 members in 1879 to its high point of 729,000 members in early 1886—was the direct result of strike victories. Later in 1886, however, the Knights sustained a disastrous defeat in the Southwest when the independent railroad brotherhoods there refused to support a Knights-sponsored strike. Subsequently, their national membership rapidly plummeted: by 1893 there were fewer than 75,000 members, and Powderly had resigned as leader. In the early twentieth century the organization ceased to exist.

As the long-run goal of the Knights was to improve the status of the American worker, most of their specific objectives could be gained only through the political action of legislative bodies: the distribution of free land, a tax on land values, a graduated income tax, currency reform, public ownership of transportation and communication industries, the creation of a federal department of labor, and an eight-hour workday. They accomplished little of that agenda—with one notable exception: immigration restrictions. Although it required dogged effort, the Knights were remarkably successful in achieving virtually every immigration reform they sought.

The most immediate immigration issue they confronted was the continuing influx from China of unskilled workers along the West Coast, primarily in California. Like the NLU before them, the Knights believed that it was impossible for unskilled American workers to compete with unskilled coolie workers who were contractually obligated for seven years or more to the Chinese employers who brought them to the United States. Indeed, many of these Chinese workers were peasants who had been literally kidnapped ("Shanghaied") by Chinese labor brokers who recruited for these employer groups.[13]

But in addition, there was the expressed fear that such Chinese workers simply could not be assimilated into American life. Drawing from a report prepared by a committee of the California legislature in 1877, Powderly wrote that "during their stay in this country, the Chinese never associate with other people, never adapt themselves to our habits, modes of dress, or our educational system; they carry their pagan idolatry into every walk in life; never pay heed to the sanctity of an oath; see no difference between right and wrong, and live in the same fashion in California as their ancestors did in China twenty-five hundred years ago." As for the women, who also came in under contract, he contended that "nearly all Chinese women brought to California were brought over for the purposes of prostitution."[14]

Thus, again like the NLU, the Knights in the late 1870s began to agitate for the repeal of the Burlingame treaty. As a result of their efforts, as well as those of other workers and elected officials all along the West Coast, legislation passed Congress in 1879 to abrogate the Treaty, but it was vetoed by President Rutherford B. Hayes. Nonetheless, President Hayes did appoint a commission to renegotiate the treaty; it was amended, and the changes approved by Congress in 1880 gave the United States the right to "regulate, limit, or suspend" but not "entirely prohibit" the entry of Chinese immigrants.[15] The adoption of this amendment paved the way for stronger action two years later. With the support of the Knights and other workers' organizations, the Chinese Exclusion Act was passed in Congress and signed into law by President Chester A. Arthur in 1882. It "suspended" immigration of all persons from China for ten years, was renewed every ten years later and made permanent in 1902. Not until 1943 was China given a minimal annual quota of 105 immigrants a year, which remained in effect until 1965.

The practice of excluding specific groups had begun in 1875 when a ban on persons who had been prostitutes or criminals, regardless of what country they came from, was enacted. But the Chinese Exclusion Act was of far greater importance than these selective exclusions. Its passage represented the first significant step taken by Congress to restrict the level of immigration to the United States.

As elated as the Knights and the independent craft unions were with the passage of this bar on Chinese immigration, they quickly recognized that the law itself was an insufficient deterrent, for Chinese workers continued to enter illegally from Canada and, through the use of fictitious names, even at West Coast ports.[16] Demands were then made to Congress to adopt a means to enforce the law.

On 2 September 1885, at least thirty Chinese workers were massacred at a coal mining site at Rock Springs in the Wyoming Territory by a group of displaced white workers. Although Powderly found this action "inexcusable" he nonetheless sought to rationalize it:

Exasperated at the success with which they had evaded the law, . . . the white workmen became desperate and wreaked a terrible revenge upon the Chinese. Had steps been taken to observe the law, and had the Chinese been as rigidly excluded as they should have been, the workmen at Rock Springs would not have steeped their hands in the blood of a people whose very presence in this country is contamination, whose influence is wholly bad, and whose effect upon the morals of whatever community they inhabit tends to degrade and brutalize all with whom they come in contact.[17]

Thus, with the nation's first significant effort to restrict immigration came a new issue that has plagued both policymakers and organized labor ever since: illegal immigration.

In a general assembly of the Knights a month later, Powderly formally addressed the subject of "the Chinese evil." He catalogued the failure of the Chinese Exclusion Act "to check the importation of Chinese into the United States" and declared that "no blame can be attached to organized labor for the outrage perpetuated at Rock Springs" because "if Congress had not winked at violations of the law, and refused to listen to the plaint of those who suffered because the laws were outraged, the men at Rock Springs would not have taken the law into their own hands." Stating that the issue was no longer merely regional but one of national importance, he insisted that "the whole people must act through their representatives and put a stop to further importation of the Chinese under any and all circumstances, for any purpose whatever, and for all time to come."[18]

The following year a committee report presented to the general assembly meeting of the Knights by a delegation from California bitterly attacked the continuation of Chinese immigration despite the law banning their entry. It summarized the past by saying that "this evil grew upon us before we were aware of its danger" and warned that "this yellow cloud of rain has overrun California . . . and it is rushing its streams to the East."[19]

But the issue of contractual workers was not limited to those who came from China. As noted earlier, contract labor continued to be widely practiced as a means of fostering immigration from Europe because the specific practice itself had not been banned. As Powderly explained: "The method by which immigration to the United States was stimulated by those who wish to take advantage of the ignorance of the immigrant was by means of advertising abroad for laborers."[20] He contended that this was done not because there was any generalized shortage of American workers but to create a surplus of labor in local labor markets in the United States. Indeed, in testimony before a New York State Senate committee in 1882, the railroad mogul Jay Gould boasted that "when I was in Europe you couldn't go anywhere but you saw agents of American land-grant companies [i.e., American railroad companies]."[21]

The Knights were quick to point out the contradictions of prevailing public policies that provided high tariffs to protect American corporations from competition with foreign products, made by cheaper foreign labor, while foreign labor itself could immigrate from Europe without any restriction. Powderly crystallized the hypocrisy by saying: "If foreign 'pauper labor' is what we are opposing when we establish a tariff, why is it that we only keep out the product of the 'pauper,' while allowing the 'pauper' himself to land free of duty?"[22]

In response to mounting criticism from both the Knights and the independent craft unions, in February 1885 Congress passed the Alien Contract Law, which banned all foreign recruitment of workers by American companies: thenceforth, "no person, company, partnership, or corporation . . . could in any way assist or encourage the importation or migration of any alien . . . into the United States."[23] But the legislation quickly proved to be another meaningless gesture for organized labor, for once more Congress had passed a law restricting immigration but had not provided any penalties or means of enforcement.[24] Hence, employers continued to recruit contract workers, who became increasingly involved in labor disputes as strikebreakers.

In a classic example, sixty-two Scottish stonecutters put under contract in 1885 to work on the mammoth state capitol building in Texas, were recruited and transported to Austin after members of the Granite Cutters' International Union boycotted the project in a wage dispute. By the time the case came to court in 1889, the work on the capitol had been completed and the workers had scattered. The contractor was found guilty of violating the Alien Contract Law, but only a token fine was imposed. In the ten years following the enactment of the statute, 400 such lawsuits were filed nationwide charging violations of its terms. In a number of these cases, either the Knights were directly involved or they passed sympathetic resolutions—as they did in the case of the stonecutters in Austin—to protest these flagrant violations of the law.[25]

Given the deficiencies of the Alien Contract Law, the Knights of Labor again pressed Congress to correct its inadequacies. The law was amended in March 1887 to give the U.S. Secretary of the Treasury the power to enforce it by examining would-be immigrants at the time of their arrival and returned forthwith to their country of origin any who were found in violation of the law.[26] But once again Congress had not specified any fine for those who actually did the recruiting, so the Knights pressed for a further legislation to fill this new loophole. In October 1888 another amendment did provide fines for offenders, plus payments to informers who furnished information that the law had been broken. And for the first time since the Alien Act of 1798 (which permitted the president of the United States to expel any foreigner but which had been quickly repealed in 1800), it permitted the expulsion of any alien who, within one year of arrival, was found to have entered the country in violation of the Alien Contract Law of 1885.[27]

The Formation of the American Federation of Labor

With the fading prominence of the Knights of Labor in the late 1880s, the fate of the U.S. labor movement reverted to the hands of the independent national unions.

In the previous decade, the nation's economy had slipped into a deep and prolonged depression that lasted from 1873 through 1879. It was a turbulent period, characterized by soaring unemployment, falling wages, and numerous strikes by both independent national unions of skilled craft workers and various railroad brotherhoods. The violence often associated with these strikes led to a series of urban riots in major cities across the country. These were usually collateral events motivated by the desperate plight of unemployed workers unaffiliated with the labor dispute, but it was the labor movement that was blamed. As labor historian Norman Ware summarized the period, "Labor became an outlaw, the wage earner a member of a subcommunity or class, separate and distinct from the general community to which he had, at least in theory, always belonged." The sinister specter of class conflict rose to tarnish the national unions whose number fell from thirty-three in 1873 to only nine in 1879.[28]

By that time, however, several former craft unions were attempting to reorganize. Initially, these efforts were overshadowed by the emergence of the Knights of Labor who had abandoned their secrecy in 1878 and were actively seeking members. But in November 1881 representatives of many of the craft unions and the Knights as well as various social reformers, met in Pittsburgh for the purpose of uniting these disparate organizations into the Federation of Organized Trades and Labor Unions (FOTLU). This was largely a paper organization that lacked a permanent governing structure. Nonetheless, at its first meeting it passed a series of resolutions on such issues as child labor, compulsory education, the eight-hour day, convict labor, and the need for a bureau of labor statistics. It also proposed an anti-Chinese resolution that called for "the use of our best efforts to get rid of this monstrous immigration."[29] The resolution was adopted with only one dissenting vote and contributed to the momentum of the Knights' efforts that culminated in the passage of the Chinese Exclusion Act the following year.

The lasting significance of the creation of FOTLU in 1881, however, was that it led directly to the creation of the American Federation of Labor (AFL) only five years later. In recognition of this evolutionary role, the AFL continues to this day to date its organizational birth as 1881, not 1886.

It was also at this historic meeting of FOTLU in 1881 that a representative of the Cigarmakers' International Union, Samuel Gompers, gained the attention of the assembled representatives. He was to become the most influential labor leader in the nation's history and, in Charles Madison's words, he "for many years fathered the anti-immigration policy of the American Federation of Labor."[30] He took this position even though he himself was born in London to a Jewish family that had emigrated in 1863, when he was thirteen years old, and had settled in New York City. A year later Gompers joined the cigarmakers' union and became active in its affairs. Despite his youth, he was soon part of the union's inner circle of intellectuals who educated him in the fundamentals of the labor movement. During the depression of the mid-1870s his local union struggled to survive both the external depression and an internal power struggle with more radical socialist elements. In 1875, Gompers formed a new local union and was elected its president. By 1878 he and his associates had gained control of the national cigarmakers' union.

It was his involvement in union affairs in the 1870s that made Gompers aware of the adverse effects that Chinese cigarmakers in California had on the wages and employment of white cigarmakers. Indeed, one result of this conflict in California had been the creation of the union label, used to this day to identify for consumers the products that are made by workers employed under union-negotiated wages and protections. It happened in 1872 when a San Francisco cigar company's employment of Chinese workers led to protests by white cigarmakers, who claimed that the Chinese would undermine prevailing work standards. They organized a consumer boycott of the company and, to distinguish which cigars were made by companies that employed unionized white workers, affixed a white label to their cigar boxes.[31]

As the membership in the Knights of Labor rose in the first half of the 1880s, the strain between the Knights (with their leadership focus on long-run political reforms), and the national craft unions (with their focus on short-run economic gains), reached a breaking point. Even though some craft union members—including Gompers—were also members of the Knights, there were mounting charges that the Knights were competing with the crafts for members. When the Knights began chartering local unions of dissidents within the national unions, the era of coexistence soon came to a bitter end. The notion that another union could encroach on the jurisdiction of established craft unions served to unify the national unions against the Knights.

After a number of clashes the national unions met in the spring of 1886 and offered a treaty which they knew the Knights would not accept. It essentially warned the Knights to desist from organizing members of the various crafts and to abstain from issuing any union labels that competed with those of an established craft. At the Knights' annual convention that October they did not take up the treaty, but they did adopt a resolution calling for all members who were cigarmakers to dissociate themselves from the old cigarmakers' union controlled by Gompers and his associates and to join a separate faction supported by the Knights which was opposed to the organizing of workers along craft lines. It was a fatal error, for it highlighted the differences in organizational goals between the Knights and the craft unionists.

Ultimately, at a simultaneous meeting of national craft unions and FOTLU on 8 December 1886, in Columbus, Ohio, they reached a common accord. The resulting federation of autonomous national unions absorbed FOTLU and created a new organization called the American Federation of Labor (AFL). At that time it represented twelve national unions, six trade assemblies, and seven local unions with a total membership of about 140,000. Samuel Gompers was elected president and held that office continuously, with the exception of the year 1894, until his death in 1924. At this initial convention the new AFL also passed a series of resolutions, one of which was a condemnation of Chinese immigration.

Consequences

The arrival of a capitalistic economic system is signaled by the development of a wage-dependent workforce. It was in the years just preceding the Civil War and the thirty years thereafter that this process of becoming a nation of employees took firm hold in the United States. Slavery came to an end; the pace of mechanization quickened, so that larger-scale enterprises began to displace smaller businesses; machines reduced the need for self-employed mechanics and artisans; and the percentage of the labor force dependent upon agriculture for employment began to fall. Local labor markets became increasingly influenced by regional and national employment trends. In this context the influence of mass immigration on the size and composition of the nation's labor supply became a center-stage issue for the emerging labor movement.

Although the organizations representing working people over this time span varied widely in their structures and goals, each such entity that appeared on the scene became immediately involved with efforts to control the flow of immigrants. They achieved the repeal of the nation's first statutory effort to encourage immigration; their fight to end the unlimited immigration of unskilled Chinese workers succeeded in suspending virtually all Chinese immigration for the next sixty years after 1882; they opposed the right of U.S. employers to recruit foreign labor abroad, and the practice was banned after 1885; and, recognizing that restrictions on immigration are meaningless unless accompanied by enforcement efforts, advocated the adoption of penalties that include fines against employers and the deportation of illegal entrants. Although diverse in the agendas of its various elements, organized labor was unified in its recognition of the adverse effects of mass immigration.

To understand how this attitude developed, it is necessary to recall that the second wave of immigration occurred at the same time as a considerable increase in the spread of machine technology. Indeed, Robert Asher contends that the escalating reaction against immigration in the post-1860 period by the "indigenous working class" was due, in part, to the fact that it was simultaneously "experiencing a severe dilution of skills and bargaining power" due to the introduction of the new technology.[32] Lebergott found that the real wages of workers did fall during the early 1860s; they recovered slightly in the late 1860s but only moved back to the pre–Civil War levels, where they remained virtually constant until the early 1880s before increasing moderately during the remainder of the decade.[33] Thus, wage trends tended to move inversely to the annual immigration flows over these same years. As shown in Table 3.2, the second-wave immigration was high during the mid-1860s before slightly receding, only to be renewed and sustained at relatively high levels from the end of the 1860s to the early 1880s. By the mid-1880s the era of second wave immigration was approaching its end. Lebergott, therefore, confirms the same conclusion reached by the labor movement of that era: the ebb and flow of mass immigration affected real wages during these years.[34] Using more complex econometrics, Timothy Hatton and Jeffrey Williamson have also found that urban real wages would have been 14 percent higher in 1890 in the absence of the mass immigration that occurred between 1870 and 1890.[35] These wage trends, combined with the spells of high unemployment that the nation experienced over this thirty-year period, clearly indicate that the labor market was demonstrating frequent signs of surplus. There was therefore ample reason for union leaders to be concerned about the adverse effects of immigration and to act to curb them.

The particularly virulent anti-Chinese policies pursued by the members and leaders of labor organizations during this era, however, were motivated also by some degree of racial bias. As Asher explains, "Most workers and working class spokesmen simply regarded the Chinese immigrants" as being "so different that they could never be assimilated."[36] Much of the most vocal and violent opposition in California was led by white workers who themselves were immigrants. The Irish workers in particular believed

Table 3.4. Union Membership of Nonagricultural Employed Labor Force, 1860–1890

Year	Union Membership	Percentage Unionized (of Nonagricultural Employed Labor Force)
1860	n/a	n/a
1870	300,000	4.9
1880	200,000	2.4
1890	372,000	2.8

Source: Lloyd Ulman, "The Development of Trade and Labor Unions," in *American Economic History*, ed. Seymour Harris, (New York: McGraw-Hill, 1961), 393.

the Chinese incapable of understanding the democratic principles for which the Irish had unsuccessfully fought in their former homeland and then come to America to find. In the San Francisco Bay area, for example, it was Dennis Kearny, an Irish immigrant, who successfully mobilized local workers in the 1870s to take political action on a statewide basis to attempt to rid California of Chinese workers.[37]

The bitter reaction against the Chinese was also due to the conditions in which Chinese recruiters transported these workers to the United States and by the degrading employment conditions imposed on them by Chinese employers. Many of the unskilled immigrants arrived in "ships as crowded and as filthy" as those used in the earlier African slave trade; (indeed, as Asian scholar Peter Kwong points out, some of the ships involved in the "coolie trade" were the same ones that had illegally transported African slaves before the Civil War.[38] Such treatment reinforced the view of white workers in port cities that the Chinese immigrants were a subservient people, expecially since "many of the Chinese labor contracts were set by Chinese contractors and were enforced through the informal political systems within the Chinese community, usually unbeknown to American authorities." Clearly, the widespread "opposition to the coolie trade . . . in the late 1870s" was a contributory reason for the enactment of the Chinese Exclusion Act in 1882.[39]

Of course, the fact that the labor movement fought in the 1880s for the passage of the Alien Contract Law, which represented the first broad legislation to apply restrictions on European immigrants, supports the conclusion that labor's restrictive concerns cannot be dismissed as being motivated only by racial bias. There were legitimate economic reasons for labor to seek political recourse to end what workers viewed as an artificial means to stimulate a rate of immigration which would not have otherwise occurred.

As for the relationship of mass immigration to union membership, Tables 3.3 and 3.4 again show the seesaw effect: as the foreign-born percentage of the population rose, the percentage of the nonagricultural labor force belonging to unions fell. To be sure, there were other causative factors, and there were significant fluctuations in membership between the decade markers used in the tables. For instance, the Knights' membership did briefly spike at over 700,000 in early 1886, but it rose to that height almost as fast as it collapsed shortly thereafter. Thus explained, such brief exceptions tend to prove the general rule; they do not contradict it.

The "Third Wave" of Mass Immigration: Unionism Strives to Survive (1891–1920)

The Setting

Between 1891 and 1920 the United States moved from being a nation of minor economic and political consequence to becoming one of significance. Domestically, the period was marked by the ascendancy of corporate domination of the business sector; manufacturing became the largest employment sector; the internal combustion engine revolutionized the transportation industry and accelerated the development of the petroleum industry; homes and industry began to be electrified; the steel business, which had been a localized collection of independent firms, was regionally and administratively consolidated through mergers to become the nation's first truly large-scale manufacturing industry; and the assembly-line method of mass production was introduced in the automobile industry. Internationally, the era witnessed the entry of the nation into World War I on the side of the subsequently victorious Allied forces in Europe.

The economic accomplishments were fostered in part by a prolonged period of pro-business legislation by the federal government, which was itself dominated and influenced by corporate interests. Tariff policy was one example of this symbiotic relationship. Tariffs had been high since the Civil War, but the McKinley Tariff Act, passed in 1890 and signed by the Republican president, Benjamin Harrison, represented protectionism run wild. Not only were rates on existing imports raised to historic heights, but the list of covered products was greatly enlarged. A populist reaction to this initiative led to the defeat of Harrison in 1892 and the election of the Democratic candidate, Grover Cleveland. Almost immediately after he assumed office in 1893, the economy fell into a deep depression. The subsequent effort to reduce the prevailing tariffs, which had been promised by the Democrats in the election campaign, proved to be a fiasco. The Wilson-Gorman Tariff Act of 1894, originally intended to cut tariffs, was so loaded with new protection measures added by Democratic congressmen from industrial states that the slight reductions authorized on some goods were more than offset by the new tariffs imposed on other goods. Outraged by what his own party had done but lacking the votes to sustain a veto, President Cleveland allowed the bill to become law without his signature.

In 1896, Republican William McKinley was elected president, and the following year the Dingley Tariff Act raised tariffs to even new heights. Its passage assured that American industry could continue to develop without the fear of foreign competition in the domestic marketplace. After a Democrat, Woodrow Wilson, was elected president in 1912, tariffs were briefly reduced by the 1913 Underwood Tariff Act. But with the outbreak of war in Europe in 1914, there was scant opportunity for foreign imports to make inroads into the American economy. And after the war, when Republicans again captured the White House in 1921 with the election of Warren Harding, higher tariffs were reinstated quickly by emergency legislation in 1921 and formally by the Fordney-McCumber Act of 1922.

Even more indicative of the nature of the times was the spread of anti-competitive practices. With government showing little inclination to regulate business, the free competition that resulted meant there would be virtually unrestricted economic opportunity. As a consequence, the business sector itself began to look for ways to control competition for its own self-interest. As the scale of production increased, corporations began to replace proprietorships and partnerships as the preferred form of business organization. By one means or another, firms merged to form bigger enterprises so that "by the late 1890s," wrote Robert Patton, "combination became a positive rage."[1] Mergers were one way to reduce the number of competitors, to restrict production, and to raise prices. The larger the size of enterprises, the more difficult it was for newcomers to enter their industries. These large businesses, in turn, began to look for ways to avoid overproduction and any cutthroat price competition that might result. These concerns led to the spread of price-fixing agreements, interlocking corporate directorates of supposed competitors, price maintenance agreements, and price discrimination tactics. Free competition, therefore, did not lead to freer competition. Rather, it fostered oligopoly, with all its countercompetitive tendencies.

In the wake of public outcries against these business practices, the Sherman Antitrust Act was passed in 1890. It was a short piece of legislation simply stating that "every contract, combination in the form of trust . . . or conspiracy, in restraint of trade or commerce . . . is hereby declared to be illegal."[2] There was scant elaboration of its terms. It did set forth serious penalties for violations, but President Harrison did not instruct the Department of Justice to take the law seriously, nor did his immediate successors, Grover Cleveland and William McKinley. Ironically, the first attempt to apply the law was made not against a corporation but against the activities of a union in 1895—even though no congressional deliberations preceding the passage of this act had ever implied that it was intended to regulate union activity.

Not until 1901, during the presidency of Theodore Roosevelt, was the law seriously applied to regulate corporate conduct. He believed that because it was impossible to return to the earlier competitive situations, before industrialization began, it was a necessary for government to regulate business conduct, and forty-three antitrust suits were filed during his administration. In 1914 the Clayton Antitrust Act, supported by the Wilson administration, added new restrictions against corporate mergers and anticompetitive pricing practices.

In the labor market, however, competition was allowed to flourish with virtually no restrictions. Following the end of the depression of 1893–97, the third wave of mass immigration rapidly accelerated and swelled the labor supply. In absolute numbers, it quickly exceeded the inflow of immigrants of the two earlier waves and continued at record levels until the outbreak of World War I interrupted the process in 1914. Still, real wages increased—mostly because of productivity improvements—throughout most of the 1897 to 1920 period, though at a very moderate rate of about one-half of 1 percent (0.5 percent) a year. But for workers and their families, the more important measure was family income. Since wage levels were low to begin with and frequent spells of unemployment interrupted income streams, labor economists Harry Millis and Royal Montgomery found that "probably three-fourths of the adult male wage earners did not earn enough prior to the war to support standard families at a minimum level and many did not earn enough to maintain families at the poverty level."[3]

Once the war broke out in Europe and immigration flows were reduced, there were slight improvements in real wages and family incomes between 1914 and 1920, but as Millis and Montgomery cautioned, "the difference was only one of degree—and certainly not a great degree."[4] The fact remained that the majority of American families in 1920 lived in poverty and many more just barely above its threshold. Most urban workers lived in crowded urban slums that lacked adequate sanitation and minimal public health services; disease spread easily, fires were frequent, and general lawlessness prevailed.[5]

At the workplace, conditions were not only bad but often perilous. The standard workday in most enterprises regularly exceeded ten hours. The Minnesota state legislature adopted a law in 1890 forbidding railroad companies to require more than eighteen hours a day of their workers.[6] In the steel industry the practice was to employ two shifts, each working twelve hours a day, seven days a week. Every two weeks the shifts switched, giving one a day off while the other worked the infamous twenty-four hour shift. Not until 1923 did the industry end this practice by scheduling three eight-hour shifts.[7]

In addition to the long hours, there was little concern for the health or safety of workers. The introduction of mechanized work (both in factories and on farms) dramatically increased the hazards, and with the advent of the assembly line in 1914 came an increase in the pace of the work. But the dangers were not just machine-related. In 1906, Upton Sinclair shocked the nation with his account of the appalling lack of concern for worker welfare and consumer health in the meatpacking industry caused by dangerous and unhygienic working conditions.[8] Every industry had its unique perils: cave-ins, explosions, lead poisoning, moving vehicles, hand-coupling of railroad cars, overhead cranes.

The problem of unhealthy and unsafe conditions was especially acute in the garment industry, which employed mostly women and children, many of whom were immigrants. They worked in factories often located in tenement buildings, and in 1911 the nation was shocked when a fire at one such sweatshop, the Triangle Shirtwaist Company, trapped and killed 148 women workers.

Since there were few safety records kept in these years to document the industrial accident rate, however, only fragments of information are available. In 1907, for instance, 4,534 workers were killed in the railroad industry alone, and another 2,534 in bituminous coal mining. The nation's occupational death toll in 1908 is estimated at 30,000 to 35,000 workers; in addition, 2 million job-related disabilities lasted three days or more. At that time the total labor force averaged about 28 million workers.

The U.S. economy was in another recession in 1914 when World War I began in the Balkans. As the fighting spread during that summer, immigration from Europe rapidly declined, since people could no longer leave. In the spring of 1917 the United States entered the war; the military draft was reintroduced, and 4 million men were called to service. The hard lessons of the past had taught the nation that wars cannot be fought unless there are government controls on production and prices in the private sector; hence, the easygoing ways of the unfettered free market that had reigned supreme since the nation began to industrialize had to be suspended. The War Industries Board was established by the federal government to coordinate the industrial activity needed for war production, to reduce civilian production, and to eliminate duplication and waste. The antitrust laws were put aside. Private businesses were asked to comply voluntarily with the directives of the board or be compelled to do so if they resisted. Scarce resources were shifted from consumer to military production. There was no general fixing of retail prices but controls were imposed on basic materials and, for short periods, on certain retail prices. Conservation of food and fuel by consumers was stressed by government leaders and hoarding of food was made a punishable crime. Fuel prices were fixed. Labor-management disputes were to be settled by mediation and arbitration, not by strikes. Union membership almost doubled from 1914 to 1920.

Against this background of government control and economic planning, capacity to produce was dramatically enlarged, and output soared to levels never before imagined. Ironically, much of the actual military production was never used. By the time the economy had tooled up to fight, the War came to an abrupt end in November 1918 when Germany's leaders unexpectedly agreed to an armistice. With no plans in place on the home front for how to demobilize the economy, the readjustment to free market conditions became chaotic. Shortages of consumer goods quickly fostered inflationary pressures. In response, there was widespread labor strife in 1919. Furthermore, there were signs that mass migrations of people from the devastated regions of Europe to the United States was about to recommence. But this time, there was a new policy response.

The Labor Force and Industrial Employment Patterns

Between 1890 and 1920 the nation's labor force grew from 23.3 million to 41.6 million workers (see Tables 3.1 and 4.1). Over this thirty-year interval, manufacturing surpassed agriculture to become the nation's single largest employment sector. Agriculture, which had been de-

Table 4.1. The Labor Force and Nonfarm Employment by Industry, 1900–1920 (in thousands)

Year	Civilian Labor Force (14 years and up)[a]	Mining	Construction	Manufacturing	Transport and Utilities	Trade	Finance	Service	Government
1900	28,376	637	1,147	5,648	2,282	2,502	308	1,740	1,094
1910	36,709	1,068	1,342	7,828	3,366	3,370	483	2,410	1,630
1920	41,340	1,108	805	10,702	4,317	4,012	902	3,100	2,371

Source: Stanley Lebergott, *Manpower in Economic Growth: The American Record since 1800* (New York: McGraw-Hill, 1964), tables A-3 and A-5. Copyright 1964 by McGraw-Hill Inc. Reprinted by permission of the publisher.

Note: The data for 1890 (cited in Table 3.1) are omitted here because slightly different definitions of categories were adopted in 1900. The Civilian Labor Force data are given for comparison only. They are taken from a different source than the nonagricultural employment data.

[a]The civilian labor force numbers were estimated by methods different than the nonagricultural employment numbers.

Table 4.2. Employment in Agriculture, 1890–1920 (in thousands)

Year	Employment in Agriculture (14 years and up)
1890	9,960
1900	11,050
1910	11,260
1920	10,440

Source: Stanley Lebergott, Manpower in Economic Growth (New York: McGraw-Hill, 1964) tables A-1 and A-6.

clining in relative terms for over a century, peaked in absolute numbers in 1907 with 11.4 million workers (see Table 4.2). With only a few exceptions, the number of agricultural workers has steadily decreased ever since. Between 1890 and 1920, manufacturing employment increased by 128 percent. It was spurred by the development of new industries such as automobile manufacturing and its complementary industries of rubber, steel, and petroleum. Their growth led in turn to major expansion in mining, where employment soared by 168 percent over this time span.

Overwhelmingly, the occupations in the industries that grew the most were those requiring unskilled, blue-collar workers. There was no particular need to be English-speaking or educated or skilled to meet hiring standards. In large numbers, laborers and operatives were needed to do primarily manual work, and these were what the third wave of immigrants provided. As immigration scholar Peter Roberts wrote in 1913, "We may yearn for a more intelligent and better trained worker from the countries of Europe but it is questionable whether or not that type of man would have been so well fitted for the work America had to offer."[10] As for human capital, as late as 1917 less than 6 percent of the adult male workforce had graduated from high school. In fact, most of the native-born labor force, like most of the immigrants, lacked formal education or skills, which implies that the two groups were similar in the qualifications they had for jobs; they were competitors. As the noted authority on immigration Oscar Handlin would conclude, "it was the unique quality" of the third-wave immigrants "that the people who moved here entered the life of the United States at a status equal to that of the older residents."[11] Such congruency between the native-born and the foreign-born at the time of their entry has never again existed since these pre–World War I years.

There was, of course, an alternative source of unskilled native-born workers who could have been recruited to fill many of these new jobs. The vast number of workers living in rural areas, mostly in poverty, were lacking in human capital endowments, but for the types of jobs that were being created they were certainly as qualified as most of the immigrants who became the chosen alternative. Many were white, but the most obvious group was the black population still trapped in the rural South since being freed from slavery (92 percent of the blacks living in the South in 1910, essentially the same percentage as on the eve of the Civil War fifty years earlier). Indeed the famed black scholar of the era, Booker T. Washington, had made this issue the central theme of his famous speech at the Atlanta Exposition of 1895. He pleaded with the assembled industrialists not to look "to the incoming of those of foreign birth and strange tongue and habits" but, instead, to turn to native-born blacks "who shall stand with you with a devotion that no foreigner can approach"; by "interlacing our industrial, commercial, civil, and religious life with yours . . . [we] shall make the interests of both races one."[12] His words, though cheered at the time, were ignored. Not until immigration was cut off during World War I were the rural poor—blacks in particular—free to fill the new occupations being created in the urban North and West.

Immigration

Following the entry of more than 5 million immigrants in the 1880s, the third wave began at a slower pace. As shown in Table 4.3, immigration for the 1890s totaled slightly over 3.6 million persons. The retarding factor was the prolonged economic recession of the mid-1890s. When a recovery began in 1897, mass immigration quickly resumed, and record annual arrivals occurred until 1914. In 1905, 1906, 1907, 1910, 1913, and 1914 more than a million immigrants entered the country each year (not until the year 1989 would legal entrants again top the million mark). Mass immigration briefly revived after World War I, in 1919–20, but came to an end in 1921 as the result of the passage of legislation that set the first ceiling on immigration from the Eastern Hemisphere in the nation's history.

Not all of the third-wave newcomers stayed; in fact, it is roughly estimated that almost one-third subsequently returned to their homelands. As the number of male immigrants exceeded the number of females by more than a 2-to-1 margin, it is likely that this was the actual intention of many men who had left their families and relatives behind; they were known as "birds of passage" because their stay in the United States seemed a temporary phenomenon. Then there were those who originally planned to stay but left because they could not adjust to the harshness of the life they encountered. And some were deported for criminal activity

Table 4.3. Immigration to the United States, 1891–1920

1891–1901	**3,687,564**
1891	560,319
1892	579,663
1893	439,730
1894	285,631
1895	258,536
1896	343,267
1897	230,832
1898	229,229
1899	311,715
1900	448,572
1901–1910	**8,795,386**
1901	487,918
1902	648,743
1903	857,046
1904	812,870
1905	1,026,499
1906	1,100,735
1907	1,285,349
1908	782,870
1909	751,786
1910	1,041,570
1911–1910	**5,735,811**
1911	878,587
1912	838,172
1913	1,197,892
1914	1,218,480
1915	326,700
1916	298,826
1917	295,403
1918	110,618
1919	141,132
1920	430,001

Source: U.S. Immigration and Naturalization Service.

or other violations of the immigration restrictions imposed in the 1890s, which during this period were enforced for the first time.[13]

The third wave was also distinguished by the shift in the immigrants' countries of origin. Before 1890, 85 percent of all free immigrants since the country was founded had come from western and northern Europe. That is, most were drawn from the same general regions of Europe as were the people who arrived during the colonial period. Beginning in the 1890s, however, the number of immigrants from those countries declined sharply, while the number from eastern and southern Europe increased dramatically. In 1896, for the first time, immigration from eastern and southern Europe exceeded that from western and northern Europe. Over the ensuing years the gap quickly widened until, in 1910, 70 percent of all immigrants to the United States that year came from the former region and only 20 percent from the latter.[14]

The largest number of the new immigrants came from Italy, followed collectively in only slightly lower numbers by those from the Slavic-speaking nations of Poland, Czechoslovakia, Hungary, Croatia, Romania, Russia, the Ukraine, and Slovenia. Additional east European immigrants came from Greece and Austria. Most of these were not Protestants but Roman Catholics, Orthodox Christians, or Jews. Also unlike the earlier waves of immigrants, most of these were from rural areas where they had usually been peasant farmers. Many were illiterate even in their own languages, not to mention in English. Typically, they had known only impoverished living standards, and had had no previous experiences with democracy, regarding government largely as an oppressive force. Most of them settled in the cities of the Northeast and the Great Lakes area of the Midwest.

Meanwhile, a new source of immigrants developed in the West: Japan. It was not until 1884 that the Japanese government permitted its citizens to work in foreign lands—the same year that the United States and Japan established formal diplomatic relations. It was also in 1884 that sugarcane growers in Hawaii (who were mostly U.S. citizens, though Hawaii itself was still an independent monarchy) initiated efforts to recruit Japanese workers for their plantations. In relatively short order a large number of Japanese workers were employed in Hawaii, so many that as their numbers increased, the United States feared Japan would take control of the island chain. Following a coup d'etat led by Americans which overthrew the monarchy in 1893, the United States unilaterally annexed the islands in 1898 and made it a U.S. territory in 1900. In the wake of these changes, Japanese workers on Hawaii began to migrate to the West Coast of the U.S. mainland in large numbers.

The occupational backgrounds of the Japanese immigrants in this period resembled that of the new European immigrants of the third wave in that both groups were from agricultural heritages. The Japanese too were typically illiterate in their own language, knew virtually no English, and had little experience with democracy. Unlike the European immigrants, though, who typically entered the urban labor market, most of the Japanese sought employment in the agricultural and food-packing sectors in California and a few other western states. Some found jobs as laborers on the railroads or in construction or mining. Relatively few worked in manufacturing. Japanese immigration came to an abrupt halt in 1908, however, as the result of a diplomatic agreement between the governments of Japan and the United States.

It was also in the 1890s and the early 1900s that immigrants from Korea first appeared on the West Coast. They too had often initially worked in the Hawaiian agricultural sector before migrating to the U.S. mainland. But Korean immigration came to a quick halt in 1905 when Japan invaded Korea, made it a protectorate for the next forty years, and prohibited emigration.

The Philippines, ceded to the United States in 1898 in the aftermath of the Spanish-American War, were another significant source of Asian immigrants to the West Coast. Immigration from these islands began during this era but it did not become numerous until the 1920s. Filipinos tended to concentrate in the agricultural sector of the California economy. But their immigration was also abruptly ended as a consequence of legislative restriction in 1934.

The last group to enter the United States in significant numbers during this period were immigrants from Mexico. As mentioned in Chapter 2, the United States acquired the region now known as the Southwest in 1848. In the process, it also acquired about 75 thousand persons of Mexican heritage and the 250 thousand Indians were also living in this territory. The Indians, as Carey McWilliams has written, are "the forgotten link in Anglo-Hispanic cultural relations in the Southwest" because they were "the real masters of the Southwest in 1848."[15] Throughout the remainder of the nineteenth century, there was very little immigration from Mexico into this vast region. But beginning in 1909 and over the ensuing decade there was a mass migration to the Southwest as a consequence of a violent civil war in Mexico. The extent of violence can be measured by the estimate of 1 million people killed of a total Mexican population of about 15 million, and many more were injured and maimed. As a consequence, 250 thousand Mexicans officially immigrated to the United States between 1910 and 1920; countless more unofficially crossed the essentially unpatrolled southern border. Most of these were also from agricultural backgrounds, and it was in the agricultural sector of the American Southwest where most sought work. Indeed, it was precisely at this same time that southwestern agriculture was expanding rapidly, thanks to the completion of an extensive system of government-supported irrigation projects in California and South Texas which opened vast areas in both states to the production of specialty crops (e.g., citrus fruits, grapes, lettuce) by private interests. Other Mexicans found construction and maintenance work on the railroads that were spreading throughout the region, or in mining. Although most of this early wave of Mexican immigrants settled in the Southwest, a significant number settled in Chicago as well.

Policy Enforcement: A Critical Digression

As the scale and importance of immigration mounted, significant changes were made in the administration of immigration policy. Until 1891, implementation of federal policy was left to state governments. The Immigration Act of 1891 represented the first comprehensive national law intended to control immigration.[16] It ended state government involvement in the design and enforcement of immigration policy. The Bureau of Immigration was established within the Department of the Treasury and took over the functions previously performed by state agencies at seaports. What would become the largest and most famous of the immigrant processing centers—Ellis Island, located in the harbor of New York City—was opened in 1891. More than two-thirds of all third-wave immigrants entered through this single center. The 1891 legislation also provided for regulation of overland immigration from Canada and Mexico, and it created several categories of exclusions: persons likely to become public charges, persons with contagious diseases, polygamists, and persons convicted of certain crimes. It also forbade the encouragement of immigration by advertisement and provided for the deportation of any alien who entered the country illegally. In 1892 the U.S. Supreme Court upheld the law and the federal government's exclusive preemption of immigration policy.[17]

Policy Administration

In 1903 the Bureau of Immigration was shifted to the newly established Department of Commerce and Labor, and the commissioner who headed the bureau was granted authority over all immigration matters. This administrative shift was implicit recognition by Congress that immigration was primarily a labor issue. Over the next few years the commissioner expressed concern over the concentration of immigrants in New York and Pennsylvania and concluded that it would be better if they were more geographically dispersed. He also warned that illegal immigration across the Mexican border was becoming an increasingly serious issue.[18]

Because of mounting concerns about fraud and carelessness in the state courts that still retained control over naturalization, the Bureau of Immigration and Naturalization (BIN) was created in 1906. The state courts still had the power to grant naturalization, but uniform national requirements were established, and all records had to be submitted to the new federal agency. Then, in March 1913, BIN was shifted to the newly created Department of Labor, and its dual functions split into two separate bureaus: one for immigration and one for naturalization. This administrative change underscored the belief among policymakers that immigration was a labor issue and that the formulation and administration of immigration policy should recognize this reality. The first Secretary of Labor was William B. Wilson, a former member of the Knights of Labor and an official of the United Mine Workers prior to his appointment to the cabinet position by President Wilson. Responsibility for immigration matters remained in the Department of Labor until it was "temporarily" shifted to the Department of Justice in 1940 for national security reasons associated with the onset of World War II.

Of passing interest is the fact that Terrence Powderly, the longtime leader of the Knights of Labor, had been appointed Commissioner of Immigration by President McKinley in 1897. He remained in that office until 1902 when, after trying in vain to wipe out the pervasive corruption that plagued the administration of affairs on Ellis Island, Powderly was dismissed by President Theodore Roosevelt. Later, Roosevelt realized that he had unintentionally made a serious mistake, for corruption was a real issue on Ellis Island. In an effort to make amends in 1907 he appointed Powderly chief of the Division of Information in the Bureau of Immigration, where he remained until 1921, when he was made a member of the bureau's Board of Review until his death in 1924.[19]

Unionism

A Focus on Craft Unions

Entering the 1890s, the leadership of the newly formed American Federation of Labor was confident it had developed a successful formula for organizing workers in the unique American setting. The AFL became a voluntary association of national craft unions. Each national union's exclusive jurisdiction entitled it to the sole right to organize the workers in that craft. Each union was also autonomous in that it alone had the authority to determine what bargaining objectives were in the best interest of its members. These objectives were primarily economic in nature, having to do with wages, hours, and working conditions in that craft. The goal was to secure short-run improvements through direct negotiations with employers rather than to seek long-run political reforms to uplift workers by legislation.

Each union's prestige and strength were derived primarily through its control over the supply of labor and, consequently, its power vis-à-vis employers. The AFL itself was not a union and therefore could exercise little direct power over the actions of individual national unions. Its primary roles were to mediate jurisdictional disputes between the member unions and to serve as a collective voice for the workers with respect to general labor interests (e.g., immigration). The federation could also form local unions in industries where no national union had clear jurisdiction, and such "federal locals," as they were called, could eventually be molded into new national unions.

The focus on crafts, of course, meant that relatively little attention was paid to organizing unskilled and semiskilled workers in broad-based industries. This does not mean that there was *no* interest in such workers. Indeed, the United Mine Workers, which joined the AFL shortly after its founding in 1890, was an industrial organization of largely unskilled workers, many of whom were immigrants. The UMW was able to organize these men through diligent efforts and because the mines were typically located in isolated rural settings where it was more difficult for employers to tap into alternative sources of labor—although many tried—when organizing ventures or strikes occurred. Typically, however, the AFL believed that if industrial workers were to be organized, they should be divided into separate groups that resembled, as much as possible, existing crafts. But since such organizing efforts were costly, duplicative, and extremely inefficient, most industrial workers were left unorganized during these years.

The AFL also felt that the American environment was not conducive to the formation of a labor party. American workers were less class conscious than workers in European countries because there had been no tradition of feudalism, and white male workers had been given the right to vote very early in the nation's history. Samuel Gompers believed as well that American workers were disillusioned with party politics and had little faith that the political system itself could be a vehicle for improving the welfare of workers, especially at a time when conservative court rulings greatly limited the power of the federal government to address social issues. During these formative years, however, there was a vocal minority of workers in a number of unions who were socialists and who vigorously protested the "no politics" position of the AFL.

The optimism of union leaders in the early 1890s was quickly shattered with the onset of an economic recession that quickly worsened to become a deep depression in 1893. Prices of stocks, products, and commodities collapsed, as did wages. Unemployment had skyrocketed to over 18 percent by 1894 and remained in the double-digit range for most of the remainder of the decade. The average nonfarm workday increased from ten to eleven hours. A wave of strikes occurred, usually broken by employers who had the support of the local police, state militia, and even federal troops. The availability and frequent use of immigrant strikebreakers in these disputes greatly exacerbated tensions in numerous communities. Yet for the wealthy it was a period of unprecedented opulence. Thorstein Veblen forever immortalized their lifestyles with his famous description of the "conspicuous consumption" of these wealthy members of what he called the "leisure class."[20]

The Homestead Strike

During the spring of 1892, one of the most famous strikes in American labor history occurred at the Carnegie Steel Corporation in Homestead, Pennsylvania.[21] At the time, the skilled workers in the industry were represented by the Amalgamated Association of Iron and Steel Workers. Concentrated largely in western Pennsylvania, the union comprised about 24,000 workers in different companies. In membership size it was the largest union affiliated with the AFL. True to the AFL's organizational features, it represented only the skilled workers (about 20 percent of the employees) at Carnegie. To staff the more numerous unskilled jobs, the steel industry "was among the first to inaugurate deliberately the practice of importing cheap labor in order to maintain low wages and thereby assuring a surplus of workers."[22] The AFL had been protesting such hiring practices by steel companies, including Carnegie, before the strike occurred, believing that these immigrant recruiting activities were blatant violations of the Alien Contract Law of 1885.

When its existing contract expired in 1892, the Iron and Steel Workers' union offered a proposal to maintain the wage rates of most of its members at prevailing levels. The company responded with a decision that it would no longer bargain with the union and it started firing union members. The strike that resulted became violent when the company sought to import strike-breakers. At least thirty-five men were killed and more than four hundred injured in the ensuing gun battle and general fighting. The state militia was called in, the strike was broken, and to all intents and purposes the union was destroyed (although it did linger on for a number of years). A few weeks later a Russian immigrant and anarchist (not associated with the union) attempted to assassinate the manager of the facility, Henry Frick. He was seriously wounded but able to fight off his assailant and became a folk hero as a consequence.

The Pullman Strike

The second historic defeat for organized labor came in 1894 when a strike occurred at the Pullman Palace Car company in Chicago.[23] Unlike workers at most other manufacturing enterprises, the employees at Pullman were required to live in a company-owned town, to purchase utility services from the company, and to shop at company stores. With the onset of the depression in 1893, workers were laid off and wages were slashed, but rents and prices at the company-owned facilities remained constant—as did dividends to the stockholders.

The Pullman workers were represented by the new American Railway Union (ARU), led by Eugene Debs. He had bucked the tide of craft unionism by organizing railroad workers into a single industrial union. Nationwide, his independent union had 154,000 members at the time. After the Pullman workers went on strike, the company closed the plant and laid off the entire workforce. When the ARU responded with a boycott of all Pullman cars used on western railroads, all operations in the region came to a halt. As the strike spread, strikebreakers were hired, and violence soon ensued. In Chicago, where violence turned into rioting, the railroads requested that President Cleveland send in federal troops to restore order, and he complied—over the protest of the governor of Illinois, John Peter Altgeld, who claimed he could control the situation.

The railroads also sought an injunction from a federal court forbidding any person to induce any railroad employee to refrain from performing his duties. When Debs defied the injunction by convening a conference of labor leaders to consider calling a nationwide general strike, he was charged with contempt of court and was jailed. The strike was broken and the union soon disbanded. Debs's conviction was subsequently upheld by the U.S. Supreme Court in 1895, even though the grounds for issuing the original injunction were not clear. The railroads contended that the actions of the union were a conspiracy to restrain trade and therefore violated the recently enacted Sherman Antitrust Act. The Court did not rule on this point; rather, since there had been violence associated with the strike, the Court upheld the issuance of the injunction as a means of forestalling additional irreparable damage to persons and property—a traditional justification for such an issuance. Debs served six months in jail and, upon his release, abandoned his belief in the prospect that unions and collective bargaining could improve workers' economic welfare. Instead, he turned his attention to political action and the pursuit of democratic socialism as the only hope for American workers.[24]

Radical Unionism

Meanwhile, in the Rocky Mountain area of the West (from Montana to the Arizona Territory), where life was hard and rugged differences were usually settled by violence, union organizing efforts took a turn toward radicalism. Unlike the miners in the East, whose ranks contained many immigrants who could be pressured by employer intimidation, the western miners were typically native-born workers and far more individualistic. Many had come to the mountains to find a personal fortune but, failing to do so, had to take jobs to survive. The mine owners were much the same breed of men in their attitudes and actions, and even the small number of immigrants who came to this region in this era tended to be ethnically homogeneous; most were from the British Isles and Scandinavia, and a high proportion had become formally naturalized citizens; hence, they were not typical of the other third wave of immigrants.[25] And in these isolated mining communities, then, there was virtually no middle class to moderate the stark class differences between mine owners and their workers.

In 1892 the first of a lengthy series of violent clashes broke out at the mines in Coeur d'Alene, Idaho.[26] It was only quashed by the introduction of federal troops and the imposition of martial law. From this group of defeated miners was formed the Western Federation of Miners (WFM) in 1893. It was intended to be an industrial union for all who worked in the western mines, regardless of their skills; it joined the AFL in 1896 but withdrew its membership the following year. All the while, throughout the Colorado mining region the WFM was losing a series of strikes usually quelled by the state militia. In 1898 the WFM changed its name to the Western Labor Union (WLU) and assumed a more militant political stance. In 1900 it endorsed socialist candidates for office and pressed for political reforms through legislation. It claimed that the AFL approach of favoring craft unions and bargaining with individual employers was obsolete in the wake of the growth of industrialism. In 1902 the WLU changed its name once more, to the American Labor Union (ALU) and formally accepted socialism as its goal and industrial unionism as the proper means of organizing workers.

Recognizing that it needed to broaden its base, the ALU was instrumental in convening of a national conference of other dissident groups favoring class struggle. Out of this famous meeting, held in Chicago in 1905, came the formation of the Industrial Workers of the World (IWW), the most profound example of grassroots radicalism that the United

States has ever produced.[27] Led by "Big Bill" Haywood, a former miner from Utah, the IWW favored direct economic action (e.g., sit-down strikes at plant sites, chain picketing, sabotage on the job) as opposed to political reforms from government (which it felt would always be controlled by corporate influences). Worker control and ownership (i.e., syndicalism) of enterprises was its ultimate economic objective.

From its beginning, though, the IWW was beset by internal dissension, bitter opposition from the AFL leadership, and severe legal and physical assault from both employers and government. Nonetheless, through its organizing efforts it publicized to the nation the appalling conditions in which the numerous unskilled workers of the nation toiled in its factories, fields, forests, mines, and on its docks. It demonstrated the imperative to organize the workers who were largely ignored by the AFL.

Most of its organizing efforts were unsuccessful, but in 1912 the IWW won its greatest victory in a strike that was a complete anomaly. It occurred not in the West or in the mines, or among the native-born workers who were supposedly its strength. Rather, it happened in the East, in the textile industry in Lawrence, Massachusetts.[28] And it was also the first time that a large number of immigrant, mostly female, workers followed radical leadership. The public revelations of their squalid and oppressive working conditions, as well as the notoriety given to the brutality used by business leaders and the local police to break their strike, forced the companies ultimately to accede to all the union's demands and even led Congress to hold public hearings on the atrocious working conditions that prevailed in the industry. The wife of President William Howard Taft attended these hearings as a way to indicate support for workplace reforms.

The days of IWW influence came to an abrupt end when it openly opposed the country's preparation for entry into World War I. When several strikes by its members occurred in the copper mines of Montana and Arizona as well as in the lumber industry in Washington state, the IWW was labeled "pro-German" and therefore subversive. In the spring of 1917 its offices were raided by the federal government and most of its leaders arrested, charged with interfering with the war effort. They were subsequently found guilty and imprisoned, except for Haywood and eight others who jumped their bail and fled to the Soviet Union. Although the IWW was later active during the Great Depression of the 1930s and still lingers on, largely as an empty-shell organization, this brief period of radicalism of American labor essentially ended in the World War I era. At its peak, the IWW probably had no more than 20,000 members but many times that number sympathized with its goals, and its efforts did lay the initial groundwork for the later organization of industrial workers.[29]

Industrial Unionism

Despite the failure of the IWW to spread the concept of industrial unionism, important steps were being made in this direction by some of the unions affiliated with the AFL. In 1900 the International Ladies Garment Workers Union (ILGWU) was founded in New York City and received an AFL membership charter that same year. It became firmly entrenched in the industry in 1909 as the result of a strike in which the women workers gained widespread public support, thanks to the revelations of the deplorable conditions, poor pay, and long hours under which they toiled, as well as of the abusive tactics used by police and company guards to break their organizing efforts. The ILGWU had been founded because the original AFL union in the industry, the United Garment Workers (UGW), had been led by native-born workers who had little sympathy for the immigrants who had come to dominate the industry's workforce by the turn of the twentieth century. In particular, the UGW leaders were fearful of the socialistic leaning of many of the Jewish immigrants who they felt were more interested in long-run political action than in bargaining with employers for short-run economic gains.[30]

A similar organization led by immigrants evolved at roughly the same time in the men's branch of the clothing industry, and it too grew out of an internal fight with the United Garment Workers. In 1910 and 1912 there were strikes in the garment industry in New York and Chicago, led by immigrant workers in protest against wage cuts and employer refusals to recognize their union. In both these instances the union leadership reached settlements with the employers, only to have them rejected by the rank-and-file workers. The internal conflict was carried over to the union's 1914 convention and then to a lengthy court fight between the insurgents and UGW's leaders. When the old guard of the UGW finally won control of the union, the insurgents bolted and established a new union, the Amalgamated Clothing Workers of America (ACWA). Under the leadership of Sidney Hillman, a Lithuanian immigrant, the ACWA quickly overshadowed the older UGW in both size and importance. But because the union was established by dissidents, not until 1934 could it affiliate with the AFL and Hillman become recognized as a national labor leader.

Similarly, the United Brewery Workers—centered in Milwaukee, Wisconsin, founded in 1886, and a member of the AFL—was another successful example of an industrial union in this era. Its success stemmed from the fact that the union stressed cooperation between skilled and unskilled workers. Although many of its members were immigrants, they were overwhelmingly from one country—Germany—and their common heritage served to unite rather than to divide them. It was also very easy for the labor movement to boycott nonunion beer and thus strengthen the union's bargaining hand.

But except for the United Mine Workers, the two garment unions, and the brewery union, there was very little organization of unskilled and semiskilled industrial workers, despite the fact that their numbers were soaring in these early decades of the twentieth century. The relative success of those four were most probably due to the special circumstances that existed in each of these industries. The main reason for the failure of efforts to create other industrial unions was the ease with which employers could recruit strikebreakers—many of whom were new immigrants—as replacements.

The AFL Experience

The AFL unions sustained a brief period of growth between 1897 and 1905, when membership in the AFL totaled close to 1.6 million. Many workers had concluded that the rapid industrialization of the economy during these years was bringing poverty to the masses of the population and wealth and power to only a privileged few. Unionism seemed to be the only way for workers to challenge this polarizing trend. But with the outbreak of sustained violence in the western mining region, the growth of socialist political parties and memberships in many parts of the nation, and the formation of the IWW, opposition by employers to all forms of unionism intensified after 1905. Most employers viewed the AFL unions with equal disdain and fear. A number of employer associations—such as the National Association of Manufacturers and the U.S. Chamber of Commerce—were formed during the period for the express purpose of fighting unionism.

During the following ten years, AFL unions called very few strikes. Instead, they relied extensively on the use of the union label and the consumer boycott to press their organization objectives. In 1906 the metal polishers went on strike against the Buck Stove Company in St. Louis. As the strike lingered on, the AFL placed the name of the company on its national boycott list. The company went to court, arguing that the boycott represented a form of restraint of trade that was a violation of the Sherman Antitrust Act, and secured an injunction. Gompers, in open defiance of the court, claimed that he had the right of free speech and the AFL had the free press rights to publicize the dispute. When he continued to advertise the boycott in the AFL's publication *the American Federationist,* he was indicted, found guilty of contempt of court, and sentenced to jail. Ultimately, the case was settled out of court, but Gompers had become convinced that the U.S. court system was stacked against all forms of unionism, not just radical unionism.

Concurrently, in 1908, another Supreme Court ruling involving a nationwide boycott (the products of the Danbury Hat Company in Connecticut) affirmed the earlier position: that the boycott was a conspiracy in restraint of trade and that an injunction could be issued to ban its implementation. Thus, organized labor was confronted with the most powerful antilabor weapon it had faced since the criminal conspiracy doctrine of a century earlier. If unions were subject to the antitrust acts, then they could do nothing to make employers recognize their existence or to bargain with them on behalf of their members.

As a consequence, the AFL concluded that it must make an exception to its "no politics" stance and seek legislative relief from the new use of court injunctions in labor disputes to protect intangible property: that is, the right to do business. Historically, under English common law, injunctions could be issued only to protect tangible property from what could possibly be irreparable damage. It was only to be used in such extraordinary circumstances. Gompers expressly noted that the same business organizations that opposed his efforts to seek legislative relief from the injunction were also those who opposed labor's simultaneous efforts to reduce the scale of immigration.[31] In 1912, Gompers and the AFL took an unprecedented step by announcing their opposition to the reelection efforts of the Republican candidate, William Howard Taft. He was labeled an "injunctionist judge" because in his earlier career he had issued injunctions in labor disputes as a judge in Ohio. Yet neither did the AFL endorse the Democratic candidate, Woodrow Wilson. Subsequently, when Wilson won the election, he said in his inaugural address that the nation needed to safeguard workers' lives, to improve their working conditions, and, most important, to give them the "freedom to act in their own interests."

The AFL rejoiced at these words and waited to see what they meant. In 1914 the Clayton Antitrust Act was passed, and labor's optimism appeared to be borne out. The act contained two relevant provisions. Section 6 stated that "the labor of a human being is not a commodity or article of commerce"; accordingly, nothing in the antitrust laws should be applied to the existence or operation of a labor union. Section 20, in turn, specifically stated that injunctions should not be issued in labor disputes unless necessary to prevent irreparable injury to physical property. The AFL hailed the legislation which it felt would now free it to renew its active organizing campaigns without judicial interference. But the Supreme Court had the final say and, in quick order, nullified the intent of both these provisions.[32] Thus, organized labor found itself right back where it was before he passage of the Clayton Act. Unions could exist, but virtually anything they did could be enjoined by an injunction.

In the ten years from 1906 to 1916, therefore, there were few labor victories, and the AFL had to fight hard simply to maintain its membership levels. By the eve of the entry of the United States into World War I, membership in the AFL unions was about 2 million and the total labor movement had about 2.7 million members (see Table 4.4). The war changed everything: with the military draft of men in effect, immigration from Asia and Europe cut off, and production demands accelerating, labor shortages quickly developed. President Wilson sought ways to avoid industrial conflict and to guarantee uninterrupted production of military goods. The most contentious issue prior to the war was the unwillingness of employers to recognize unions. This issue was muted for the time being by the principles set forth following the convening of the War Labor Conference of labor and business leaders. Among these principles were provisions for the recognition of unions by employers. To avoid strikes, however, arbitration would be required when disputes arose.

As war-related industries expanded in size and employment, so did union membership. By 1919 some 4 million workers belonged to unions, and the AFL, in particular, was once more confident that it had a bright future. But these hopes were quickly dashed, for not only did the government quickly reduce its military spending but all the temporary governmental interventions into the economy ended. Inflation of prices quickly ensued. Of 3,630 strikes in 1919, with major strikes occurring in the railroad, coal, and steel industries, most represented defeats for organized labor. Typically, the central issue was the refusal of the companies to recognize the unions as representatives of the workers.

The Steel Strike of 1919

The most disastrous defeat for organized labor in 1919 was in the steel industry. The industry giant by this time was the U.S. Steel Corporation, formed in 1901 through the mergers of several large competitors (including the Carnegie Steel Company that had been the subject of labor's last serious attempt to organize the steel business in 1892). The plan the AFL set forth to organize the industry did not to deviate from its existing principles: workers were to be divided into separate groups that most

Table 4.4. Union Membership of Nonagricultural Employed Labor Force, 1890–1920

Year	Union Membership (in thousands)	Percentage Unionized of Nonagricultural Employed Labor Force
1890	372	2.8
1897	455.4	3.6
1898	523.9	4.1
1899	680.7	4.9
1900	932.4	6.5
1901	1,184.40	7.8
1902	1,519.10	9.3
1903	1,930.00	11.4
1904	2,018.50	12
1905	1,947.10	10.8
1906	1,930.60	10.1
1907	2,060.10	10.5
1908	2,051.70	10.9
1909	1,994.90	9.9
1910	2,168.50	10.3
1911	2,333.90	10.9
1912	2,488.50	11.1
1913	2,665.60	11.7
1914	2,611.40	11.7
1915	2,597.60	11.5
1916	2,773.30	11.2
1917	3,090.40	12.1
1918	3,561.40	13.9
1919	4,259.20	15.7
1920	4,823.20	17.6

Sources: 1890: see Table 3.3; 1897–1920: Leo Troy and Neil Sheflin, *U.S. Union Sourcebook* (West Orange, N.J.: Industrial Relations Data and Information Sources, 1985), A-1.

closely resembled existing crafts, with two unions agreeing to pick up any residual workers. A coordinating committee was established, and ultimately, twenty-four different unions became involved.

Much of the initial impetus to launch the organizing campaign actually came from foreign-born workers who had arrived in the country before the outbreak of war in Europe in 1914.[33] They had been "Americanized" during the war years by various appeals to patriotism and national unity conducted by the government and industry, and they saw unionism as a logical exercise of the participatory democracy ideals that these national leaders had earlier espoused. Native-born workers soon joined the cause.

But once the war was over, the steel industry's management reverted to its historic posture of not recognizing unions. In response, workers throughout most of the industry walked out on strike in late September 1919. Numerous clashes between strikers, private guards, and local police occurred at various plant sites. Industry officials sought to link the strike with radicalism. The fact that immigrant workers had played an instrumental role in the organizing drive at U.S. Steel was directly linked to the charge of radicalism, the implication being, of course, that unionism was basically an anti-American idea that had been transported to the United States by immigrants.[34] William Z. Foster, designated by the AFL as secretary-treasurer of the steelworkers' organizing committee, fervently rejected this charge, stating that unions only "organize them [immigrants] after they get here, we don't bring them here." Furthermore, he pointed out that "American unions fought for over a third of a century to keep them out"; it was big business—especially steel industrialists—who pressed "to bring them in."[35]

Nevertheless, as the issue of radical influence came to dominate strike coverage, it destroyed any hope of a settlement. The focus shifted from the actual working conditions and the refusal of industry leaders to deal with unions to the refusal of the company to deal with radicals who, it was alleged, favored syndicalism or socialism. The charge also effectively neutralized any prospect that the federal government could intervene to help reach a settlement.[36] By late October 1919 the industry had begun to hire large numbers of strikebreakers (many were black workers who, while immigration was curtailed during the war years, had migrated to the North in large numbers to find jobs). As various plants re-opened and tactical and financial divisions occurred among the multiple unions involved, support for the strike began to deteriorate. In early January 1920 the strike was officially called off by union leaders; for all intents and purposes, it had been broken weeks earlier. It was a disastrous defeat for the labor movement. The AFL had tested its strength and lost. The only benefit for the workers who remained employed was that the negative publicity during the strike over the continued use of the twelve-hour workday in the industry did result in its reduction by management to eight hours a day in 1923.

As this period came to an end, then, so did the growth of unionism. In fact, the very future of the labor movement was once more in doubt. Yet for the first time, some major employers were questioning the efficacy of the "open door" immigration policy that they had long championed as a means of checking unionism.

Consequences

Like all previous efforts to establish an organized labor movement, the newly formed AFL was confronted immediately with the adverse effects of mass immigration. It is true, of course, that the AFL and other independent unions faced additional obstacles during these years, stemming from the overtly antiunion tactics employed by both business and government. But it was the essentially open-border immigration policy that kept the supply of unskilled labor in a state of constant surplus.

When the federal government finally assumed total responsibility for the formulation and enforcement of immigration policy in 1892, the stage was set for labor leaders to press at the national level for the imposition of an immigration policy that had limits and accountability. Gompers boasted that "the labor movement was among the first organizations to urge such policies," for as he explained, "we immediately realized that immigration is, in its fundamental aspects, a labor problem."[37]

In one form or another, immigration was the subject of continual criticism at all of the early conventions the AFL. Not until 1896, however, did the leadership formally raise the issue: a resolution to reduce the level of immigration was first proposed at its annual convention that year. Speaking in support, Gompers stated that "immigration is working a great injury to the people of our country."[38] But instead of adopting the resolution, the convention authorized the creation of a committee on immigration to make recommendations. Subsequently, it reported that several actions were necessary to eliminate what Gompers called "the existing evils" associated with the nation's immigration policy: stricter enforcement of the existing exclusionary bans against the entry of criminals and paupers; punishment by imprisonment of wealthy violators of the Alien Contract Act who were willing to pay the fines in order to break the laws; and a literacy test (in the applicant's native language) as a prerequisite for admission to the United States.[39] Legislation calling for such a test had been proposed in 1896 by Henry Cabot Lodge, Republican senator from Massachusetts, and had passed in Congress, only to be vetoed by President Cleveland. The following year, 1897, the AFL convention did formally pass a resolution favoring the adoption of a literacy test as a means to reduce the level of unskilled immigration, even though there was strong opposition from some of the delegates.

As the economy in 1898 pulled out of the lengthy recession that had begun in 1893, the issue of general immigration restrictions receded in prominence. At the AFL convention of 1898 the delegates rejected an effort to support general immigration restrictions but let stand the earlier support for a literacy test to screen would-be immigrants. But the immigration issue itself was not left dormant. Instead, attention shifted once more to the issue of Chinese exclusion. The exclusionary legislation passed in 1882 required reenactment every ten years. It had been extended in 1892 and was up for renewal again in 1902. But the issue had become more complex since its initial passage in 1882, for the United States had in the interim acquired both the Hawaiian and the Philippine islands. There were fears in the AFL that if any changes were made in the wording of the original treaty, it might be possible for Chinese to take up residence in Hawaii or the Philippines as a means of subsequent entry to the United States.

It was at this juncture that the AFL's positions on literacy tests and Chinese exclusion became intertwined. Labor did not want to appear anti-worker by supporting tests that would disadvantage would-be members of the working class while not being likely to affect affluent immigrants at all. Hence, the AFL sought to draw a distinction between class discrimination and the behavior of certain nationalities. Gompers stated that the opposition of American labor to Chinese immigration was based not on nationality per se but rather on the fact that the Chinese "had allowed civilization to pass them untouched and uninfluenced" and permitted themselves "to be barbarously tyrannized over in their own country" so as "to menace the progress, the economic and social standing of the workers of other countries."[40] It was for this reason, he argued, that Chinese immigration needed to be forbidden.

By logical extension, there was also a need for a literacy test to reduce immigration from eastern and southern Europe. As Gompers explained:

> Our problem was part of the larger national problem, for the majority of immigrants no longer came from Western Europe where language, customs, and industrial organization were similar to those of the United States but from the countries of Eastern Europe where low standards of life and work prevailed. As these immigrants flooded basic industries, they threatened our standards.[41]

To be sure, there was a strong element of ethnocentrism in these words that argued for the more selective (i.e., discriminatory) immigration policy. But, there was also legitimate advocacy for self-interest as Gompers contended:

> This flood of immigrant workers drifted to so called "unskilled work." Practically all of the basic industries were revising their productions methods to substitute machine work in the place of previously indispensable craft skill. In the early years of this period of transition, the idea developed that the workman should be only a machine tender and, hence, an unskilled workman. For this sort of work the immigrants were considered desirable.[42]

Thus, the economic forces that were restructuring the workplace were also critical factors in shaping labor positions on immigration. But despite criticisms that can be made of the rationales used by Gompers and others in the labor movement to press for discriminatory restrictions, the bottom line for their actions is best summed up by historian A. T. Lane: "Numbers alone, no matter what the countries of origin, would have created a problem for trade unions."[43] The literacy test was viewed by the AFL as a means to reduce the level of immigration—and since the vast preponderance of immigrants during this period were coming from Southern and Eastern Europe, it was inevitable that any effort to reduce the scale of immigration would most heavily impact these immigrants.

Following the renewal of the Chinese Exclusion Act in 1902, the issue of restrictions of Japanese immigration quickly surfaced, albeit from an entirely unexpected source. Prior to 1900 there were virtually no Japanese immigrants on the mainland of the United States, although, as noted earlier, there had been considerable Japanese immigration to Hawaii. Soon after its annexation their mainland numbers rose sharply as Japanese immigrants began to migrate from Hawaii to the West Coast. In response, a grassroots movement of worker groups in San Francisco in 1900 began to agitate to have the Japanese included in the pending renewal of Chinese exclusion in 1902. It did not happen. Then, at its 1904 convention held in San Francisco, the AFL demanded that the Chinese Exclusion Act be amended to include immigrants from Japan.[44] Separate legislation was introduced in Congress in 1905 to do this, but it died because of opposition by the Roosevelt administration. Meanwhile, there were petitions to Congress from the state legislatures of California, Nevada, Idaho, and Montana demanding a cessation of Japanese immigration, and organized labor on the West Coast supported all these efforts, as did the AFL leaders in Washington.[45]

The issue suddenly erupted on the national scene in 1906 when the San Francisco School Board ordered all Japanese children to attend the Oriental School located in Chinatown. Local labor unions had strongly supported this move.[46] Samuel Gompers gave his support after the decision had been made.[47] President Roosevelt, who was attempting to formulate a policy reflecting U.S. commercial interests in the Far East, labeled the action of the school board "wicked absurdity," which comforted the Japanese government but did not mitigate the attitudes in California. Softer tactics were required, and the president invited the school board members to Washington for discussions. At their meeting he promised to end Japanese immigration in return for the board's rescinding the ethnic classification policy. It agreed, and legislation (although it never specifically mentioned the word "Japan") was quickly passed by Congress in 1907 to stop the migration of Japanese workers from Hawaii to the mainland.[48]

The larger issue, however, was how to stop immigration from Japan itself directly to the continental United States. Secretary of State Elihu Root proposed that the government of Japan itself impose restrictions forbidding its citizens from emigrating to the United States, which, in return, would not enact any formal legislation to exclude Japanese citizens. That "Gentlemen's Agreement" was finalized through an exchange of diplomatic correspondences by the two governments in February 1908 and became effective at once. Roosevelt thought it imperative that this immigration issue be quickly resolved in a nonconfrontational manner, lest it affect the security of U.S. business interests in the Philippines and China, since Japan was emerging as the regional power center.[49]

Against this backdrop the AFL renewed its active support for a literacy test at its 1905 convention and continued to so do at each convention until such legislation was finally enacted in 1917.[50] In response to mounting concerns by organized labor and other groups about the adverse economic effects of third-wave mass immigration, Congress took up the literacy test issue in 1906. The bill required literacy in one's native language as a condition of entry and proficiency in English as a condition of naturalization. Supporters of the bill were unable at the time to pass the literacy test for entry, but they did succeed in making proficiency in English a condition for naturalization (which it continues to be to this day).[51]

There were considerable political risks associated with any effort to address the issue of immigration directly. The powerful Speaker of the House of Representatives at the time, Joseph Cannon (R-Illinois), feared that the subject could split the Republican Party, which had dominated the national political scene since the Civil War era, and he had the complete power to control what issues could come before the House until 1910, when his absolute power was constrained. Cannon's aversion to the issue was shared by President Roosevelt. Not only did Roosevelt fear the divisive effects on his party, but he was also concerned that public debate could disrupt the ongoing secret and delicate negotiations to restrict Japanese immigration. Hence, when the literacy test resurfaced, Roosevelt joined with others to block the move, and he lent his support to an alternative congressional proposal that called for a careful investigation of the entire issue of immigration. Most Republicans felt that this would be an effective way to bury the issue.

Because there was strong public support for changes in immigration policy, however, and because he knew there was suspicion that politicians would not take the study seriously, Roosevelt sought to mollify such concerns by suggesting a variance in the normal congressional investigative procedures: he suggested that the work be done by a commission of outside experts. Ultimately, a compromise was reached whereby the commission would be composed of nine members: three from the House, three from the Senate, and three outside experts appointed by the president. The plan immediately received widespread endorsement, and in February 1907 legislation was enacted that created the Immigration Commission. Senator William Dillingham (R-Vermont) was chosen as its chairman. The AFL strongly supported the legislation.[52]

The American public developed high expectations that the commission would produce a body of verifiable facts about the effects of immigration, facts about which there would be little to debate and which would serve as a basis for comprehensive reform legislation. Subsequent reviews of its work have strongly criticized its methodologies and its impartiality.[53] Nonetheless, the undertaking has been described as "one of the most ambitious social science research projects in the nation's history up to then, barring only the census."[54]

The Dillingham Commission issued its final report in 1911. It disclosed that immigrants accounted in 1910 for over half of all operative workers in mining and apparel manufacturing; over half of all laborers in steel manufacturing, bituminous coal mining, meatpacking, and cotton textile milling; over half of all bakers; and about 80 percent of all tailors. Moreover, immigrants were disproportionately concentrated in the large urban centers in the Northeast, in the Great Lakes region of the Midwest, and along the West Coast. In major cities such as Buffalo, Chicago, Detroit, Milwaukee, Minneapolis, New York, Portland, and San Francisco, foreign-born men constituted more than half of the male labor force.[55] Accordingly, in these occupations, industries, and urban centers, immigration was determining wage levels and working conditions. The effects were to depress wages, cause unemployment, spread poverty, and make it difficult for workers to form unions.

Subsequent studies have confirmed the adverse economic effects of third-wave immigration on the American labor market. Economists Timothy Hatton and Jeffrey Williamson, for example, have found that in the absence of the large-scale immigration that occurred after 1890, the urban real wage would have been 34 percent higher in 1910. Parenthetically, they observed that "with an impact that big, no wonder the Immigration Commission produced a massive report in 1911 which supported quotas!"[56] Likewise, economists Harry Millis and Royal Montgomery wrote of this era that organized labor was correct in its assessment of adverse economic impact "as labor markets were flooded, the labor supply was made more redundant, and wages were undermined."[57]

Had the commission limited its inquiry purely to the economic effects, it would have supplied sufficient evidence for the need to adopt significant immigration reforms. Unfortunately, it went on to link the economic effects with sociological and anthropological attributes designed to distinguish the third-wave immigrants from those of the two earlier waves of mass immigration. Using various pseudoscientific theories pertaining to "superior" and "inferior" races, it concluded that the recent immigrants were "inferior" and possessed personal attributes that would make it very difficult for them to assimilate. The mixture of legitimate economic arguments with dubious ethnocentric arguments has plagued all efforts to discuss and to legislate immigration reforms ever since.

The Dillingham Commission recommended not only that the nation restrict the level of immigration, since a much slower rate of entry was preferable to the high rate it was experiencing, but also that the nation should be more selective in encouraging and discouraging newcomers.

Following the release of the report, there were immediate efforts to respond to its recommendations. In 1912, Congress again took up a bill requiring literacy tests for immigrants. The AFL strongly supported the proposal, which Gompers considered to be "the accepted method of setting up restrictive standards."[58] By this time, even the socialists who were usually at odds with Gompers over political tactics had taken up the banner of reducing immigration. Socialist labor leaders in Milwaukee, for instance, openly stated that their advocacy of the worldwide solidarity of labor did not mean that workers in other nations had a right to come to Milwaukee to look for jobs.[59] But the legislation met strong opposition from the National Association of Manufacturers, lobbyists for various steamship lines that transported immigrants to the United States, and the aforementioned Speaker of the House Joseph Cannon. "No measure was more hotly contended," Gompers would later write.[60] In the end it did finally pass Congress in 1912, but when it reached the desk of President Taft, he vetoed it. Thus, for the third time, Congress had passed legislation to impose a literacy test as a means of reducing the immigration of unskilled workers, only to have it vetoed by the sitting president.

In late 1914 similar legislation was again adopted by Congress, only to be vetoed in 1915 by President Woodrow Wilson. The AFL took up the cause of responding to Wilson's objections. Gompers showed that various liberal groups who were opposing immigration restrictions, supposedly for "idealistic" and "sentimental" reasons, were in fact being supported financially by various corporations opposed to the bill while other businesses organizations opposing the legislation did so because they had "found profit in employing cheap immigrant workers."[61] In the next session of Congress the literacy test legislation was reintroduced. Once more it passed Congress, only to be vetoed by President Wilson, but this time Congress mustered the two-thirds vote needed in both houses to override the veto, and the Immigration Act of 1917 became law.[62] Its passage marked the beginning of serious efforts to screen immigrants so as to reduce the entry of large numbers of unskilled and poorly educated job seekers. This legislation also created the "Asiatic Barred Zone," which banned immigration from virtually all Asian countries.[63]

Following the end of World War I there were reports from U.S. consulates in Europe that, in light of the vast destruction there, millions of persons were planning to emigrate to the United States. As the actual numbers began to mount in 1920 (see Table 4.3), it also became apparent that many immigrants were still coming from eastern and southern Europe and that the literacy test requirement was not having the expected impact. One reason, it turned out, was that it was possible to prepare people to take the test; in Italy, for example, special schools were established to teach peasants the basic fundamentals needed to pass it. As there was by this time widespread public support (including that of labor leaders) for restricting immigration, on the basis of the earlier findings of the Dillingham Commission, the House of Representatives quickly passed a bill in late 1920 calling for a suspension of all immigration for one year. In response, the Senate adopted a bill calling for the imposition of an annual numerical ceiling on immigration, with preference given to those of western and northern European ethnic backgrounds. The Senate bill was adopted at the end of the congressional session. President Wilson, who by this time was seriously ill and in his last days in office, gave the bill a pocket veto by refusing to sign it.

His successor, President Warren Harding, who took office in March 1921, had no qualms about the need for such legislation. Hence, Congress quickly adopted a slightly revised version of the earlier Senate bill, and Harding signed the Immigration Act of 1921 into law on 19 May 1921.[64] It imposed the first statutory ceiling on immigration in U.S. history (about 350,000 persons a year) and it contained ethnic quotas limiting the number of immigrants from any nationality to be admitted in any year to no more than 3 percent of that nationality who lived in the United States in 1910. The act was considered to be "temporary" until more carefully constructed legislation could be drafted and enacted. The era of the "open border" was over; thereafter, statutory law would govern the immigration entry process.

Table 4.5. The Foreign-Born Population, 1890–1920

Year	Foreign-Born Population (millions)	Percentage of Total Population
1890	9.2	14.8
1900	10.3	13.6
1910	13.5	14.7
1920	13.9	13.2

Source: U.S. Bureau of the Census, *Historical Census Statistics on the Foreign-Born Population of the United States, 1850–1900,* Population Division Working Paper no. 29 (Washington D.C.: U.S. Department of Commerce, 1999), table 1.

In reflecting on the period from 1890 to 1920, one finds the relationship between union membership and immigration somewhat mixed. As shown in Table 4.4, most of the growth in union membership occurred in two separate spurts, from 1897 to 1905 (when immigration was increasing sharply) and from 1916 to 1920 (when immigration declined sharply). In the years between (1906 through 1915), unionism had only modest gains (concentrated largely in only four industries: railroads, construction, clothing, and coal mining), while immigration soared. Other factors, such as the speed of industrialization (on the labor demand side) and the events associated with World War I (on the supply side), influenced both union membership and immigration trends. Accordingly, this is the only era in the development of American unionism where the seesaw effect between union membership and immigration levels is clouded. Certainly, organized labor in this period felt that its activities were restrained by mass immigration, and it reacted accordingly. Labor leaders supported every piece of restrictive legislation taken during this period, and sometimes, in fact, initiated the actions.

Ironically, over these thirty years the percentage of the population that was foreign-born actually declined from its historic high of 14.8 percent in 1890 to 13.2 percent in 1920 (see Table 4.5). But this downward trend can be easily explained by the reduction of immigration flows that occurred during the World War I era, 1914–18.

Likewise, union membership and its percentage of the labor force grew significantly between 1890 and 1920 (see Table 4.4). But, as discussed, for most of this period unions were fighting a desperate battle just to survive. It was only after immigration was constrained by World War I that union membership surged into significant growth.

Thus, as always, both historical factors and institutional actions provide the necessary basis for understanding seemingly strange statistical findings. The numbers never speak for themselves.

Mass Immigration Ceases;
Unionism Takes Off (1921–1965)

The Setting

The mass immigration that the nation experienced with little interruption for over a century came to a halt during the late 1920s. The events associated with World War I had already slowed the process before the decade began; legislation adopted in the 1920s, an economic depression in the 1930s, and international conflict in the 1940s reinforced the trend and confirmed its reality. By 1965 the percentage of the population that was foreign-born had fallen to 4.4 percent, the lowest level in the nation's history. Over this same interval, union membership rose to levels of absolute numbers that had never been experienced before and, with nearly one in three nonagricultural workers belonging to a union, the labor movement achieved a higher unionized percentage of the labor force than has ever been experienced since.

Similarly, the evolution of public policy over these same years reflected a conviction that the nation's destiny rested increasingly with the productive capabilities of its native-born population. It was therefore in the national interest to focus attention on the human-resource development and well-being of the labor force. This era witnessed the enactment of the most progressive worker and family legislation the nation has ever adopted.[1] At the federal level, laws were passed guaranteeing the right of workers to join unions and to bargain collectively; to receive minimum wages; to limit daily and weekly working hours before overtime rates are obligatory; to restrict child labor; and to expand publicly supported education and

[81]

training opportunities. Beneficial worker legislation manifested public commitments to pursue full employment policies; to promote equal employment opportunity; to provide vaccination and nutrition programs for the young; to guarantee minimum incomes for dependent children, the disabled, and the blind; to combat the causes of poverty; and to provide retirement income and health insurance for the elderly. In response to federal prodding, all states adopted unemployment compensation and enacted worker compensation programs to provide family income when workers lose their jobs or are injured or killed on the job.

Against this backdrop of social advancement, the nation became the world's preeminent industrial power. In retrospect, the forty-five-year period 1920–65 was one of supreme human achievement. The nation turned inward, with respect to policy development and it was well that it did. There was a lengthy legacy of stifled opportunities, discriminatory behavior, and underutilized talent among the citizenry that needed to be addressed. There had been far too much indifference to human suffering and a dangerously widening gulf in the distribution of income among the segments of society. All these issues had been ignored for far too long, and the lack of attention was endangering the nation's prospect for domestic tranquillity. By the mid-1960s the quality of life for working people, not the quantity of workers, finally emerged as the primary concern for public policy formulation.

The cessation of mass immigration over these years also made it easier for the third-wave immigrants and their descendants to become assimilated and for the process of social elevation to occur. With the end of mass immigration it was obvious to these immigrants that their ethnic cultures and sentiments would not be renewed by succeeding waves of similar immigrants. As sociologist Richard Alba observed about this era, "The shutting off of the immigrant flow made clear to the second and third generations that their future lay in the new society."[2]

Social and economic advancement over these years was not, of course, continuous or uninterrupted. There was opposition all the way and periods of backward steps. Indeed, the whole era began with little evidence of the progressive changes for workers and their families that were to come. In 1920 the Supreme Court dismissed an antitrust case against U.S. Steel which had been pending for many years and this brought an end to the "trustbusting era." In its decision the Court ruled that "bigness is not badness" and that U.S. Steel had gained industry dominance through merger tactics that were not in and of themselves illegal. Warren Harding became president in 1921 with a promise to return the nation to an era of "normalcy" (a word that did not previously exist). In 1921 and 1922 the nation slipped into a recession, only to rebound in 1923 with a veritable explosion of output by the expanding goods-producing industries. The assembly-line method of mass production spread to a host of manufacturing industries. The automobile industry, where it had been introduced, mushroomed into one of the largest in the world, and with its growth came the complementary expansion of the steel, petroleum-refining, rubber, glass, and road-building industries. Massive new manufacturing businesses emerged to produce such items as electrical appliances, electrical machinery, aviation equipment, and radios.

The surge in productivity, which resulted from the introduction of new production methods and machinery, led to falling prices and a tightening of the urban labor market. During the decade of the 1920s, real wages for nonagricultural workers tripled.[3] Thus, the increase in capital formation enhanced not only the capacity to produce but also the capacity to consume.

The 1920s were of consequence also because of a mass movement of the population from rural to urban areas. Historian Arthur Link described this migration as "the most important internal demographic change of the decade."[4] Six million rural people moved to the urban sector, and the rural population sustained a net loss of 1.2 million persons—the first such net decline ever experienced in the nation. With immigration partially constrained, millions of native-born persons previously trapped in rural poverty were released to seek wider employment opportunities and higher incomes in urban America. Most of those who migrated to the cities were poor whites, but a sizable number were blacks from the rural South.[5] (Black outmigration had begun only a few years earlier, during World War I, when mass immigration had been initially constrained.)

But all was not well during this period of seemingly general prosperity. There was a mounting concentration of wealth and property in the hands of a few. The distribution of income, already a problem before the decade began, became decidedly more unequal in the 1920s. In 1929, 42 percent of all families had incomes of less than $1,500 a year and, in total, accounted for only 13 percent of all family income. Conversely, the upper one-tenth of one percent (0.1 percent) of all families had incomes in excess of $75,000 a year and also accounted for 13 percent of all family income. The distribution of income for one-member families was even worse. On the basis of these figures, the Brookings Institution estimated that 60 percent of the population was living in poverty in 1929.[6] Indeed, the rural economy was in a state of virtual economic collapse throughout the decade. Mechanized farming had translated into agricultural surpluses that led to declining prices that translated into falling wages and reduced employment for farm workers.[7]

In 1929, national income, the volume of production, and stock prices soared to historic heights—but suddenly the spell of prosperity broke. On 24 October, 1929, stock market prices plummeted. Despite a few brief rallies, the stock market lost half its market value within three weeks and, by 1932, 90 percent of its former value. The stock market crash generated a sharp note of caution throughout the entire business sector. Sharply curtailed purchasing led to production cutbacks, which led to the mass layoff of workers. President Herbert Hoover and his advisers were at a loss to know how to respond. Believing that the primary cause of the economic collapse was overproduction in both the manufacturing and agricultural sectors of the economy, the Hoover administration first sought voluntary restraints by business to reduce both layoffs and wage cuts. Receiving little response, the government turned to stronger measures, undertaking a fruitless effort to balance the federal budget. It condemned the use of public works projects but nonetheless initiated such federal projects.[8] Yet in response to falling tax revenues, the administration not only tried to reduce aggregate government spending but actually secured the passage of the Revenue Act of 1932, which raised taxes to the highest level the nation had ever experienced during peacetime.[9] Moreover, in 1930 the Smoot-Hawley Tariff Act raised already high tariffs even higher, and as other countries responded in kind, exports were crippled. As economist John Kenneth Galbraith has lamented, the administration's actions represented "the triumph of dogma over thought," for the economic advice Hoover received and implemented "was invariably on the side of measures that would make things worse."[10]

Aside from the fact that the nation was taken by complete surprise, the most unique feature of the Great Depression "was that it was overwhelmingly an experience of joblessness."[11] Numerous economic downturns before had severely affected employment, but none had brought unemployment of such magnitude or duration as that of the 1930s. There were 4.3 unemployed workers (8.9 percent of the labor force) in 1930; 8.0 million in 1931 (16.3 percent of the labor force); 12.1 million in 1932 (24.1 percent of the labor force) and 12.8 million in 1933 (25.3 percent of the labor force).[12] Even these figures tell only part of the story of hardship, for millions of those persons who did have jobs were working only part time and therefore had severely reduced incomes. The payroll of the powerful U.S. Steel Corporation is illustrative: in 1929 it had 224,980 full-time employees; as of 1 April 1933 that number was zero, as its employment rolls had fallen to about 100,000 workers, all of whom were employed part time.[13] Nonetheless, over the course of the decade, the labor force actually grew by an average of 400,000 people per year as persons from all walks of life desperately sought a way to earn income for themselves or their families. Immigration, in contrast, fell to low levels that had not been experienced in any decade in over a hundred years. For the first time since the early years of the republic, immigration became an inconsequential influence on the growth of the labor force.

With the inauguration of President Franklin D. Roosevelt in March 1933 and the subsequent implementation of the job creation policies of the New Deal, unemployment slowly began to recede. The Roosevelt administration adopted the view that the heart of the problem was underconsumption, and it initiated job creation programs to stimulate aggregate spending. It also sought to reduce the production of agricultural surpluses by adopting programs to restrict output and guarantee minimum prices on specific farm goods. But in retrospect, even these unprecedented policy initiatives can be seen as grossly inadequate, for even at the lowest unemployment rate reached in the decade, in 1937, there were still 7.7 million out of work (a 14.3 percent unemployment rate). Older workers (with higher salaries), married women, and minorities were among the first to be laid off and the last to be rehired. Unskilled workers, in general, were quickly fired and skilled workers downgraded to fill their positions. Homelessness, poverty, malnutrition, family breakups, and personal despair plagued communities in every region.[14] Bank failures and bankruptcies of farms and business enterprises were commonplace.

In addition to the horrendous economic and financial effects, there was the social impact. The old order was destroyed. No longer was there confidence in the supremacy of businesses, or admiration for business heroes, or a belief in the unqualified benefits of a free market system with minimal government regulation or intervention. In its place, wrote Irving Bernstein, emerged a presumption "that the American worker should never again suffer the economic and social devastation visited upon him by the unemployment of the thirties."[15] The joblessness of the era created an overpowering yearning for security, and in response the New Deal provided new income maintenance programs, statutory worker protections, and labor laws to promote trade unionism—most of which still exist to this day.

It was not until 1940 that the physical volume of industrial production in the nation equaled the level that had existed in 1929. Even then there were still 8.1 million unemployed workers (with an unemployment rate for the year of 14.6 percent), for technological improvements in production enabled output to increase with reduced labor input. The Great Depression did not end until 1941, when the country entered World War II defense spending stimulated the expansion of the economy, and the reinstated military draft tightened the civilian labor market.

It was fortunate that the increase in the demand for labor associated with military rearmament occurred at a time of high unemployment; the transition was far less difficult than if all the needed workers and soldiers had had to be recruited from the ranks of a fully employed economy. During the war years, 18 million men were screened for the U.S. military draft and about 11.4 million were actually inducted. Of those called into military service, 60 percent were employed at the time or would have been, under normal circumstances.[16] Not only did their positions have to be filled, but additional workers were needed to meet the expansion of production. Even with the substantial withdrawal of young men for military service, the labor force expanded by 5 million workers over the course of the war years. With immigration virtually nil, employers had to look to domestic sources previously ignored (women, youth, the disabled, and the elderly); previously restricted or excluded by artificial barriers of discrimination (black workers); and underutilized (many workers of all races in rural areas).

Of the multiple factors that led to the victory of the Allied forces over the Axis powers of Germany, Italy, and Japan, none was more important than the ability of the U.S. economy to expand its production dramatically. The gross national product of the country increased by an astounding 125 percent over the war years. For it to do this, the passive principles of free market economics had to be set aside in favor of the active policies associated with economic planning. The War Production Board was set up in January 1942 to organize the production of military goods. The factories producing cars and trucks and most consumer durable goods were converted to making war goods exclusively. Factories preparing or processing nondurable goods (food and clothing) continued to do so, but military orders took priority.

Besides the conversion of existing facilities, new construction of plants was required and new machinery needed to fill them. Although most of the war production was done in the established industrial centers of the Northeast and California, significant new facilities were added in Texas, Utah, Nevada, Washington, and Oregon. Ownership of the production facilities remained in private hands, but what was produced was largely determined by the federal government. Most contracts went to the nation's largest firms—Boeing, General Motors, U.S. Steel, Dupont, General Electric—as only they could handle the required scale of output. These firms, in turn, subcontracted large amounts of work to thousands of smaller firms that produced parts and subassemblies. Channeling the raw materials to these subcontractors in a manner that would avoid waste, excessive inventories, and labor shortages was an enormous administrative problem.

In order to prevent inflation in the wake of such heavy public spending, prices and wages were essentially frozen, as were rents. High tax rates were imposed on profits. Many essential consumer goods (such as gasoline, tires, sugar, and shoes) were rationed. Under these circumstances, the stabilization efforts were remarkably effective, as the cost of living increased by only 31 percent between 1939 and 1945.

To handle labor-management disputes and to avoid strikes, the National War Labor Board (NWLB) was established and processed almost 18,000 cases. As a way of easing some of the unavoidable tensions that occurred as a result of the pressure to maintain production while wages were frozen, the NWLB allowed various "fringe benefits" to be introduced to compensate workers for their efforts. The board also had the power to arbitrate the inevitable grievances that arose. Except in coal mining, there were surprisingly few strikes, and those were usually of short duration—even in the coal industry.

When the war ended in August 1945, there were dire fears that the full employment the nation had achieved would come to an end and that the economy would be plunged back into deep depression. It did not happen. Instead, pent-up demand and the accumulation of forced savings during the war generated enormous expenditures by consumers. Inflation became the chief enemy of stability. Wage controls and most rationing ended shortly after the war. Rent controls remained in place for several years and were gradually phased out on a community-by-community basis as local housing stocks were increased. Taxes were reduced.

President Harry Truman favored the retention of price controls until the volume of peacetime production was sufficient to meet demand at the controlled prices, but the more conservative Congress favored quick abandonment of price controls in order to stimulate profits and expand production to eliminate consumer scarcities. Congress put forth a bill to extend the president's authority in the matter for one year, but it greatly emasculated his actual power and allowed many prices to be increased right away. Truman vetoed it—and with no price controls in place, prices immediately skyrocketed. Truman then accepted another bill, similar to the one he vetoed, but one that allowed him to end controls when he saw fit. When the administration attempted to use its authority to force price reductions, however, many producers—especially meat producers—withdrew their products from the market. As public indignation mounted, the administration surrendered. In October 1946, Truman announced the abandonment of all controls except those on rent which were only gradually reduced. As could have been expected, prices quickly soared, and within one year the cost of living increased by 27 percent—almost as much as it had during the entire war period.

Against this inflationary background a wave of strikes occurred in the years 1945–48. There were major strikes in the automobile, steel, rubber, coal (which went on strike three times) industries, and a nationwide railroad strike was only narrowly avoided. In 1946 alone there were 4,630 strikes involving more than 5 million workers.[17] Unionism, while riding a crest of popularity with workers (in 1946, one of every three nonagricultural workers was a union member), raised fear of union power in the business community and, because of the wave of strikes, apprehension among those elements of the general public who did not belong to unions. As a consequence, when the Republicans captured control of both houses of Congress in 1946, they successfully passed the Labor-Management Relations Act (or Taft-Hartley Act) in 1948, over President Truman's veto. It introduced regulations governing union conduct and placed restrictions on collective bargaining.

As for the economy itself, the United States emerged from World War II with its productive capacity not only unscathed but enormously enlarged. Moreover, as the result of extensive investment by the federal government in research and development, the nation's production enterprises had at their industrial disposal the most advanced science and technology on the planet. In February 1946 the world's first electronic computer became operational, and only two years later the transistor was invented. A new age was dawning, though no one at the time could conceive of the technological transformations that lay ahead.

Meanwhile, as a form of compensation and to ease the transition of young men and women who had served in the military during the war, the provisions of the Servicemen's Readjustment Act of 1944 (popularly called the GI Bill) had gone into effect. For those veterans who chose to avail themselves of it, the program provided funds to cover the up to four years' tuition for various forms of education and training, plus a monthly living allowance. In total, 7.8 million men and women enrolled in the program. Their lives and those of their families were dramatically altered by the wide array of better jobs for which they were able to qualify and the higher incomes they could receive.[18] This government program still stands as one of the most beneficial human resource development policies the nation has ever enacted.

As for the military itself, there were immediate pressures to reduce its scale, and steps were taken to do so. The draft ended in 1946, but it was reinstated in 1948. By this time, the Cold War with the Soviet Union had commenced in response to the spread of Communism in eastern Europe and, in 1949, in China after the fall of the Nationalist Chinese regime that year. Furthermore, the United States joined with other forces from the United Nations to repel an invasion by the Communist government of North Korea into South Korea in 1950. The United States had become an integral part of the world community. Rearmament commenced, and high levels of expenditures on military equipment and manpower as well as defense-oriented research became ongoing facts of economic life.

During the Korean War years, wage and price controls were reinstated but ceased when the war stalemated and a truce was arranged in 1953. Although the remainder of the 1950s was a period of general prosperity, there was a mild recession in 1954 and a more serious one from the middle of 1957 to the early 1960s. The postwar years 1947–68, however, represented the only period in American history in which there was a significant movement toward greater income equality within the nation: over this time span, the U.S. Bureau of Census calculated that there was a 7.4 percent decline in family income inequality during a time when family income for everyone was rising.[19] Thus, all income groups shared in the growth of income, but the greatest gains were made by those in the lowest income ranks.

During the 1950s there were signs of future problems even though they were not immediately recognized or addressed. For one thing, the recessions of the decade sparked concern that there might be new causes for unemployment that would not be solved by reliance on government spending or tax reduction. Specifically, it was argued that "automation" (a word coined in the automobile industry in 1947 to denote new automatic control processes) represented a new form of technology that might create largely skilled jobs but was destroying unskilled jobs. A special committee studied the issue in 1959 but came to no firm conclusions.[20] It was simply too early to tell what the impact of the computer-led technology on the workplace would be.

Likewise, when Rosa Parks, a black woman in Montgomery, Alabama, refused to move to the back of a public bus in December 1955 and was arrested, and Martin Luther King initiated a consumer boycott in protest, the national ramifications were not immediately recognized. Until this time the civil rights struggle by black Americans had been fought mainly in the courts, not in the streets. But the long-neglected issue of the ill treatment of black Americans was beginning to surface.

Then on 4 October 1957 the surface tranquillity of the period was shattered when the Soviet Union launched the world's first earth-orbiting space satellite, Sputnik I. The smug feeling of superiority about U.S. scientific and technological abilities was suddenly called into question, and the caliber of the nation's educational system came under immediate attack. In January 1958 President Dwight Eisenhower appealed to Congress to recognize that education was critically important to national security. The National Defense Education Act was enacted later that year, and a broad range of educational reforms designed to improve the quality of education were adopted nationwide.

With the coming of the 1960s these long-simmering domestic issues came to the fore. In 1961, with the unemployment rate hovering around 7 percent, the newly elected administration of President John Kennedy made its reduction a primary domestic goal. The cause of the high unemployment rate became the subject of a major debate: one school of thought held that it was because taxes were too high; another argued that it was due to structural changes in the labor market caused by the spread of computer-driven technology. The administration favored tax reductions, whereas Congress tended to prefer structural remedies, such as retraining and upgrading the employment skills of workers threatened with technological displacement.[21] Meanwhile, the civil rights movement had blossomed into a full-scale protest movement. The Kennedy administration proposed legislation to address both these domestic issues but was unable to force Congress to act on most of its agenda.

All of this suddenly changed with the tragic assassination of President Kennedy in November 1963 and Lyndon Johnson's accession to office. Johnson, one of the most vivid personalities and astute politicians ever to be president, quickly broke the legislative logjam. Between 1964 and 1966 the most ambitious domestic reform agenda in the nation's history was proposed, and it was all enacted. Taxes were cut, but the issues of structural change in the labor market were also addressed. Legislation to provide retraining; to improve elementary, secondary, and higher education; to combat poverty, to protect the environment, and to provide health care for the elderly and the poor population was passed in rapid succession. In addition, pathbreaking federal legislation pertaining to civil rights was adopted to address employment discrimination, segregation of public facilities, and the denial of voting rights. It was in this same vein that immigration reform, designed to end the overt ethnic discrimination that had been in place since the 1920s but not to increase the level of immigration, was passed in 1965. It was a brief period when serious governmental efforts were made to confront an accumulation of issues that had been ignored for too long.

The Labor Force and Industrial
Employment Patterns

Between 1920 and 1965 the U.S. labor force increased significantly in size, from 41.7 million to 75.6 million workers (see Table 5.1). But of greater consequence was the shifting pattern of industrial employment that occurred on the labor demand side of the equation. In 1920, employment in manufacturing exceeded, in absolute numbers, employment in agriculture for the first time (see Tables 5.1 and 5.2). Agriculture, which had dominated employment since the beginning of the republic, had been declining in absolute numbers of workers since 1907 and had fallen precipitously since 1950. Manufacturing emerged as the largest single employment sector of the economy and remained the leader throughout this entire era. But its growth pattern was erratic. Indeed, throughout the 1920s, manufacturing employment remained virtually constant; the expansion and spread of assembly-line technology during that decade enabled productivity and output to increase significantly but did not lead to any increase in jobs.[22]

The advances in technology spawned a demand by employers for capital formation, which greatly enlarged the capacity of the economy to produce. Real wages rose sharply in the 1920s, but because actual wage levels were low to begin with, the increases still did not keep up with productivity. Hence, the demand for products could not match the supply of products. Underconsumption, made worse by the widening inequalities in the distribution of income, set the stage for the depression years of the 1930s. During the 1930s, employment in all the goods-producing industries, as well as transportation and public utilities in the service sector, declined over the entire decade (see Tables 5.1 and 5.2).

The outbreak of World War II reversed all these industrial employment trends except for agriculture. Manufacturing employment in particular experienced unprecedented growth. The expanded military needs for vast quantities of standardized items comported perfectly with the evolving state of assembly-line technology. Steel and wheeled vehicles were the backbone of the land warfare requirements, and they dominated military procurement. As the automobile industry was the dominant manufacturer of metal products when the war began, it was radically transformed, and Detroit became the production center of the economy.[23] But with the need for other mass-produced items as well—such as uniforms, armaments, tents, and medical supplies—manufacturing enterprises in other industrial centers also experienced employment growth. Likewise, the shipbuilding and aircraft industries dramatically expanded in scale.

Table 5.1. The Labor Force and Nonfarm Employment by Industry, 1920–1965 (in thousands)

Year	Civilian Labor Force (14 years and up)[a]	Total Nonfarm Employees	Mining	Construction	Manufacturing	Transport and Utilities	Trade	Finance	Service	Government
1920	41,720	27,434	1,180	850	10,702	4,317	4,012	902	3,100	2,371
1930	48,783	29,424	1,009	1,372	9,562	3,685	5,797	1,475	3,376	3,148
1940	56,180	32,377	925	1,294	10,985	3,038	6,750	1,502	3,681	4,202
1950	64,749	45,222	901	2,333	15,241	4,034	9,386	1,919	3,382	6,026
1960	73,126	54,347	709	2,882	16,762	4,017	11,412	2,684	7,361	8,520
1965	75,635	60,770	628	3,211	17,984	4,031	12,585	3,043	8,903	10,046

Sources: 1920–1960: Stanley Lebergott, *Manpower in Economic Growth: The American Record since 1800* (New York: McGraw-Hill, 1964), tables A-3, A-5. Copyright 1964 by McGraw-Hill Inc. Reprinted by permission of the publisher; 1965: *Economic Report of the President: 1999* (Washington, D.C.: U.S. Government Printing Office, 1999), Tables A-1, C-1.

[a]The Civilian Labor Force data are given for comparison use only. They are taken from a different source than the nonagricultural employment data.

Table 5.2. Employment in Agriculture, 1920–1965 (in thousands)

Year	Employees in Agriculture (14 years and up)
1920	10,440
1930	10,340
1940	9,540
1950	7,507
1960	5,723
1965	4,361

Sources: 1920–1960: Stanley Lebergott, *Manpower in Economic Growth* (New York: McGraw-Hill, 1964), table A-6. 1965: *Economic Report of the President: 1999* (Washington, D.C.: U.S. Government Printing Office, 1999), table B-35.

Thus, it was the manufacturing sector that sustained the largest increases in employment during the war years, growing by 6 million workers between 1940 and 1944. With over 17 million workers in 1944, manufacturing alone accounted for 41 percent of all employment of nonagricultural workers in the nation. That boost represented the first increase in manufacturing employment since the 1917–18 era of World War I. The occupations that experienced the greatest growth in manufacturing were in the unskilled and semiskilled work. Public and private training programs were initiated and extensive efforts were made to redesign job requirements to accommodate less skilled workers. But the underlying explanation for the ability of the industry to accommodate so many unskilled workers was that the assembly-line technology used for the mass production of standardized items did not require much in the way of human capital.

In this environment, many women, minorities, youth, disabled persons, and rural workers were absorbed into the industry's expanding workforce. With immigration virtually nonexistent, the tight labor market forced employers to look to domestic sources for needed workers. When they searched, they found them—though it took some serious prodding by government as well as appeals to patriotism for some employers in the private sector to abandon the prejudicial barriers that had kept them from considering some of these native-born workers for employment. The opposition of some craft unions and the railroad brotherhoods also had to be overcome.[24] Indeed, the roots of the drive to end employment discrimination in the labor market, which would culminate in the equal employment opportunity provisions of the Civil Rights Act of 1964, can be traced directly to these pathbreaking events of the World

War II era.[25] Once formerly excluded or marginalized groups had been given access to primary labor market jobs, there was no way to keep them out in the years that followed. The dice of social change had been cast. Moreover, the employment accommodations made in the 1940s demonstrated that there had been for many years a viable domestic alternative to reliance on mass immigration as a source of workers in a growing economy.

Following the war, the pent-up consumer demand for durable goods and housing kept the momentum for manufacturing strong. The revival of military spending associated with the Korean War of 1950–53 and ongoing defense spending caused by the Cold War perpetuated the trend.

Yet by the late 1950s and early 1960s there were signs of structural changes occurring in the labor market. Employment in the goods-producing industries—especially in manufacturing—began to lag behind the rapid growth of employment in the service industries. Moreover, within all the goods -producing industries, employment in the production occupations (i.e., blue-collar jobs) began to fall while employment in the nonproduction occupations (i.e., white-collar jobs) began to rise. These changing proportions reflected what appeared to be a significant change in job requirements: increasingly, jobs that required skills, training, and education across the occupational spectrum were increasing while those that did not require human capital endowments were either declining or, at a minimum, not increasing proportionately. The overall unemployment rate began to creep upward, but the unemployment rate of certain segments of the labor force increased more rapidly than did that of others. Specifically, the severity and duration of unemployment was identified with those who lacked skills and education.[26] It was also recognized that because of different industrial trends, certain urban and rural communities (called "distressed areas") had inordinately high unemployment rates, regardless of the state of the overall economy.[27]

At the time, it was unclear whether these differential experiences were simply a temporary aberration associated with underconsumption or symptoms of a more fundamental structural transformation of the labor market: one associated with the introduction of computer technology and the shifting consumer tastes of an affluent society. In retrospect, it is apparent that the latter was the case. The labor market was in the process of being radically altered and the days of domination by employment in goods-producing industries with a multitude of blue-collar occupations that required little in the way of human capital preparation were coming to a rapid end. An entirely new labor market was dawning.

Immigration

At the end of World War I, there were diplomatic reports that mass immigration from Europe was poised to resume; in fact, immigration levels were already rising (see Tables 4.3 and 5.3). Congress, in response, hastily passed the Immigration Act of 1921, and President Warren Harding quickly signed it, establishing the first ceiling ever placed on immigration at about 358,000 immigrants a year (plus immediate family members: spouses and minor children). The legislation supplemented the bans on virtually all immigration from Asia (except for the Philippines, a U.S. colony at the time) by establishing a limit on the number of immigrants of any other nationality for any one year at 3 percent of the number of persons of that nationality of the Eastern Hemisphere (essentially Europe), who had been living in the United States in 1910. The effect was to reserve about 200,000 of the available slots for immigrants from northern and western European countries. (The ceiling did not apply to the Western Hemisphere, except those Caribbean Basin countries still under the direct European control.) The task of actually setting the specific quotas for individual countries proved to be extremely difficult, however, as nine new nations were created in Europe following the war, and thirteen other nations had their prewar borders changed.

The Immigration Act of 1921, viewed as a temporary measure intended to last only for one year, was extended by a joint resolution of Congress until 1924 while a permanent immigration law was being crafted. The Immigration Act of 1924 incorporated all the essential principles of the earlier act but was even more restrictive.[28] A transition period was specified from 1924 to 1927 to allow the details to be worked out, but the process became so complicated that it was 1929 before the law actually went into full effect.

The law established the "national origins quota system." As enacted in 1924 it set the annual admission quota at 2 percent of the number of foreign-born persons of each nationality who were residing in the country in 1890 (again, the legislation did not apply to immigrants from the Western Hemisphere). This translated into an overall ceiling of 164,667 immigrants (plus immediate relatives) who could be admitted each year. The exact ceilings for each country were to be determined jointly by the secretaries of labor, commerce, and state.

As noted, it took five years to work out the methodologies for setting the country quotas. The use of 1890 census data was roundly criticized as being blatantly discriminatory against those nationalities that had dominated the third wave of immigrants (i.e., those from eastern and southern

Table 5.3. Immigration to the United States, 1921–1970

1921–1930	**4,107,209**
1921	805,228
1922	309,556
1923	522,919
1924	706,896
1925	294,314
1926	304,488
1927	335,175
1928	307,255
1929	279,678
1930	241,700
1931–1940	**528,431**
1931	97,139
1932	35,576
1933	23,068
1934	29,470
1935	34,956
1936	36,329
1937	50,244
1938	67,895
1939	82,998
1940	70,756
1941–1950	**1,035,039**
1941	51,776
1942	28,781
1943	23,725
1944	28,551
1945	38,119
1946	108,721
1947	147,292
1948	170,570
1949	188,317
1950	249,187
1951–1960	**2,515,479**
1951	205,717
1952	265,520
1953	170,434
1954	208,177
1955	237,790
1956	321,625
1957	326,867
1958	253,265
1959	260,686
1960	265,398
1961–1970	**3,321,677**
1961	271,344
1962	283,763
1963	306,260
1964	292,248
1965	296,697

1961–1970 (cont.)	3,321,677 (cont.)
1966	323,040
1967	361,972
1968	454,448
1969	358,579
1970	373,326

Source: U.S. Immigration and Naturalization Service.

Europe). The use of the 1910 census, on the other hand, had been criticized as being equally discriminatory against the nationalities that had dominated the first and second waves, as well as those living in the country when it became independent (i.e., those largely from northern and western Europe). Consequently, when the final version of the law went into effect in 1929, it represented an entirely different selection methodology: it established an admissions quota system based on the national origins of both the native-born and the foreign-born populations as enumerated in the 1920 census. Each country's specific quota was the same proportion of the total ceiling (set at that time at 150,000 immigrants a year) as the proportion of the people who, by birth or descent, represented that nationality in the population as counted in the 1920 census. The only exception to the formula was that each nationality (except those specifically excluded) was assured a minimum quota of 100 immigrants, so the actual total became 154,277 persons a year (plus immediate relatives) who could be admitted. The calculations totally excluded the descendants of slaves, of Indians, and of most Asians (who either were excluded by legislation or were ineligible under existing law to be naturalized).

The effect of including the native-born nationalities in the design of the selection system was to greatly favor immigrants from northern and western Europe: they received 82 percent of the total available quota slots each year; eastern and southern European countries, 14 percent; and the remainder of the Eastern Hemisphere nations (parts of Africa and the Philippines in Asia) received 4 percent. Even more precisely, Great Britain alone received 65,000 of the total slots available each year. But since accurate statistics as to nationality were not available from the earlier censuses or from colonial records, the list of names used to compile the actual country quotas was haphazard and the entire process, wrote W.S. Bernard, scientifically "indefensible."[29] Yet with only slight modifications made in 1952, the national origins quota system remained in effect until 1965.

The Immigration Act of 1924 also contained a provision that had the effect of legislatively excluding immigration from Japan, which the Gentlemen's Agreement had greatly reduced but had not entirely stopped; many noncitizens of Japanese ancestry continued to migrate to the mainland from Hawaii. During the 1923 congressional session, there was strong agitation from groups in California as well as from such diverse organizations as the American Legion and the AFL for a total ban. The language used to accomplish this purpose was cleverly drawn so as not to mention Japan but yet to apply specifically to Japan.[30]

Secretary of State Charles Evans Hughes tried in vain to have Congress enact a small quota of not more than 250 immigrants a year for Japan rather than to pass a total exclusion.[31] And Calvin Coolidge, who had succeeded to the presidency when Harding died in office, indicated that he would have vetoed the provision as bad foreign policy if it had been presented to him as an individual bill. But since it was not, this exclusion became law and remained in effect until 1952. The principle of total exclusion of persons from a specific country had begun with the Chinese, a weak power at the time, and now had been applied to Japan, a proud, sensitive, and influential state. The United States had unilaterally abrogated the Gentlemen's Agreement. When the ban took effect, Japan declared a day of national mourning and humiliation.

The effect of the legislation of 1921 and 1924 was to sharply reduce immigration from Europe after 1921, but it did not immediately accomplish the main objective of its supporters. As shown in Table 5.3, of the 4.1 million immigrants legally admitted during the decade of the 1920s, 1.8 million entered after the legislation of 1924 went into effect. The main reason for the continuation of high levels of immigration was that the law did not apply to the Western Hemisphere: in the 1920s there were over 900 thousand immigrants from Canada and another 459 thousand from Mexico. It was also during the 1920s that immigration from many countries in the Caribbean began to accelerate.

Although some critics of immigration thought that the countries of the Western Hemisphere should have been included in the 1924 legislation, the decision not to do so reflected both the fact that up to that time, immigration from those nations had not been significant, and concern that the imposition of such restrictions might adversely affect U.S. relations with neighboring nations. There was also the practical problem that, given the lengthy U.S. land borders with Canada and Mexico, it would have been futile to impose restrictions on entry without some means of enforcement. Further, as there had been scant immigration from many countries of Central and South America, there was an insufficient base on which to establish individual country quotas. For all these reasons, no numerical ceiling was placed on Western Hemisphere immigration until

1965, although individual immigrants from this region were subject to the general qualifications and specific exclusions that applied to all immigrants.

Another reason that immigration continued to grow during the 1920s, despite the enactment of restrictive legislation, was the surging number of illegal entrants. From the time the nation began to impose screening restrictions on would-be immigrants in the 1870s, countless numbers of supposedly excludable persons still sought to enter and were usually successful—thanks to those extensive land borders with Canada and Mexico. The United States was able to secure some assistance from Canada but Mexico offered little help. Of particular concern was the frequent use of the Mexican border as a means of entry for illegal immigrants from China.

In 1904 the Bureau of Immigration assigned seventy-five inspectors to patrol the 1,945-mile southern border on horseback, but these initial efforts proved too meager to be real deterrents. Over the years the situation worsened: with the passage of the quota laws in 1921 and 1924, the problem was greatly exacerbated by the efforts of Europeans who could no longer enter in unlimited numbers. Consequently, in 1924, Congress established the U.S. Border Patrol as a uniformed enforcement agency in the Department of Labor to deter the entry of illegal immigrants and to deport those found in the United States. Congress provided funds to hire 450 persons to perform these duties. Nearly all who were originally appointed were chosen from a register of applicants for federal jobs as railway postal clerks, since there was no civil service register in existence at the time for these new positions.[32]

Because of illegal entries, the "real" level of immigration in the 1920s was no doubt higher than the official figures cited in Table 5.3. Some economists have made the mistake of assuming that the quota laws of the 1920s must have had the immediate impact of reducing the supply of labor, thus explaining the sharp rise in real wages that occurred in this decade.[33] But since immigration levels remained quite high throughout the 1920s (especially if one considers additional numbers of illegal immigrants), and since it was not until 1929 that the Immigration Act of 1924 became fully effective, a different explanation is most likely: that it was the effect of accelerating technology in the 1920s driving down product prices, rather than any perceived "shortened supply" of labor, that accounted for the actual real wage gains of the 1920s.

There is no debate that with the advent of the Great Depression in 1929 immigration levels plummeted. Not only were the low quotas in full effect by then, but the bottom had fallen out of the labor market. Abundant jobs and rising wages gave way to mass unemployment and falling wages. As shown in Table 5.3, immigration for the decade of the 1930s fell to levels lower than any experienced for more than a century. Not even the low quotas assigned to the countries of eastern and southern Europe were met. It is likely that more people emigrated from the country in 1933, than immigrated. Some state and local governments, burdened by high relief costs, pressured Mexican immigrants, who had come in large numbers in the 1920s, to return to their homeland.[34]

Also in the 1930s a new immigration issue surfaced that would have major policy consequences in subsequent years: the issue of refugee accommodation. Before the passage of the Immigration Act of 1924 there was no need to be concerned about how the United States might respond to the needs of persons who sought to escape persecution in their homelands; if they could get to the United States, they were generally admitted. But once quotas were set for some countries and total bans on others, the era of automatic admission ended; the Immigration Act of 1924 contained no provisions for exceptions to its terms. In the 1930s, however, as the events in Europe and Asia which would culminate in World War II began to percolate, there were people in Germany and Italy who feared the actions of their own governments and citizens of neighboring nations who either sensed imminent danger or were already experiencing invasions. Many of these people sought to emigrate to the United States.

But as the United States had just ended a century of virtually continuous mass immigration and was in the throes of the worst economic collapse in its history, the country was in no political mood to be accommodating. To be sure, some 250 thousand refugees from Axis or Axis-occupied nations who were admitted between 1933 and 1941—about half of all the immigrants over this time span. Perhaps two-thirds of these refugees were Jews, but in all they came from twenty-one different countries.[35] They were admitted, however, not because they were refugees per se, but because they were eligible within the quotas provided by the law.

It is not surprising, then, that the characteristics of the immigrants of the 1930s represent a series of anomalies. Of the 528,431 legal immigrants of that decade, Germany was the largest single source country (which had not been the case since the 1880s), accounting for 22 percent of the total flow. Most of these immigrants were people who, under normal conditions, would not have wanted to leave their native lands but felt they now had no choice. They were not the rural peasants who had dominated the mass flows of the third wave, which had ended only a little over a decade earlier. Instead, they were mostly from urban middle and upper classes. There were large numbers of white-collar workers, businessmen, manufacturers, and professionals, including physicians, scholars, and scientists.[36] These were not typical people who would choose to enter the working class of the nation or seek blue-collar jobs.

As indicated in Table 5.3, immigration levels declined even more during the war years. Few would-be immigrants could escape the fighting in much of Europe and Asia, and even if they could, the military draft in effect for all U.S. men between eighteen and thirty-five years old was not much of an incentive. Even agriculture, the one industry that sought foreign labor to meet the perceived shortage of unskilled workers during the war years, had to rely on special legislation—not part of the nation's existing immigration system—to gain the temporary admission of workers from Mexico and the British West Indies.[37] When the planting and harvest seasons were over, these agricultural workers were expected to return home, and most did; some stayed, albeit illegally. (These "temporary" worker programs were continued after the war and became a subject of extensive controversy—especially with organized labor.)

When the war ended in 1945, the immigration system became the subject of renewed criticism. The issue was not the low level of immigration. There was little interest in going back to the pre-1924 days of unregulated entry. Rather, the concerns were the inflexibility of the system and its overtly discriminatory features.

The immediate catalyst for controversy was the issue of refugee accommodation, which rapidly worsened after the war. Millions of Europeans had been displaced from their native countries during the years of conflict. Many did not wish to resettle in eastern Europe where the Soviet Union, with its variant of totalitarian Communism, was in the process of taking political control of their homelands. To make matters worse, the devastation of the war had left the west European countries to which refugees were now fleeing in no position to accommodate such large inflows.

President Truman, realizing that the responsibilities of world leadership had been thrust upon the United States, sought to act accordingly. But he could function only within the confines of the immigration laws. In December 1945, he ordered the admission of 80 thousand refugees, mostly from eastern and southern Europe, by declaring that these persons were filling, retroactively, their countries' unused visa slots from the war years. Truman also successfully pressed Congress to pass the Displaced Persons Act of 1948, which admitted another 205 thousand refugees from east European countries. This ad hoc legislation, the first refugee measure ever enacted by Congress, accomplished its purpose by allowing these countries—which all had very low annual quotas—to mortgage up to half of their future admission quotas for a specific number of years in favor of immediate admissions. In the long run, therefore, the ethnic composition of the nation—which the national origins system sought to preserve—would not be altered, for refugees arriving from those countries would be subtracted from the number who would have entered anyhow in the future. In 1951 the legislation was amended again to admit an additional 188,542 European refugees under essentially the same mortgaging arrangement.

But there were just so many contortions of the existing system that could be performed. The issue of refugee accommodation was a main reason that President Truman initiated an effort to overhaul the nation's immigration system. He believed the overtly discriminatory features that were at the heart of the prevailing law did not befit a nation that had become a world leader.

The Great Depression years, followed by the war years, had caused a greater reduction in the levels of annual immigration than even the restrictionist advocates of the Immigration Act of 1924 had sought. From the time the national origin quotas took effect in 1929 until 1949, only 27 percent of the authorized quotas had actually been used. Even counting the nonquota immigrants from the Western Hemisphere, the total for the period was only 75 percent of what the overall quota would have allowed. Indeed, given the fact that there was considerable emigration during the 1930s, immigration had simply ceased to be of consequence to the American economy. Symbolically, its numerical insignificance at the time was marked by the closing of Ellis Island, the historic immigrant gateway, in 1954. In aggregate terms, the importance of immigration to the American economy was diminishing with every passing year and continued to do so until the mid-1960s.

Indeed, in the postwar years, the nation's immigration system was confronted with a startling paradox: the ethnocentrism of the national origin quotas was distorting the administration of the entire system. Some countries such as Great Britain, which were entitled to a high percentage of all authorized visas, could not fill their annual quotas; whereas countries such as Italy and Greece, which had low annual quotas, had massive backlogs of applicants.

Under these circumstances there was considerable interest, not only in the White House but also in Congress and among the general populace, to move away from an admissions system based on ethnic and racial selectivity. They favored both a nondiscriminatory system based on humanitarian principles (to assist persons confronted with the threat of persecution) and one geared toward admitting immigrants who had human resource attributes that could benefit the nation. In other words, they sought an immigration policy designed to meet defined national interests.

The Immigration and Nationality Act of 1952

In response to prodding by President Truman, in 1947 the Senate initiated a congressional study of the extant immigration system. But its report of April 1950 completely dismissed the goals advocated by Truman and other reformers. Instead, it argued for the maintenance of the status quo: "The committee believes that the adoption of the national origin system quota formulas was a rational and logical method of numerically restricting immigration in such a manner as to best preserve the sociological and cultural balance of the United States."[38] On the basis of these findings, Congress adopted the Immigration and Nationality Act of 1952 over President Truman's stinging veto.[39] The new law perpetuated, with only slight modification, the prevailing low level of immigration as well as the national origins admissions system on all immigration from the Eastern Hemisphere. It did, however, make an important change with respect to Asia: all the overt exclusions against Asian immigrants were eliminated (i.e., the "Asian Barred Zone" was repealed), and the individual countries of that vast region were each given a small annual quota, raising the overall ceiling for the Eastern Hemisphere to 156,700 entrants (plus immediate family members).

In his veto message, President Truman assailed the legislation's lack of attention to actual reform:

The basis of this quota system was false and unworthy in 1924. It is even worse now. At the present time this quota system keeps out the very people we want to bring in. It is incredible to me that, in this year of 1952, we should again be enacting into law such a slur on the patriotism, the capacity, and the decency of a large part of our citizenry . . .

In no other realm of our national life are we so hampered and stultified by the dead hand of the past as we are in this field of immigration.[40]

Although the new legislation made only minor changes in the overall quota system, it made major changes in how priorities were assigned. A four-category preference system was established. The first category, which was allocated 50 percent of all visas, was assigned to eligible immigrants on the basis of their educational attainment, technical training, special experiences, or exceptional abilities that were deemed to be of benefit to the United States. The act also introduced the concept of labor certification as a prerequisite for the admission of these immigrants, but it was to be administered in a passive manner: that is, the secretary of labor was empowered to certify that the admission of these non-family-related immigrants would not adversely affect the wages or working conditions of citizens who were employed in the same occupations or industries. The U.S. Department of Labor, therefore, was obligated to refuse certification if it anticipated any adverse economic impact to American workers.

Clearly, Congress was giving official recognition to the idea that immigration policy should be used primarily as an instrument of human resource policy, meant to be congruent with actual labor market needs. In turn, the other three categories of admission, which were of lower order of priority, were provided to various categories of adult relatives of persons who were already citizens or permanent resident aliens. The Immigration and Nationality Act did not alter the admission status of would-be immigrants from countries of the Western Hemisphere. They remained exempt from coverage by either the overall ceiling or national origin quotas.

Throughout the remainder of the 1950s there was considerable controversy associated with the nation's immigration system because none of the real issues had been addressed by the 1952 legislation. Refugee accommodation was a constant problem throughout the Eisenhower administration; on several occasions, ad hoc pieces of legislation had to be rushed through Congress to deal with the topic.[41] Moreover, from 1952 until 1965 the nation's immigration system found itself still trapped in a paradoxical situation: only 61 percent of the system's total quota slots were actually issued, yet tens of thousands of persons were seeking entry but could not be admitted because they were from countries with low quotas.

As the number of nonquota immigrants from the Western Hemisphere began to rise during the 1950s and to approximate the number of quota immigrants admitted each year, and as various groups of refugees were continuing to be admitted outside the quota provisions, it was apparent that the immigration law was out of step with the events it sought to regulate. In fact, only one of every three immigrants to the United States between 1952 and 1965 was admitted under the terms of the national origins system. Moreover, the national origins restriction was crippling the intentions of the new preference system created in 1952: the first-preference immigrants—those admitted because they had desired human capital attributes—accounted for only 1 percent of entrants between 1952 and 1965. The reasons were twofold. First, the preference system by definition did not apply to immigrants from the Western Hemisphere, who were not numerically restricted. Second, countries from the Eastern Hemisphere with large quotas (e.g., Great Britain) often had unfilled slots; hence, there was no need to apply the preference system to immigrants from these countries because there were insufficient applicants anyhow. Thus, the only persons subjected to the first-preference requirements were skilled and educated persons from Eastern Hemisphere nations that had low quotas, causing long backlogs of such applicants. Hence, the whole notion that the legal immigration system should be designed to meet labor market needs was being undermined by the very law that created this intention.

It should be noted (for later discussion) that the Immigration and Nationality Act repealed the Alien Contract Law of 1885 (see Chapter 3), which forbade the recruitment of foreign workers under contractual terms. In the 1990s this issue would become a major concern for organized labor. At the time, however, its significance was not recognized.

The Immigration Act of 1965

With the election of President John Kennedy in 1960, the subject of immigration reform was once more placed on the national agenda. The issue was not raised in the presidential campaign that led to his victory, nor was it of central concern in his immediate legislative agenda. But Kennedy, as a member of Congress for the preceding fourteen years, had strongly supported all the ad hoc measures to admit various groups of refugees, and in 1958 he had published a short book praising the contributions of immigrants to American life. According to his brother Robert Kennedy, the intention of that book was to provide an understanding that "was essential to any future effort to eliminate the discrimination and cruelty of our immigration laws."[42]

On 23 July 1963, Kennedy formally transmitted to Congress a legislative proposal to revise the nation's immigration system in which he stated that "the most urgent and fundamental reform I am recommending relates to the national origins system of selecting immigrants." He recommended that it be replaced by a system giving first priority to "the skills of the immigrant and their relationship to our need," regardless of where that immigrant was born. He acknowledged that this preference existed under prevailing law but pointed out that it could not function within the restrictive confines of the national origins system. His proposal did not call for an increase in the level of immigration—"there is, of course, a legislative argument for some limitations upon immigration. We no longer need settlers for virgin lands"—but noted that even the most liberal bill pending in Congress at the time would raise the annual immigration quota from the existing 156,700 visa slots to only 250,000. Therefore, he reiterated, "the clash of opinion arises not over the number of immigrants to be admitted, but over the test for admission." It was the test, the national origins selection method, that he sought to change.[43]

Following the assassination of President Kennedy on 22 November 1963, President Lyndon Johnson began the process of enacting the Kennedy policy agenda, almost all of which had been previously stalled by a recalcitrant Congress. Johnson accomplished the feat—and much more.

Not until mid-1965, however, was Congress able to get to the Johnson administration's immigration reform proposals. The original bill called for a five-year phaseout of the national origins system but proposed that the high priority given under the existing law to human capital characteristics remain intact. Half the visa slots each year would be reserved for immigrants who had skills, talents, or work experience that were currently needed by the U.S. economy, just as President Kennedy had proposed. The other half would go to various categories of adult immigrants who were relatives of citizens or permanent resident aliens. The preferences would apply only to Eastern Hemisphere nations. There was nothing in the proposed bill that was intended to raise the level of immigration by any significant amount. As Secretary of State Dean Rusk testified before Congress in support of the proposed bill, "The significance of immigration for the United States now depends less on the numbers than on the quality of the immigrants."[44] Likewise, Senator Edward Kennedy (D-Massachusetts), the floor manager of the bill in the Senate, stated, "This bill is not concerned with increasing immigration to this country, nor will it lower any of the high standards we apply in the selection of immigrants." Kennedy also tried to reassure skeptics that "our cities will not be flooded with a million immigrants annually," that "the ethnic mix of this country will not be upset," and that the pending bill "would not cause American workers to lose their jobs."[45] Presumably, these assurances were made at that time because they would not be desirable policy outcomes.

Since Congress had finally passed the historic Civil Rights Act of 1964 only months earlier, it was not difficult to find political agreement about ending the overt racism of the national origins system. But agreeing on what to replace it with was entirely another story. Congressional leaders let it be known to the Johnson administration that any new legislation had to contain two new components. First, there must also be a ceiling on

Western Hemisphere immigration; they feared that the absence of such a limit, combined with the extraordinarily high population growth of Latin America, would otherwise lead to an uncontrollable influx from this region in the near future. Second, the labor certification requirements for non-family-related immigrants had to be strengthened to protect American workers.

The administration was forced to accede. The final bill, therefore, contained an annual ceiling of 120,000 immigrants a year from countries of the Western Hemisphere, to take effect on 1 July 1968.[46] It was the first time general restrictions had ever been placed on Western Hemisphere immigration. The bill also reversed the previous logic of the labor certification requirement: thereafter, all non-family-related immigrants would have to get positive certification from the Department of Labor that their presence would not adversely affect the wages or working conditions of American workers before they could receive a visa.

A new ceiling was set for Eastern Hemisphere immigrants at 170,000 visas a year, which, combined with the new Western Hemisphere ceiling, meant that the number of visas available each year would total 290,000. In addition, besides immediate family members (defined as spouses and children under the age of twenty-one), parents of U.S. citizens were for the first time to be admitted without restriction. For the Eastern Hemisphere only, a seven-category preference system was set up, which significantly altered the original intention of the reform movement. The new system gave highest admission priority to family reunification: four of the seven categories, to which 74 percent of the available visas were to be allocated, pertained to the admission preferences for family reunification. Of particular consequence was the creation of a new admissions category for adult brothers and sisters of U.S. citizens. The two labor market categories established were not only downgraded to lower priorities but reduced to only 20 percent of the annual allotment of visas. A new seventh preference level was created for refugees—the first time that U.S. immigration law had contained such a specific admission category—who were allotted 6 percent of the annual visa slots. Thus, 80 percent of the visas issued each year would be allocated without regard to the human capital attributes of the would-be immigrants (i.e., those pertaining to family and refugee admissions). (Western Hemisphere immigrants would be admitted on a first come, first served basis up to the newly established annual ceiling.)

The drastic change in the priorities for admission were made by Congress in response to the lobbying pressures of various groups (e.g., the American Legion and the Daughters of the American Revolution) strongly opposed to the abandonment of the national origins system. Aware that they could not block the reform drive on this fundamental issue, they sought to make the changes in admissions criteria more symbolic than real. They believed that stressing family reunification would make it possible to retain virtually the same racial and ethnic priorities that the national origins system had fostered, even if the selection device itself was abolished. It seemed unlikely that many persons from Asia or southern and eastern Europe would be admitted under the new system because the prohibitions imposed during the prior forty years had prevented the entry of so many people from those countries that the few who were admitted would not likely have many living relatives in their homelands who could now qualify. Conversely, those previously favored over the preceding forty or fifty years would most likely still have living relatives in their homelands who would qualify. Representatives of various Asian American organizations vigorously protested the shift to an emphasis on family reunification for this very reason. The Department of Justice also opposed this change in priorities, estimating that Asian immigration might hit a high of about 5,000 immigrants a year before falling to an even lower annual level.[47]

Nevertheless, the Johnson Administration was forced to accept these changes as the price of ending the much despised national origins system. To satisfy the private interests of some citizens rather than serve the national interest, the principle of family reunification became the cornerstone of the new immigration system and remains so, even though it does not rest on a morally sound foundation.[48]

On 3 October 1965, President Johnson signed the Immigration Act of 1965 into law.[49] It was, said Elizabeth Harper, "the most far reaching revision of immigration policy since the imposition of the first numerical quota in 1921."[50] Its primary intention was to eliminate the overtly discriminatory features of earlier immigration legislation, and in this regard it has been an unqualified success. Nor was it intended to significantly increase the level of immigration. Yet the new law set in motion a process whereby mass immigration would once more become a distinguishing feature of the U.S. economy. A sleeping giant of economic policy had been awakened out of the nation's distant past.

Policy Administration: A Brief Digression

Significant changes occurred in the administration of U.S. immigration policy during the 1920–65 era. In June 1933 the separate Bureau of Im-

migration (which included the Border Patrol) and the Bureau of Naturalization were consolidated by Roosevelt's Executive Order 6166 to form a
single federal agency, the Immigration and Naturalization Service (INS).
The agency remained in the Department of Labor, but because of the decline in the level of immigration in the 1930s, the department's staff and
funding were sharply reduced.[51]

Although the scale of immigration declined, however, the complexity
associated with its day-to-day administration and enforcement of immigration matters continued unabated.[52] The refugee issue in particular was
an extremely time-consuming concern. But with the nation in the midst
of the Depression, the Department of Labor was also on the front lines of
major domestic policy issues. It was involved with the various job-creation
programs of the New Deal. It was also deeply concerned with the polarized state of labor-management relations, seeking ways to institutionalize
a formal collective bargaining system. And it was working to have a host of
labor protection proposals relating to child labor, minimum wages, maximum hours, and unemployment compensation enacted by Congress.

As a consequence, Secretary of Labor Frances Perkins began to agitate
behind the scenes for relief from the department's immigration responsibilities, which she saw as diverting attention and scarce resources from
other pressing domestic needs. Indeed, by 1940, 60 percent of the department's limited personnel were involved with the administration of
the immigration system.[53] Moreover, as it became clear that the United
States was going to become involved in a war in Europe and probably with
Japan as well, national concern with immigration issues shifted from employment impact to internal security matters: it was feared that immigration would become an entryway for enemy spies and saboteurs. Hence, a
fateful decision was made. On 20 May 1940, President Roosevelt recommended that Congress shift the INS from the Department of Labor to the
Department of Justice. The transfer was made not for efficiency but out of
national security concerns. Roosevelt made it clear that after the war,
Congress should reconsider where the administration of immigration
matters should be properly housed.[54]

Interestingly, Attorney General Robert Jackson opposed the move of
the INS to his department. Secretary of Labor Perkins strongly favored
the shift, as she had found her office "swamped" by immigration issues.
But after leaving government service Perkins concluded that Justice was
not the right agency to have responsibility for the for the administration
of immigration policy.[55] The Department of Justice has multiple other duties, and as a consequence, immigration matters are often treated as a
neglected stepchild. Moreover, the agency has no expertise in employ-

ment or labor market issues, and it is a highly politicized agency that often looks to expedient solutions to controversial issues without concern for long-run consequences. Nonetheless, the responsibility for the administration, enforcement, and formulation of immigration policy has remained with the Department of Justice since 1940.

Unionism

Having been handily defeated in its efforts to organize the steel industry in 1919, the labor movement began the 1920s on a sour note and, over the decade, everything went downhill from there. President Calvin Coolidge set the tone for the period by declaring, "The chief business of the American people is business." The seeds of opposition to unions were deeply planted. The labor movement was viewed as immoral, illegal, and dangerous to the American way of life. These were, as Irving Bernstein has aptly described them, "the lean years" for America's unions.[56]

There were multiple approaches to the assault on unionism. A psychological attack that centered on the advocacy of the "open-shop" (also called the American Plan) was led by the National Association of Manufacturers. Allegedly, the open shop was one where equal hiring opportunity would prevail for all, regardless of whether workers belonged to a union or not. In most instances, this claim was fraudulent propaganda, for open-shop firms usually refused to hire or to retain workers who belonged to or attempted to join unions.

Many individual firms initiated human relations policies to make the workplace more pleasant. They organized company activities for their employees—athletic leagues, glee clubs—bands, and some, like the Goodyear Rubber Company, built workers' clubhouses with bowling alleys, gymnasiums, card rooms, swimming pools, and beauty shops. The idea was that workers would reward a paternalistic employer by not joining unions.

Other firms set up company unions, systems of self-government designed to expropriate the key attributes of a collective bargaining system. Typically, workers were allowed to elect a shop chairman and to form joint labor-management committees to discuss shop issues. Under the old system, workers had been seen as "outsiders" to the workplace, with no rights or privileges that management was obliged to respect. With company unions, workers became participants—but, as far as employers were concerned, each firm was a separate island. There was to be no contact with workers in other companies in the same labor market or the same industry; company union membership was restricted to the employees of the firm. The company paid all the organizational costs, but the topics about which the union's representatives could negotiate were carefully prescribed. As a rule, they were limited to individual worker grievances, plant safety, and production efficiency. Management reserved the right to hire and to fire workers; strikes were prohibited; and most important, no discussion of wages or hours was allowed. The major weakness of company unions was the absence of any real power for workers.

Many businesses were also putting into practice the principles of scientific management as conceived by Frederick W. Taylor. As the size of the enterprises and the scale of production were rapidly increased, it was soon evident that the organization must replace the individual as the source of authority; the individual executive of, say, a family-owned enterprise simply could not efficiently direct a large corporation. Hence, the management function was turned over to professionals. But in this period of transition, many new professionals—who were often engineers—were just as unprepared to deal with the issues of employee relations as were the former owner-managers. Nonetheless, the new management officials—reflecting Taylor's views—believed that existing workplace practices were administratively wasteful. Employees sought to do as little as possible yet to be rewarded as much as possible; employers, on the other hand, sought to get as much effort from their workers as possible yet pay them as little as possible.

Such a struggle, as seen by Taylor and his followers, was grossly inefficient. They thought that management should resolve the impasse by reorganizing so that the employer could determine the actual contribution of workers and reward them accordingly. To do this, management needed to quantify, systematize and coordinate the production process through such measures as job analysis, time-and-motion studies, piece rates, and incentive pay systems. Wage rates, accordingly, were not something to bargain over but something to be determined by actual work performance. Obviously, the union movement was appalled by such an approach; interestingly, even many old-line managers objected to the substitution of studies and measurements for their time-tested dictatorial methods.

Another assault on unions during the 1920s and early 1930s was a full-scale legal attack launched by the nation's court system. On 20 June 1920, former President William Howard Taft was appointed Chief Justice of the Supreme Court. He held this position until February 1930 and was the chief architect of the antiunion decisions that followed (as noted earlier, the AFL had opposed Taft in his unsuccessful effort to be reelected president in 1912). President Harding, despite his brief two years in office, appointed not only Taft but also three other conservative justices to the Court.

As there was still no statutory law at the federal level to guide the Court, labor law was based entirely on common law (i.e., judge-made decisions).

At the time, unions were considered to be lawful private associations, but the courts imposed severe limitations on their activities: on the use of consumer boycotts, picketing, and even the right to strike. In 1921 the Supreme Court essentially nullified the antitrust laws' exemption of unions that the Clayton Act had provided.[57] The labor injunction, which was supposedly for use only under extraordinary conditions, became the ordinary device used regularly by courts to restrict union activity and to forestall union organization.[58] As a consequence, the gulf between labor and the law became perilously wide. It was the general belief of most workers and all union leaders that the common man could not receive justice in any court in the country.

Finally, if none of the foregoing tactics worked, many companies turned to the use of brute force—terror and intimidation—to forestall the spread of unionism. Professional strikebreakers were employed; labor spies were hired to infiltrate unions; labor missionaries were sent to workers' homes to warn family members of the dangers of union support by their breadwinners; public officials were bribed to make it hard for union organizers in their communities; private police forces were established to hassle workers; and even night-riding vigilante groups were used to physically subdue union activists.[59]

As shown in Table 5.4, union membership declined in absolute numbers and as a proportion of the employed labor force throughout the 1920s and early 1930s. Major membership losses occurred in the coal mining and textile industries.

In 1924, the AFL sustained its first major change in leadership when Samuel Gompers died. He was replaced by William Green, the son of English immigrants, who accepted all Gompers's views about the organization's structure *except* the preeminence of craft unions. As a former miner, he had sympathy for industrial unionism, but he was not a strong leader. During his long tenure in office (which was until 1952), power tended to flow to the AFL executive council with its strong personalities and craft union advocates. Green avoided militancy toward the business community, preferring to stress organized labor's role as an auxiliary to business and as a supporter of capitalism.

But with the advent of the Depression in 1929 and the years that followed, the plight of unionism became desperate (see Table 5.4). The situation was so bad that George Barnett, president of the American Economic Association, delivered in 1932 what he believed to be a eulogy for the American labor movement:

Table 5.4. Union Membership of Nonagricultural Employed Labor Force, 1920–1965

Year	Union Membership (in thousands)	Percentage Unionized of Nonagricultural Employed Labor Force
1920	4,823.3	17.6
1921	4,398.3	18.0
1922	3,754.2	14.5
1923	3,476.2	12.2
1924	3,411.2	12.2
1925	3,685.1	12.8
1926	3,742.2	12.5
1927	3,844.9	12.8
1928	3,790.2	12.6
1929	3,750.5	10.0
1930	3,749.6	12.7
1931	3,559.7	13.4
1932	3,400.2	14.4
1933	3,491.0	14.7
1934	4,002.7	15.4
1935	3,649.6	13.5
1936	4,140.7	14.2
1937	5,706.1	18.4
1938	5.961.7	20.4
1939	6,491.3	21.2
1940	7,296.7	22.5
1941	8,728.6	23.9
1942	10,187.1	25.4
1943	11,673.6	27.5
1944	12,129.8	29.0
1945	12,254.2	30.4
1946	12,935.7	31.1
1947	14,067.1	32.1
1948	14,271.9	31.8
1949	13,935.8	31.9
1950	14,294.2	31.6
1951	15,139.4	31.7
1952	15,632.0	32.0
1953	13,310.0	32.5
1954	15,808.5	32.3
1955	16,126.9	31.8
1956	16,446.0	31.4
1957	16,497.7	31.2
1958	15,570.5	30.3
1959	15,438.3	29.0
1960	15,516.1	28.6
1961	15,400.5	28.5
1962	16,893.9	30.4
1963	17,133.4	30.2
1964	17,597.2	30.2
1965	18,268.9	30.1

Source: Leo Troy and Neil Sheffin, *U.S. Union Sourcebook* (West Orange, N.J.: Industrial Relations Data and Information Services, 1985). Pp. A-1–2.

The past ten years have seen changes of amazing magnitude in the organization of American society. It is of one of these fundamental alterations that I wish to speak this evening. There are doubtless other changes of a more spectacular kind but I doubt whether any other is of more permanent import, both in practical results and in theoretical interest. The change to which I refer is the lessening importance of trade unionism in American economic organizations.[60]

But the announcement of the passing of the labor movement proved to be premature, for it was in 1932 that the first sign of a change in the antiunion posture of government occurred. After several years of effort, Congress finally passed the Norris-LaGuardia Act, which was signed into law—though not with enthusiasm—by President Herbert Hoover.[61]

Drafted by a panel of distinguished professors of economics and labor law, sponsored by two Republican congressmen, the legislation was far more comprehensive in its scope than any that labor leaders had dared to expect. This legislation gave statutory recognition to the right of workers to organize and to bargain collectively with representatives of their own choosing. And it prohibited a number of antiunion tactics—most important the use of court injunctions in labor disputes to restrict peaceful union activity.

During the presidential campaign of 1932, candidate Franklin Roosevelt spoke of the need to address the problem of "the forgotten man at the bottom of the economic pyramid." Following his election, labor anxiously waited to see what he would propose. New Deal labor policy was rooted in the principle that workers should have the unrestricted right to organize and to bargain collectively, which was quickly incorporated in the National Industrial Recovery Act (NIRA) that became law in June 1933. Intended to be the foundation of the administration's recovery program, the NIRA established codes of control over the entire industrial structure of the nation. It was, in reality, a broad program of national economic planning. The AFL leadership and other labor leaders rejoiced at the code supporting collective bargaining. Its words constituted an infusion of new breath for the flagging labor movement. Union organizers set forth to restore old membership levels and to form new unions in industries where labor had never been organized. The mine workers, under the leadership of John L. Lewis, were especially invigorated and, within a year, the UMW's membership had tripled. Lewis and others sought to expand the crusade to industries such as steel, automobiles, and rubber.

But many employers simply ignored the mandate of the NIRA to recognize unions, and many organizing efforts failed when confronted with strong opposition. Unfortunately, the legislation had not created a formal agency to enforce its terms. Then, on 17 May 1935, the Supreme Court declared the entire NIRA unconstitutional. An infuriated Roosevelt labeled the action "a horse and buggy decision" totally out of step with current reality. He immediately extended his full support to a much stronger bill that had been languishing in Congress: the National Labor Relations Act (NLRA) sponsored by Senator Robert Wagner (D-New York). It was quickly passed and was signed into law on 5 July 1935. It had strong labor support, for not only did it reiterate the right of workers to form unions and to bargain collectively; it also required that management recognize a duly certified bargaining agent and bargain in good faith with that certified union. Furthermore, it created a statutory agency, the National Labor Relations Board (NLRB), to hold certification elections and to hear complaints of violations of the act. It also specified a number of unfair labor practices by employers.

The thesis of the NLRA (also called the Wagner Act) is that because there is a fundamental inequality in the power of the individual worker and the power of a corporation when it comes to contractual relations, workers have the right to bargain as a group, and management cannot legally stop them from doing so. Two years later, on 12 April 1937, the Supreme Court upheld the constitutionality of the Wagner Act, and collective bargaining was affirmed as the law of the land.[62] Moreover, with this historic decision, the Court held that the federal government could regulate activity in any industry that "affects" interstate commerce, not (as previously) just those "engaged in" interstate commerce. As to what industries "affect" interstate commerce, they are whatever industries Congress declares do so (agriculture, for example, was specifically exempted from coverage by the Wagner Act). The following year, 1938, the Supreme Court also upheld the Norris-LaGuardia Act with its comprehensive protections against the use of injunctions in peaceful labor disputes.[63]

Meanwhile, the long-simmering internal feud within the labor movement over the strategy for organizing industrial workers came to a head. Lewis was convinced that the time was ripe "to organize the unorganized." At the 1935 convention of the AFL, he took the issue to the floor. He insisted that the traditional approach of dividing workers into their separate crafts or specialties and attempting to organize them on that basis (as had been unsuccessfully attempted in the steel industry in 1919) was doomed to failure. He argued for organizing the mass production industries into a single union for each separate industry.

Lewis and his supporters lost their convention fight following a lengthy and tumultuous floor debate, but in the days following, the dissidents held a meeting. Calling themselves the Committee for Industrial Organization (CIO), they announced an ambitious plan to commence organizing campaigns in steel, automobiles, rubber, and radio manufacturing. William Green and the AFL responded by charging that the CIO constituted a form of dual unionism—a practice considered a mortal sin in trade union circles.

But the CIO campaign proved wildly successful. Local unions popped up in businesses that had never before been confronted with the prospect that their workers might organize. But creating local unions was one thing; getting employers to recognize their existence was another. Most employers initially disregarded the Wagner Act requirement that they do so, because they were confident it would be struck down by the courts.

In early 1936 the first of the famous sit-down strikes occurred in the rubber industry, and later the tactics were repeated in the automobile industry. In both cases, facilities were occupied for several weeks by workers, supported by mass picketing outside the plants. The disputes ended only when most of the companies extended recognition to the CIO unions. The sit-down strikes were an illegal invasion of private property and were so ruled by the Supreme Court in 1938. The use of such an extreme tactic, however, has to be viewed as a reaction to the array of militant antiunion tactics that had been used by employers over the preceding years.

In the steel industry, the CIO won a dramatic victory against its ancient foe, U.S. Steel, without a fight. In March 1937, after secret negotiations between Lewis and the president of the firm, Myron Taylor, the company announced that it would unilaterally recognize and bargain with the CIO organizing union. Within the next month, fifty-one other steel companies signed similar agreements.

Yet a number of smaller, independent steel companies held out and declared that they would operate only as open-shop employers. The result was a full-scale antiunion campaign. Violence occurred at a number of plant sites in steel towns between organizing pickets, company-hired guards, and strikebreakers. The conflict hit its peak on Memorial Day, 30 May 1937, at the Republic Steel plant in South Chicago when a peaceful picket line was halted by police. Several objects were thrown; the police opened fire; and unarmed workers fled across an open field. When the smoke cleared, ten workers had been killed and a hundred others injured—most of them shot in the back. There was a nationwide outburst of both disbelief and outrage, as the whole incident had been captured on film. This event, immortalized in labor history as the "Memorial Day Massacre," brought to a close the era of bloody battles over the issue of union recognition.[64] Ironically, the incident had happened only weeks after the Supreme Court had upheld the constitutionality of the Wagner Act. Still, the CIO had sustained its first defeat. These steel companies continued to resist unionization until 1941, when they were specifically ordered by the Supreme Court to recognize the union.

The AFL leaders were shocked by the successes of the CIO organizing campaign, they had believed that industrial workers could not be organized or bargain effectively within firms because they could not control the supply of labor, and therefore, industrial unions could not acquire sufficient strength to prevent nonunion competition from undermining their bargaining positions. Nevertheless, the CIO showed that with determined effort, and with the support of government policies that were being upheld by the courts, many such firms could be organized.

In the fall of 1937, however, the twelve national unions that were supporting the CIO efforts were expelled by the AFL at its annual convention. In May 1938, Lewis met with the leaders of expelled unions and the twenty other newly formed industrial unions (or organizing committees) to form a new labor federation. Keeping the now famous CIO initials, they founded the Congress of Industrial Organizations and elected Lewis its first president.

The CIO was established on many of the same principles as its former parent organization, the AFL. It was totally committed to the advancement of the economic status of workers through the use of collective bargaining within the structure of a democratic capitalist system. Its differences were its greater reliance on the use of political action to gain government support for the beneficial worker legislation, and its substitution of industrial autonomy for craft autonomy as its structural foundation. It retained the principle of exclusive jurisdiction of each member union to determine what to pursue at the bargaining table in the best interest of its members.

Amazed at the success of the CIO, the AFL did not retreat into a shell but opted to change its ways and actively recruit members, regardless of whether they fitted into established craft molds. Semiskilled and unskilled workers were sought—especially by the machinists and the teamsters. Other AFL unions broadened their scope to become semiindustrial unions, while still others embraced members of multiple crafts. Full-scale "raiding" efforts were made to attract workers that the CIO unions had already organized; industrial unions were chartered to compete for members in such CIO strongholds as steel, autos, meatpacking, and paper manufacturing. By 1940, as a consequence, membership in AFL-affiliated unions had increased to 4.2 million (up from 2.9 million in 1937), while membership in the CIO unions had fallen to 3.6 million (down from 4.0 million in 1937).[65]

But of greater importance is the fact that by 1940, 22.5 percent of the nonagricultural labor force was unionized (see Table 5.4)—the highest percentage that the labor movement had yet achieved. And the dramatic turnaround in the fate of unionism had occurred despite the fact that the nation was still in the grasp of a major economic depression. It should also be emphasized that this growth in union membership occurred during the decade in which immigration levels had been of no numerical consequence for the first time since the rise of the union movement itself.

When World War II brought the necessity of uninterrupted production, there were some "wildcat" strikes, but for the most part they were quickly settled. The only exception was in the coal industry: on two occasions in 1943 the nation's mines were seized by the federal government. But ultimately an agreement was reached that allowed the mine workers to receive wage increases proportional to the increase in prices that had occurred before the government got its national price regulation system into effect.

By the end of the war in 1945, over 30 percent of the nonagricultural labor force was unionized and membership was also at an historic high (see Table 5.4). The growth in union membership had occurred largely because of the expansion of the industries in which unions were already established when the war began: autos, steel, aircraft, electrical manufacturing, mining, and transportation. As wartime demand had expanded in these sectors, so did their work forces, and so did union rosters.

When the war ended, there was an unprecedented wave of strikes. The pledges not to strike were over and there was an accumulation of unresolved and unsatisfactorily settled grievances in every industry. More important, however, the sudden abandonment of government controls over prices and wages led to a surge in inflation. The multiple strikes caused alarm in many parts of the nation concerning the rapid growth of organized labor and the whole system of collective bargaining that had been created to resolve industrial differences. It was against this backdrop that the Taft-Hartley Act was passed over President Truman's veto. It accepted the principle that collective bargaining was a desirable method of dispute settlement, but it placed restraints on union activities. It required unions to bargain in good faith and outlined a series of unfair labor practices that labor could not use. It allowed states to preempt federal jurisdiction over labor management relations and to adopt so-called right-to-work laws, which restrict the right of unions to bargain for union security clauses in collective bargaining agreements. It also required union leaders (but not employers) to sign non-Communist affidavits, and it set up provisions by which the president can declare a national emergency in certain strike situations and secure an injunction to force workers back to their jobs. The use of injunctions in a peaceful labor disputes, of course, invoked especially bitter memories for union members and their leaders.

Yet despite the passage of this legislation, which labor bitterly opposed, union membership continued to rise in the postwar years. Once more the growth was largely associated with the continuing expansion of many industries in which they had already established a presence. The continuing demand for consumer goods and for housing, plus the return to war in 1950, this time in Korea, fueled the growth of the goods-producing sector of the economy. By the mid-1950s almost one-third of the labor force were still union members.

In the early 1950s the labor movement went through a significant change in leadership: in late 1952, the presidents of both the AFL and the CIO died within weeks of each other. George Meany, from the plumbers' union, was chosen to succeed William Green as president of the AFL (since 1924); Walter Reuther, of the autoworkers, was elected to replace Philip Murray as president of the CIO (since 1940). With the election of new leaders, the stage was set to end the bitter rivalry that had existed between the two organizations since the 1930s, in late 1955 they merged to form the AFL-CIO. Together, they had over 14 million members in affiliated unions.

Entering the 1960s, membership in trade unions continued to rise in absolute numbers and was keeping up proportionately with the increasing size of the employed labor force. The unionized percentage of the labor force remained at slightly over 30 percent. At the time, no one anticipated that 1965 would be the last year that the percentage would be that high. But it was.

Consequences

It was an influential coalition of diverse groups whose actions secured passage of the legislation that brought an end to the third wave of mass immigration. Protestant church leaders feared that the large inflow of Roman Catholics, Jews, and members of Orthodox sects would threaten the Protestant character of the nation. Sociologists, anthropologists, economists, and social workers—whose views had earlier lent credibility to the findings of the Dillingham Commission's report—reiterated that uncontrolled immigration was creating insoluble assimilation problems in urban centers. Business leaders, for the first time, joined the chorus, expressing fears—based on the 1919 steel strike—that immigrant radicals and Communists were infiltrating the labor force. Extremist groups such as the Ku Klux Klan fueled the drive with their emotional worries about allowing more Catholics and Jews into the nation. But it was the labor movement that most consistently and vocally supported the imposition of a low ceiling on annual immigration admissions. Once more, the AFL itself assumed a leadership position in the articulating to American workers the importance of halting virtually unlimited immigration.[66] In summarizing labor's motivation, Philip Taft concluded that it was "fear of competition for a job and not fear of another race or religion."[67]

Indicative of the depth of this perspective were the views of A. Philip Randolph, cofounder of *The Messenger* magazine (which promoted trade unionism and socialism) and later president of the Brotherhood of Sleeping Car Porters (AFL), as well as a prominent black leader in the civil rights movement. Randolph crystallized the views of working people about the need to bring an end to the era of mass immigration. Not only did he support the passage of the Immigration Act of 1924; he wished it had been made even more restrictive. That year he wrote, "Instead of reducing immigration to 2 percent of the 1890 quota, we favor reducing it to nothing. . . . [T]his country is suffering from immigrant indigestion." He synthesized organized labor's position by explaining that "the excessive immigration is against the interests of the masses of all races and nationalities in the country—both foreign and native"[68] Scholars who have studied the subsequent economic impact of the legislation have confirmed Randolph's assessment of its importance for workers. Historian Joseph Rayback called the Immigration Acts of 1921 and 1924 "the most significant pieces of 'labor' legislation enacted during the post–World War I era." Labor economists Harry Millis and Royal Montgomery observed that "from the international viewpoint the morality of the postwar immigration policy of the United States may be questioned, but of its economic effect in raising real earnings there can be little question." Stanley Lebergott has said of the real wage gains that followed immigration reductions that "political changes in the supply of labor can be more effective in determining wages than even explicit attempts to fix wages."[69]

Freed from having to contend with the seemingly endless annual increases in the labor supply caused by immigration, the union movement could devote its attention to the challenges posed by employers and government to its survival. Likewise, it was also finally able to confront its own internal differences over the proper strategies for organizing industrial

Table 5.5. The Foreign-Born Population, 1920–1965

Year	Foreign-Born Population (millions)	Percentage of Total
1920	13,920	13.2
1930	14,204	11.6
1940	11,594	8.8
1950	10,347	6.9
1960	9.738	5.4
1965	8,549	4.4

Sources: 1920–1960: U.S. Bureau of the Census, *Historical Census Statistics on the Foreign-Born Population of the United States, 1850–1990,* Working Paper no. 29 (Washington D.C.: U.S. Department of Commerce, 1999), table 1.
1965: Jeffrey S. Passel, "30 Years of Immigration and U.S. Population Growth," (paper presented at the annual meeting of the Association for Public Policy Analysis and Management, Washington D.C., November 1995).

workers. As a consequence, the labor movement began its ascendancy in the early 1930s. Table 5.5 shows the decline in the size of the foreign-born population that occurred between 1920 and 1965. When compared with the earlier data on union membership (see Table 5.4), the mirror-image effect is manifestly clear: as the foreign-born population declined in percentage terms, union membership rose in both absolute and percentage terms. From the end of World War II to 1965 the percentage of employed workers who were union members stabilized at about one-third of the nonagricultural labor force. Meanwhile, the foreign-born percentage of the population fell to the historically low level of 4.4 percent of the total population in 1965.

Not until after World War II did the union movement again become involved with immigration matters. And when it did, its interests were focused clearly on the mechanism for restricting immigration, not on any need to increase immigration levels. In 1946 the AFL convention did express its support for President Truman's actions to admit a fixed number of displaced refugees from Europe by using accumulated unfilled quota slots from the war years. But the AFL was quick to insist that "such action in no way modifies the existing immigration laws which have always had the support of the American Federation of Labor."[70]

The first joint convention of the newly merged AFL and CIO in 1955 did adopt a resolution recognizing that the Immigration and Nationality Act of 1952 needed to be amended because the selection system was hampering the ability of the law to meet even its own low admission levels.[71] Given that unfilled quota slots in countries with high allotments coexisted with extensive backlogs of applicants for countries with low allotments, the AFL-CIO, without being specific, called for a selection system that would enable the existing admission ceiling to be reached. It did not recommend that the ceiling be raised.

In June 1956 the AFL-CIO executive council endorsed a pending bill in Congress proposed by Senator Herbert Lehman (D-New York) to replace the national origins system with one designed to reunite families, bring in needed technical and professional workers, admit refugees, and further the nation's foreign policy objectives. The bill also provided for a modest increase in the annual number of immigrant visas from 157,000 to 250,000 a year. No action was taken on the bill by Congress. At its 1957 convention, in turn, the AFL-CIO endorsed the admission of 31,000 Hungarian refugees who had been admitted by the Eisenhower administration over the past year who had fled their country after an abortive attempt to overthrow the Soviet-dominated puppet government in power at the time. Also, the AFL-CIO strongly criticized the continuation of the Mexican Labor Program (popularly known as the *bracero* program) that had been created in 1942 ostensibly as a temporary wartime measure but was still in existence as a way to admit agricultural workers for temporary seasonal work in the Southwest. The AFL-CIO charged that because employers regularly undermined the wage and work standards that were supposedly guaranteed under the law, the program exploited its workers.[72]

In 1959 the AFL-CIO condemned the practice of the commuting border crossers from Mexico who were serving as strikebreakers in labor disputes in U.S. cities along the Mexican border. Known as "greencarders," these Mexican nationals had achieved permanent resident status that allowed them to live and work in the United States, yet they elected to live in Mexico and commute daily into the United States to work. Because of the real income differences between the two countries, they had the dual benefit of the higher U.S. wages and the lower Mexican living costs. Union organizers along the border found that the commuting workers were therefore less willing to join unions or to go on strike than were those who both lived and worked on the U.S. side of the border.[73]

Immigration issues continued to be of concern to the AFL-CIO during the late 1950s and early 1960s, but they were very specific in nature. When the Kennedy Administration set forth its message in support of immigration reform in July 1963, the AFL-CIO endorsed the initiative.[74] Labor shared the view that the intention of the entire immigration reform movement at the time was to end the overt discrimination of the national origin system and only slightly increase the level of annual immigration.

In 1965 the position of the labor movement was strong. Its membership level, as a percentage of the labor force, was close to a record high; annual immigration admissions were of no particular significance; and the percentage of the population who were foreign-born was at a record low. Then the Immigration Act of 1965 became law, and everything changed.

Mass Immigration Returns; Unionism Declines (1965–2000)

The Setting

As subsequent events were to reveal, the year 1965 was a turning-point for both the development of American trade unionism and the history of immigration to the United States. When the year began, union membership was holding constant at about the same proportion of the labor force (30 percent) it had been since the end of World War II, twenty years earlier. Union membership was rising in absolute numbers but not in relative terms. The proportion of the population who were foreign born (4.4 percent) was, in contrast, at the lowest level ever recorded in the nation's history. But all this was about to change. Since 1965 the unionized percentage of the labor force has plummeted while the foreign-born percentage of the population has soared. As the year 1965 began, however, there was absolutely no indication that either of these reversal trends was imminent.

In fact, organized labor anticipated at the beginning of 1965 that it was on the verge of a new era of membership growth. The labor market was tightening (i.e., unemployment was falling), and the economic signs of general prosperity were everywhere. The most immediate source of optimism for American unionism was the composition of the new Congress that was just taking office, following the November 1964 elections. It was composed of the most heavily Democratic majority and most liberally oriented membership elected since the mid-1930s, and as events would later show, the Eighty-ninth Congress did enact a package of legislation more progressive in both scale and scope than any before it. It encompassed such crucial issues as voting rights, federal aid for education, environmental quality, immigration reform, and health care—to name only a few accomplishments. Crucial to the achievement of this record was the reelection in 1964 of President Lyndon Johnson with the largest electoral majority of any contested election until that time. Johnson had already demonstrated the year before his commitment to social change by his advocacy and support of both the landmark Civil Rights Act of 1964 and the ambitious Economic Opportunity Act of 1964 (the "War on Poverty" legislation).

In its 1964 election platform the Democratic Party set forth its ambitious legislative goals, among them a plank indicating a commitment to labor law reform. It promised to strengthen the bargaining position of unions by seeking repeal of the controversial provision in the Taft-Hartley Act that permitted states to pass so-called right-to-work laws. This provision, known as Section 14(b), allowed a state government to prohibit unions from negotiating with companies in that state for the inclusion of a "union shop" clause in collective bargaining agreements. A union-shop clause says that no one in a certified bargaining unit *must* belong to a union as a condition of employment but that after a specified period of time (usually ninety days) all employees must join the union as a condition of *continued* employment. Employers can hire anyone they please, but the new workers—who receive all benefits of the collective bargaining agreement that is in place—must at some point join the union (or at least pay union dues). Section 14(b) represented a reversal of the usual practice whereby state laws are preempted by permissive federal laws, for under federal law, union-shop clauses are perfectly legal bargaining objectives. At that time, twenty states, mostly in the South and the Rocky Mountain area, had availed themselves of the opportunity to enact such restrictive laws. Rightly or wrongly, organized labor later regarded 14(b) as one of the key factors that had caused the unionized percentage of the labor force to stagnate since the time of its enactment in 1947.

On 4 January 1965, President Johnson delivered his State of the Union speech and, true to his word, publicly stated to the assembled Congress and to a nationwide television audience, "I will propose changes in the Taft-Hartley Act, including Section 14(b)."[1] Organized labor was thrilled, and the AFL-CIO executive council quickly listed the repeal as "its No. 1 legislative objective."[2] On 18 March 1965 the administration formally forwarded a message to Congress specifically urging such action. A bill to accomplish this feat easily cleared the Labor Committee of the House of Representatives in June 1965 and passed the full House on 26 July 1965 by a 221–203 vote.

In the Senate, however, the proposal encountered strong opposition when it finally reached the floor. Despite President Johnson's reiteration of his strong support for repeal only days before the debate commenced, a filibuster against its passage was led by the powerful minority Leader of the Senate, Everett Dirksen (R-Illinois). After a week of talking, a cloture vote was called for on 11 October 1965, but the Senate voted 47–45 to continue debate. Counting those who were absent but had publicly announced their positions, the vote would have been 50–50 if all senators had been present.[3] Sixty votes were required to invoke cloture, however, and given the press of other legislative issues, the bill was withdrawn. It was a stinging defeat for organized labor and one of the few presidential proposals of the Johnson administration that did not pass that year.

Immigration Reform

As fate would have it, only the week before the cloture vote on 3 October, President Johnson signed into law the historic Immigration Act of 1965. Although it is technically a lengthy series of amendments to the Immigration and Nationality Act of 1952, it constituted a major overhaul of that legislation. It brought an end to the national origins admission system that had been in effect for more than forty years. Unknown to anyone at the time, its passage also served to launch the fourth wave of mass immigration (see Table 6.1). President Johnson had strongly supported the legislation and it also had the unqualified backing of the AFL-CIO.[4] Both the President and organized labor rejoiced at the ending of the overt discrimination that had characterized the nation's immigration admission system since 1924 but neither anticipated that its enactment would lead to the revival of mass immigration. They believed the words of one of its co-sponsors, Senator Phil Hart (D-Michigan), who said that this bill, if passed, "would not open the flood gates, as charged. There will be only a slight increase in annual numbers but nothing significant."[5] Such was not to be the case.

Civil Rights Legislation and Civil Disorders

Despite the optimism that surrounded the enunciation of Johnson's Great Society policy agenda in early 1965 and the rapid-fire passage of many of its key proposals, other events that year contributed to the unleashing of unprecedented domestic turmoil. In August a full-scale civil

Table 6.1. Immigration to the United States, 1961–1998

1961–1970	**3,321,677**
1961	271,344
1962	283,763
1963	306,260
1964	292,248
1965	269,697
1966	323,040
1967	361,972
1968	454,448
1969	358,579
1970	383,326
1971–1980	**4,493,314**
1971	370,478
1972	384,685
1973	400,063
1974	394,861
1975	386,194
1976	398,613
1976 TQ[a]	103,676
1977	462,315
1978	601,442
1979	460,348
1980	530,639
1980–1990	**7,338,062**
1981	596,600
1982	594,131
1983	559,763
1984	543,903
1985	570,009
1986	601,708
1987	601,516
1988	643,025
1989	1,090,924
1990	1,536,483
1991–1998	**7,605,068**[b]
1991	1,827,167
1992	973,977
1993	904,292
1994	804,416
1994	720,461
1996	915,900
1997	798,378
1998	660,477

Source: U.S. Immigration and Naturalization Service.
[a]Transitional quarter when the start of the fiscal year was shifted from 1 July to 1 October.
[b]Total is for only 8 years.

disorder erupted in the black ghetto community known as Watts in south-central Los Angeles, California. After the National Guard intervened and the smoke from days of fire bombing, shooting, and looting finally cleared, thirty-four people had been killed, hundreds injured, and more than 4,000 arrested. Although the pretext for the outbreak was bystander scuffling associated with the arrest of a drunk black driver by a white police officer, the underlying issue was the perceived economic schism separating the lives of blacks and whites in the city. It was the worst race riot in the United States since one in Detroit in 1943 had also killed thirty-four people.

The fact that the Watts disorder occurred less than two months after the equal employment opportunity section (Title VII) of the Civil Rights Act of 1964 went into effect (on 1 July 1965) and at a time when the national unemployment rate was relatively low (and still falling) shocked much of the nation. Most whites had believed that race relations were improving and that an era of racial harmony was in the offing. But Watts was only the beginning. In 1966 there were forty-three urban riots (including two major disorders in Chicago and Cleveland), all stemming from racial incidents. In 1967, 164 disorders, including massive riots in Detroit and Newark, collectively led to eighty-three deaths, almost 2,000 people injured, thousands of arrests, and widespread property destruction. At this point, President Johnson appointed a blue-ribbon panel of distinguished citizens to study the causes of the civilian riots and to make recommendations for changes.

In March 1968 the National Advisory Commission on Civil Disorders issued its famous report.[6] It found that "white racism" was at the root of the divisive forces separating whites and blacks. Whites, it stated, controlled all the major societal institutions that impinge on black life, and unless these institutions empathized with the plight of the blacks, the inequalities of the past would be replicated into the future, and there would be little chance for societal tranquillity. It would take a major infusion of programmatic efforts, supported by sufficient funds, to redress the past denial of equal opportunity before black citizens could compete for jobs and income on an equal footing. It would also require affirmative efforts by those in charge of these institutions to eliminate suspicions based on past acts of bad faith, and also to fill the information void that centuries of separation had created. It would be the labor market—with its jobs and income opportunities but also with its commensurate requirements for adequate human capital preparation—that would determine whether the obstacles to equal economic opportunity could be overcome. The fact that the national unemployment rate was at the lowest level (3.6 percent in 1968) since World War II meant little by itself; put bluntly, the view of the black community was "We had full employment back on the plantations."[7] Access to the full strata of jobs and income opportunities was the goal, not just greater access to the bottom rungs of the economic ladder.

Less than a month after the release of the commission's report, the Reverend Martin Luther King Jr. was assassinated in Memphis, Tennessee. He had gone there to support the efforts of its black garbage collectors to secure recognition of a labor union that they sought to form. In reaction to his death, another wave of riots broke out in urban centers across the country, adding urgency to the policy recommendations offered by the Commission on Civil Disorders.

It was against this backdrop of domestic turmoil that on 1 July 1968 the provisions of the Immigration Act of 1965 went into full effect. The one thing that black Americans, especially those living in central cities, did not need was an infusion of new competitors—mostly persons who were themselves from racial and ethnic minorities—for jobs, housing, educational opportunities, and social services. But over the ensuing decades, that is precisely what happened. The unanticipated return of the phenomenon of mass immigration has made the inclusion of black Americans as equal participants in the achievements of the economy ever more difficult.

The Beginnings of the Women's Movement

The equal employment provisions of the Civil Rights Act of 1964 did not apply just to blacks. In fact, the legislation did not specifically mention any one race, ethnicity, religion, or gender; therefore, others who felt they too had been the focus of past discrimination were also empowered to exercise their newly protected rights. Among these other groups, no efforts have been more significant than those of women. The quest of women for broader participation in the labor market and in society in general had been highlighted in 1963 by the publication of the *The Feminine Mystique* by Betty Friedan.

Women had not initially been included in the legislative bill that later became the Civil Rights Act of 1964. They were added by a floor amendment in the House as a southern ploy designed to defeat the bill: how could legislation to ban segregated facilities on the basis of race still permit certain public facilities to be separate for men and women? Recognizing the malicious intent of this amendment, the Women's Bureau of the U.S. Department of Labor at first opposed adding gender discrimination to the pending legislation. But once the issue had been raised, there was no denying that women too had been historically denied equal access to employment. After some soul searching, then, employment protection for women was formally included in the final bill.

With these protections now guaranteed by law, women flooded into the labor market in numbers not seen since the wartime emergency era of the early 1940s, and since the late 1960s two-thirds of all new entrants into the labor force have been women. Their increasing participation has contributed to the surging growth in the supply of labor that the United States experienced over the remainder of the twentieth century. But the women's movement did not only involve a larger number of job aspirants; as with racial and ethnic minorities, it has been characterized by the rising aspirations of women for access to the entire range of occupational and industrial employment choices.

The Aftermath of the Vietnam War

It was also in the mid-1960s that the Johnson administration made its fateful decision to escalate U.S. involvement in the war in Vietnam. The war led to a brief upswing of job creation in the blue-collar occupations and in the goods-producing industries (especially manufacturing); both increased in numbers in the late 1960s after having been in a state of decline for over a decade. Defense expenditures rose dramatically, and the ripple effect contributed to lowering unemployment. Then the tenfold escalation of the scale of the military draft to 400,000 inductees a year in 1965 occurred just as the initial wave of the postwar baby boom generation was turning eighteen, the primary labor force entry age for full-time job seekers. Thus, the labor market was spared for several years the task of accommodating record numbers of youthful and inexperienced male job seekers. But as the war lingered on and as casualties soared, domestic dissension over continued military involvement spread, and the prolongation of the military effort triggered a series of protest demonstrations. These events, combined with the fact that the war had degenerated into a virtual stalemate, led to Johnson's decision not to seek reelection in 1968.

The newly elected Nixon administration that took office in 1969 soon concluded that the war was unwinnable, given the political constraints imposed on its military conduct, and sought a way to disengage. It was not until April 1975, however, that all U.S. forces were withdrawn and the government of South Vietnam collapsed.

As a consequence of the involvement in Southeast Asia, the largest inflow of refugees that the United States had yet received—over a million people—began. They came not only from South Vietnam itself but also from neighboring Cambodia and Laos, and their ranks were soon swelled by many ethnic Chinese who had been expelled from Vietnam shortly after the Communist government of North Vietnam seized control of the South.

The Advent of Economic Globalization

It has also been in the post-1965 years that the United States firmly committed itself to a complete reversal of its historic anti–free trade policies, and the era of economic globalization commenced. For most of the twentieth century the scale of international trade was almost inconsequential, but the United States consistently sustained a favorable balance of trade (i.e., exports exceeded imports). With the advent of globalization, however, the scale of international trade has dramatically increased but the balance of trade has been completely reversed. Since 1976, imports have annually exceeded exports, and the gap has consistently widened. In 1946 (before the new era formally began) the United States exported $11.8 billion worth of goods and services while importing $5 billion (for a favorable balance of trade of $6.8 billion); by 1997, exports had grown to $679 billion, but imports had soared to $877 billion (for an unfavorable balance of trade of $198 billion for that year alone).[8]

International trade in goods and services can be linked directly to immigration because they both alter the supply of labor and change the skills mix of the economy.[9] With respect to imports, it is the output produced by foreign labor that comes to the United States rather than the foreign workers themselves, but the employment effects are essentially identical. Since the imported goods are the embodiment of the labor required to produce them abroad, enhanced import trade can reduce the demand for domestic labor with occupational skills similar to those of the workers who produce the imports. Conversely, enhanced trade that stimulates exports can increase domestic employment for workers in certain industries. Thus, if there is truth in the proposition that exports create jobs, it is also the case that imports destroy jobs—and the United States has been running a trade deficit every year since 1976. Moreover, the types of jobs created by expanded exports are not the same as those eliminated by expanded imports. There are winners and there are losers: certain industries, workers, and localities benefit from enhanced international trade, while others are adversely affected. It has been low-skilled and semiskilled workers—especially those in manufacturing—that have been the main losers of jobs.

The U.S. economy and its labor force have entered an entirely new phase of economic development. For the first time they are in direct competition with the productive output and the prevailing labor conditions of other nations. As noted in earlier chapters, the American economy had traditionally functioned on the basis of protectionism: high tariffs served to shield both employers and workers from the competition of imported goods.

It was when Franklin Roosevelt assumed office in 1933 that the first tentative steps toward reducing trade barriers commenced. These initial steps involved reciprocal trade negotiations between the United States and other individual countries, predicated on a "you reduce your tariffs on specific goods and we will reduce ours" policy. The outbreak of World War II brought an abrupt end to these tentative efforts.

Following the war the United States emerged as not only the only major nation whose productive capabilities had been unscathed but with its capacity to produce enormously expanded. It was in the country's self-interest to look for expanded export markets. Likewise, given the devastation experienced by other industrial nations, it seemed that enhanced trade could restart these other economies (i.e., they could produce exports for other nations, including the United States, to import). It was also believed that the virulent protectionism of all nations during the previous decades had contributed to the worsening of the Depression of the 1930s and to the rise of Nazism and fascism in Europe, which led World War II.

Consequently, in 1947 the United States joined with twenty-two other industrialized nations of the free world to form the General Agreement on Tariffs and Trade (GATT) and to support the creation of the International Monetary Fund (IMF), the World Bank, and a host of other aid programs to assist the economic recovery of countries in Europe and Japan as well. The initial GATT system was based on the precepts of reducing tariff barriers to trade, establishing fixed currency exchange rates, and maintaining domestic autonomy for the participating nations. In the late 1940s and the 1950s almost all trade was in commodities and manufactured goods, which were transported by sea. The specific barriers to enlarged trade were either tariffs or import quota restrictions on such goods. Between 1947 and 1967, tariffs were reduced by 73 percent among the GATT nations (from an average of about 40 percent in 1947 to about 7 percent in 1967).

By the mid-1960s, the concerns over trade gradually shifted to a broader array of trade barriers—in particular, to a host of nontariff practices that had been devised to circumvent the effects of the reductions of tariffs. The subjects of coverage were also expanded to include intellectual property, technology- sensitive goods, and a wide array of services.

With the revival of the economies of western Europe by the 1960s, the system of fixed international exchange rates of currencies came under mounting pressure. The integration of world capital markets meant that balance-of-payment deficits of individual countries raised the prospect of currency devaluations, which in turn triggered speculative capital outflows from such countries. In response, governments often felt the need to take restrictive action to stop the outflows or to avoid being forced to formally devalue (or, in some instances, revalue) their domestic currencies, which most were reluctant to do. Then, in 1971, the United States (confronted with its first trade deficit in the postwar era) unilaterally announced that it would no longer convert dollars into gold at a fixed price of $35 an ounce (which it had done since 1933). As a consequence of these developments, the era of fixed exchange rates ended, and world trade relationships entered uncharted waters. World currencies would thereafter float and be determined by market pressures.

Economic volatility has often been the result as domestic prices and production levels of nations can now be affected by developments outside the control of individual governments. Indeed, in some instances, international financial speculation by private groups has been able to influence the values of some national currencies (and the standards of living in those countries).

Soon, many firms around the globe began to establish subsidiaries in their major overseas markets, blurring the definition of what constituted a domestic enterprise. Consequently, the rules governing foreign investment as well as relationships with foreign consumers became entwined with trade itself, which now involved multilateral negotiations. By 1993 the number of participating GATT countries had grown to 125. That year, the Clinton Administration led the international movement for freer trade by completing the so-called Uruguay Round of negotiations, which had been dragging on for seven years and had missed two earlier agreement deadlines. Not only did these negotiations lead to an average reduction of 34 percent in the tariffs in place at the time, but they capped these reductions so that member nations agreed to give up the possibility of future increases above the bounded levels. The agreement also limited the ability of signatory nations to place restrictions on permissible trade imports, and it targeted many existing restraints—such as those on apparel and textiles—to be phased out by 2005. Agricultural import restrictions are also supposed to be phased out and replaced by tariffs of mutual restrictiveness, but final agreements for this have yet to be reached.

GATT was administered over the years through little more than talk among government officials until it was amended in 1994 by the creation of a formal bureaucracy known as the World Trade Organization (WTO), headquartered in Geneva, Switzerland, which 139 nations had joined by 2000. The WTO is intended to be a referee in disputes over trade practices among nations, and can impose financial sanctions to enforce its rulings. These rulings, made by specially convened panels of trade experts who meet in secret, can be reversed only by a consensus of the WTO member nations, which is quite unlikely. A country, therefore, can refuse to abide by a WTO ruling (to retain the appearance of maintaining its sovereignty), but it must negotiate compensation with the aggrieved nation or absorb any retaliatory trade sanctions imposed by the aggrieved nation which the WTO approves.

In 1993 the Clinton administration also succeeded in gaining the approval for Congress of the North American Free Trade Agreement (NAFTA), involving Canada, the United States, and Mexico. Effective 1 January 1994 these three nations agreed to phase-in the elimination of tariffs on both industrial and agricultural products; to protect intellectual properties; and to liberalize financial, land transportation, and telecommunication services between them.

One outcome of these trade agreements is that the nation's employers (and, by derivation, the nation's workforce) are now subject to the effects of direct foreign competition. In domestic competition the ground rules (environmental standards, worker protections, and safety regulations) are essentially uniform, but the nations of the world assign vastly different meanings to all these concerns. To what degree such differing perspectives can be reconciled with evolving trade mechanisms is yet unknown.

When the WTO met in Seattle, Washington, in December 1999 to set the agenda for the next round of negotiations, the meetings became the target of extensive and violent street demonstrations, and no formal agreements were reached. Among the most vocal protesters were leaders of the AFL-CIO and members of its many affiliated unions. They claimed that the WTO provides a means for multinational corporations to escape strict accountability for their conduct and to avoid adherence to strong labor protections and collective bargaining requirements, since companies can now flee to less-developed nations where such laws are either nonexistent or only minimally enforced.[10] They saw both the WTO and NAFTA as means of exporting jobs—especially those involving low-skilled and semiskilled U.S. workers—and importing cheaper goods, often produced by lower-paid and less-protected workers.

The labor movement claims that it favors fair trade, not free trade. It points out that certain practices from which globalization profits—such as the use of prison labor or slave labor or child labor, and the toleration in some countries of rampant discrimination and the prohibition of free unions—are not natural trade advantages based on legitimate productivity differences; they are artificial advantages perpetuated by manmade institutions that exploit labor for corporate gain, not human betterment. The ultimate objective of all economic policies should be to raise the standard of living for everyone, not just for those few on the higher rungs of the nation's economic ladder.

The Pace of Scientific and Technological Change

Of all the change-creating forces that have impinged on the U.S. labor market since 1965, none has had a greater impact than the technological progress that the economy has sustained. As a direct result of extensive governmental expenditures on research and development during World War II, the postwar years witnessed the evolution of an interlock between science (understanding) and technology (application), blurring the difference between the two.[11] The explosion of scientific knowledge has led to a race by the private sector to find ways to apply new findings for commercial advantage.

No area has had greater significance than that surrounding the development of computer technology. The world's first electronic computer went into operation in the United States in 1946; by the year 2000 there were more computers in the country than people. Before 1965, the transformation of the economy that the computer would bring was largely a matter of speculation; by the end of the twentieth century it had become a stark reality. Production and distribution of both goods and services would never again be what it had been before.

The advent of the computer meant the development of an electronic "mind" capable of performing numerous routine production operations. With the introduction of a vast array of mechanical and electronic substitutes for the human neuromuscular system, it is now possible to link computer-driven machines into self-regulating systems that can perform an enormous variety of tasks. In the process, the prophecy made in 1950 by Norbert Wiener, the intellectual father of the computer revolution, that in the future any "man who has nothing but his physical power to sell has nothing to sell which is worth anyone's money to buy" has been a continuing trend.[12]

Originally, the application of computer technology was centered on the goods-producing industries, but as it evolved it also dramatically altered the skill mix in the service sector. The new technology of the post-World War II era is creating additional jobs, but the employment growth is disproportionately concentrated in occupations that require extensive training and education.[13] The ratio of employment in nonproduction (i.e., white-collar) occupations to total employment has dramatically increased in every industry. Conversely, these trends mean that production and nonsupervisory jobs (i.e., the blue-collar occupations that often provided high pay, good fringe benefits, and unionized job protections for workers with relatively low human capital endowments) are vanishing.

The most rapidly growing occupations in the 1980s and 1990s were those in the professional, technical, and administrative occupations, and their growth is expected to continue in the twenty-first century.[14] These occupations tend to have the highest educational and training requirements in the entire job spectrum. Most require computer skills. On the other end of the spectrum, the relatively unskilled occupations of private household workers, laborers, and farmworkers sustained either negative or minimal growth rates, and all experienced declining shares in the nation's workforce. The semiskilled operative occupations, the traditional bastion of good-paying blue-collar jobs and of union membership, has sustained barely any growth.

A confirmation of these trends can be found in the movement of real wages. Workers in the occupations that require extensive education and skill preparation received significantly higher wages over the decades of the 1980s and 1990s, while those in jobs that do not suffered significant declines.[15] Whereas the technology of the pre–World War II era stressed physical and manual skills for job seekers, the emerging information society creates jobs that require communication skills and place a premium is placed on cognitive abilities such as reading, writing, numeracy, and fluency in spoken English.

Unlike anything in the nation's lengthy experience from its founding through the 1940s, the labor market of the last half of the twentieth century assumed an entirely new character. No longer can employment be assumed as a result of people simply coming of age and making themselves available for work. Preparation for work has become essential for placement and influential for advancement. Unemployment and low income are less likely to be generalized across the labor force and more likely to be associated with those persons lacking human capital endowments or living in economically depressed areas.

Although some academics had earlier warned of the coming imbalance and the need to shift the focus of government policy away from fiscal policy (i.e., taxing and spending remedies) toward human resource development policies,[16] it was not until 1987 that the Department of Labor embraced the notion that the United States was facing a serious skills imbalance in the workplace.[17] A mismatch was developing between the requirements of the jobs that were expanding and the qualifications of the future workforce to meet them.

A study conducted in 1989 by the Commission on Workforce Quality and Labor Market Efficiency confirmed that there was a skills gap, due largely to the lack of preparedness of the new labor force entrants but also to the rapid obsolescence of the skills of much of the experienced work force. The retraining of the experienced labor force, moreover, was hindered by the fact that the basic reading and computational prerequisites for effective programs "are well beyond those currently possessed by many experienced workers." With at least 30 million functionally illiterate adults in the nation, the commission warned, unless comprehensive education and training reforms were soon initiated, job vacancies for skilled workers would increase along with the rising number of unemployed job seekers and labor force dropouts—a disproportionate number of whom would be minorities. Under such circumstances, employers would actively recruit skilled immigrant and nonimmigrant foreign workers or be tempted to relocate abroad to find the skilled workers needed. Such outcomes, the commission feared, "could lead to social and political conflict" within the nation by those left out.[18]

Another report in the same vein, issued in 1990 by the Commission on the Skills of the American Workforce, found that real wages for 70 percent of the nation's workforce had actually declined by more than 12 percent since 1969; hence, it was increasingly essential for most families that there be two wage earners. It too warned that if substantial changes in human resource development did not occur, "either the top 30 percent of our population will grow wealthier while the bottom 70 percent become progressively poorer or we will all slide into poverty together."[19]

By the late 1990s the dire predictions of a dichotomy in the distribution of wages had become a stark reality. In 1997 the Department of Labor reported that between 1980 and 1996 the cumulative change in real wages for adult full-time workers, (after adjusting for inflation) increased by 10.7 percent for those in the top 10 percent of the wage distribution but decreased by 9.6 percent for those in the bottom 10 percent. Even more worrisome was the fact that for all adult workers for that sixteen-year period, median real wages had fallen by 3.6 percent.[20] Robert Reich, secretary of labor at the time, explained that the trend toward a two-tiered society—a few winners and a large group left behind, was occurring because many workers "lack the learnable skills to prosper in an economy convulsing with change."[21]

The Labor Force and Industrial Employment Patterns

Between 1965 and 2000 the civilian labor force of the United States virtually doubled in size, from 74.4 million to 137.9 million workers. As noted above, the dramatic growth in the nation's supply of labor came from three sources: the maturing of the baby boom generation (i.e., those born between 1946 and 1964) into their working-age phase; the massive entry of women into the paid labor force, and the revival of mass immigration.

Paralleling the rapid growth of the labor force has been the dramatic change in the demand for labor: as shown in Table 6.2, most of the growth in employment has occurred in the service industries. The goods-producing industries (mining, construction, manufacturing), historically the employment centers of the heavily unionized sector of the economy, in 1965 accounted for 36 percent of all nonagricultural employment; by 2000, they accounted for only 25 percent. Manufacturing, the largest employment sector of the economy in 1920, was by 2000 the fourth largest. There were essentially the same number of persons employed in manufacturing in 2000 as in 1965, however, for despite the stagnation of employment in manufacturing, the annual value of manufactured production continues to lead all sectors of the economy and is projected to continue to do so into the twenty-first century.[22] This increase in output with the same labor input is due, of course, due to the productivity advances associated with the spread of automated technology.

The most rapid growth in employment has occurred in personal services, retail trade, and government sectors of the economy. Prior to 1965, none of these three industries had been highly unionized.

Immigration

With the enactment of the Immigration Act of 1965 as an amendment to the Immigration and Nationality Act of 1952, the objective of immigration reform seemed to have been accomplished.[23] The long-criticized national origins system had been repealed and a new admissions system established based largely on family reunification. Immediate

Table 6.2. The Labor Force and Nonfarm Employment by Industry, 1965–1999 (in thousands)

Year	Civilian Labor Force (16[a] years and up)[b]	Total Nonfarm Employees	Mining	Construction	Manufacturing	Transport and Utilities	Retail Trade	Wholesale Trade	Finance, Insurance, Real Estate	Service	Government
1965	74,455	60,765	632	3,232	18,062	4,036	9,250	3,466	2,977	9,036	10,074
1970	82,771	70,880	623	3,588	19,367	4,515	11,047	3,993	3,645	11,548	12,554
1975	93,775	76,945	752	3,525	18,323	4,542	12,645	4,415	4,165	13,892	14,686
1980	106,940	90,656	1,025	4,469	20,363	5,155	15,292	5,281	5,162	17,740	16,171
1985	115,461	97,519	927	4,673	19,260	5,238	17,356	5,717	5,955	22,000	16,394
1990	125,840	110,330	735	5,205	19,064	5,838	19,790	6,361	6,833	28,209	18,295
1995	132,304	117,203	580	5,158	18,468	6,165	21,173	6,412	6,830	33,107	19,459
1999	137,943	128,136	521	6,021	18,266	6,839	22,556	7,046	7,616	38,922	20,273

Source: U.S. Department of Labor, *Employment and Earnings,* Annual Data in January editions.
[a]The minimum age for inclusion in the labor force was raised to 16 in 1967. The 1965 figure has been adjusted accordingly.
[b]The Civilian Labor Force data are given for comparison only. They are taken from a different source than the employment data.

family members—spouses, children under twenty-one, and parents of U.S. citizens—would be admitted without limitations. Members of the extended families of U.S. citizens and permanent resident aliens were allotted 74 percent of the total number of admissions permitted each year. Admissions to meet legitimate labor market needs were allotted 20 percent. A new category for refugees was given 6 percent. Immigration admissions were increased over the 156,700 slots available since 1952 to 290,000 (plus immediate family relatives). But the increase in the number of visas did not seem to be of particular significance, given the sizable growth in the labor force that had occurred since 1952.

Once this new legislation was enacted, policymakers believed that they could now shift their attention to other aspects of the Great Society's domestic agenda and to the mounting military involvement in South Vietnam. Such hopes were quickly dashed.

The Collapse of Refugee Policy

Just five days before President Johnson signed the new immigration law into effect, Premier Fidel Castro of Cuba unilaterally announced that any persons—except young men of military age—who were dissatisfied with life in Cuba could go to the port city of Camarioca and be picked up by anyone from the United States who wanted to take them. Soon a flotilla of boats set forth from South Florida. President Johnson, in step with the Cold War politics of the era, jumped at the opportunity to embarrass the Communist government of Cuba: he announced that all Cubans who wished to come to the United States could do so. As the numbers quickly soared to more than 5,000 persons in the first month and the means of transport were dangerous, a more regulated and safer method was deemed necessary. With the intermediary assistance of the government of Switzerland, an agreement was reached to replace the use of leisure boats with an "air bridge" between Havana and Miami: a chartered airplane would transport Cubans to the United States on a daily basis.[24] The process continued until 1973, when Cuba finally realized the economic cost of this human capital hemorrhage and ended it. Over the intervening years, 270,000 Cubans had been admitted to the United States as refugees.

To accomplish this feat, President Johnson had to sacrifice adherence to the newly adopted refugee provisions of the Immigration Act of 1965. As there were only 17,400 visas annually available for refugees worldwide, the Cubans exceeded the ceilings imposed by the legislation. And when the Administration sought to count the annual flow of Cubans as part of the newly created annual ceiling of 120,000 immigrants and refugees to be admitted from the entire Western Hemisphere, a federal court ordered that it could not do so.[25] As a consequence the Cubans were admitted in excess of the hemispheric ceiling as well, by the use of the "parole" authority of the president to admit individuals for "emergent" reasons that are in the "national interest." This provision of the Immigration and Nationality Act had first been used by President Eisenhower in 1956 and later by President Kennedy in the early 1960s as a way to admit refugees before the nation's immigration law had any formal refugee provisions. The Immigration Act of 1965 supposedly ended the need for recourse to an arcane authority that was never intended to be applied to foreign nationals on a group basis.

Over the years, however, subsequent administrations continued to use the parole authority, despite the intentions of the Immigration Act of 1965 to place a firm ceiling on annual refugee admissions. As the air-bridge era of Cuban refugees ended, so did the Vietnam War, and a massive wave of refugees from Southeast Asia quickly ensued. Presidents Gerald Ford and Jimmy Carter also relied on the parole authority to admit most of these refugees, whose numbers each year far exceeded the available refugee slots under prevailing law. For all intents and purposes, the refugee terms of the Immigration Act of 1965 were abrogated by these actions.

The Explosion of Illegal Immigration

As previously noted, illegal immigration had been a perpetual problem for the United States ever since it first sought to screen immigrants in the 1870s and to limit immigrant admissions in the 1920s. But two events in 1965 led to a virtual explosion of illegal immigrants which the country has still not been able to control (see Table 6.3).

First, as of 31 December 1964, President Johnson terminated the aforementioned Mexican Labor Program the *bracero* program) which had been in effect since 1942.[26] The AFL-CIO had long been a critic of the *bracero* program and had been fighting for its repeal for years. Moreover, in 1962 a grassroots community organization known as the Farm Workers Association (FWA), led by Cesar Chavez, commenced efforts to organize farm workers in the Southwest. The FWA became the National Farm Workers Association in 1964; in 1965, as the United Farm Workers (UFW), it became a chartered AFL-CIO affiliate with Chavez still its

Table 6.3. Illegal Immigrants Apprehended, Fiscal Years 1961–1997

1961–1970	**1,608,356**
1961	88,823
1962	92,758
1963	88,712
1964	86,597
1965	110,371
1966	138,520
1967	161,608
1968	212,057
1969	283,557
1970	345,353
1971–1980	**8,321,498**
1971	420,126
1972	505,949
1973	655,968
1974	788,145
1975	766,600
1976	875,915
1976 TQ[a]	221,824
1977	1,042,215
1978	1,057,977
1979	1,076,418
1980	910,361
1981–1990	**11,883,328**
1981	975,780
1982	970,246
1983	1,251,357
1984	1,246,981
1985	1,348,749
1986	1,767,400
1987	1,190,488
1988	1,008,145
1989	954,243
1990	1,169,939
1991–1997	**9,457,393**[b]
1991	1,197,875
1992	1,258,650
1993	1,327,259
1994	1,094,718
1995	1,394,554
1996	1,649,958
1997	1,536,520

Source: U.S. Immigration and Naturalization Service.
[a]Transitional quarter when the start of the fiscal year was shifted from 1 July to 1 October.
[b]Total is for only 7 years.

leader. Ending the *bracero* program was essential to any hope for the new union to succeed in California. Briefly in the late 1960s the reduced flow of *braceros* did permit the UFW to win some organizational victories and gain membership. But by the mid-1970s a new surge of illegal immigrants from Mexico reversed the trend, and since then the union has barely been able to survive.[27] In Texas and elsewhere in the Southwest, the termination of the *bracero* program did not slow the process of Mexican farm workers crossing the border to seek jobs in agricultural enterprises. They had been coming for twenty-two years; they knew where the available jobs were; and absent any real deterrence, they just kept coming—albeit now as illegal immigrants.[28]

The second contributing event was the numerical ceiling imposed for the first time on immigration from the entire Western Hemisphere. For years, as outlined in Chapter 5, there was neither quota nor ordering system established for Western Hemisphere immigration; entry visas were given on a first come, first served basis. With the passage of the Immigration Act of 1965, however, long backlogs of applicants quickly developed.

In response, the law was amended in 1976 to apply the same seven preference categories that ordered admissions from the Eastern Hemisphere to the Western Hemisphere. Mexicans could now be legally admitted only if they were family relatives of U.S. citizens or permanent resident aliens, or if they could obtain a labor certification that they could fill a job for which U.S. workers were unavailable. The amendment also placed the ceiling of 20,000 visas a year from any one country, previously applied only to the Eastern Hemisphere, on all countries in the Western Hemisphere. Mexico, which had been accounting for about 60 percent of all the hemispheric visas prior to this change, was now subject to that same ceiling. Many Mexicans, however, decided not to play by these rules; they simply came anyhow.

Because the backlogs were far longer for applicants from the Western Hemisphere than from the Eastern Hemisphere, another amendment was adopted in 1978 that eliminated the separate hemispheric ceilings. With this change, the United States had what reformers for decades had sought: a single worldwide ceiling of 290,000 visas a year with no advantages offered to anyone of any nationality or from any geographic area.[29]

In response, however, illegal immigration soared, primarily because the legislation had no enforcement deterrence. The agency responsible for enforcing it, the Immigration and Naturalization Service (INS), was poorly funded and chronically understaffed. Worse, the law had a massive loophole. In 1952, powerful Texas agricultural interests had succeeded in pressuring Congress to add to the Immigration and Nationality Act an amendment stated that although it was a felony offense for a foreign national to enter the United States without inspection at a border entry point or for anyone to knowingly harbor an illegal immigrant, anything that a U.S. employer did in his or her role as an employer did *not* constitute harboring. In short, the "Texas Proviso" meant that it was illegal for any foreign national to enter or to seek work in the United States, but it was *not* illegal for a U.S. employer to hire such a person.

Moreover, because of the costs involved in prosecuting apprehended illegal immigrants, the vast majority were given a choice: Do you want to contest your apprehension in court (and, if found guilty, be convicted of a felony offense that could preclude possible legal entry in the future), or do you want return voluntarily to your homeland? Most Mexicans, who constituted over 90 percent of those apprehended at the time as illegal immigrants, chose to return to Mexico—and then simply repeated the process of illegal entry.

The nation's immigration law, therefore, was soon recognized as a toothless tiger. There were no penalties on employers who hired illegal immigrants (indeed, many employers sought such workers, knowing that they would work hard for low wages and be docile). Likewise, there were essentially no penalties on illegal immigrants found in the United States except for the inconvenience of being taken back to their country of origin.

Response to Policy Chaos

Only a decade after passage of the Immigration Act of 1965, then, U.S. immigration policy was in chaos. Far more refugees were entering each year than the law specified, and massive illegal immigration was making a mockery of any pretense that prevailing immigration policy could control the flow of immigrants.

It was also the case that the family-based legal immigration system was producing unexpected consequences. It was anticipated that the admission system created in 1965 would perpetuate the characteristics of the immigrants that had come before: that is, most would be from western Europe. What was not considered was that the national origins system had never been applied to the countries of the Western Hemisphere. Over the long interval when European immigration had been restricted and Asian immigration banned, immigration from Latin America and the Caribbean—Mexico in particular—had become an institutionalized process. Hence, the greatest beneficiaries of the family reunification system were the families of persons with Latin American relatives. Mexico emerged as the leading source of legal immigrants in the 1960s and has maintained that annual distinction, with scant exceptions, ever since.

Likewise, the enormous post-1965 inflow of refugees from Cuba and Southeast Asia led to even more immigrants from both Latin America and Asia. Both regions became primary sources of legal immigration as the family reunification system kicked in, allowing relatives to join those persons originally admitted as refugees who had become permanent resident aliens or naturalized citizens.

Also, as a result of changes in technology, there was a dramatic increase in the use of the employment-based admission categories by educated persons from Asian countries—Taiwan, Japan, India—who had training in computer programming, mathematics, statistics, and science. (Many had actually learned their skills in the United States, having come earlier as foreign students to study at American universities; others, at Asian universities that have historically emphasized science and mathematics as being less politically controversial than social science and humanities.) The rapidly expanding technology industries in the United States began active recruitment of such trained persons, who, in turn, were able to use the family-based entry system to admit their relatives.

The inadvertent consequence of the changes in the immigration admission system in 1965, therefore, was that Latin America, Mexico, the Caribbean, and Asia became the primary sources of the expanding fourth wave. As of 1997, 27 percent of the entire foreign-born population of the United States were immigrants from only one country—Mexico; over half came from Latin America (including Mexico); and 27.1 percent came from Asian countries. Indeed, 92 percent of the total Asian-born population in 1997 had entered the United States after 1970. Conversely, Europe and Africa, the two continents that supplied virtually all the immigrants of the earlier eras, accounted for only about 20 percent of the nation's foreign-born population in 1997.[30]

Immigration policy, despite the contrary expectations and promises of those who supported the Immigration Act of 1965, had become a lever to change the racial and ethnic composition of the U.S. population. It was influencing the social and economic character as the country as well. Many of the illegal immigrants, refugees, and family-based legal immigrants—lacking skills, education, and fluency in English—began to swell the ranks of workers at the bottom end of the labor market: the unskilled and semiskilled occupations. In many ways their paucity of human capital attributes resembled that of previous immigrants in the nineteenth and early twentieth centuries. But the difference was that in those earlier times the labor market was creating largely unskilled and semiskilled jobs, whereas in the post-1965 era, the labor market was being radically transformed by technology and globalization.[31] Thus, the post-1965 immigration experience represented a two-faced Janus in its impact. On one side it was supplying large numbers of persons at the bottom of the labor market (where employment opportunities were receding and where many low-income native-born—especially black—workers were struggling); on the other side, though to a more limited degree, it was also supplying occupations at the top of the labor market where highly skilled and educated workers were in great demand.

For all these reasons, immigration reform resurfaced in the 1970s as a subject of national concern. President Jimmy Carter initiated the response in 1977 with a legislative package designed to curtail illegal immigration. It proposed to repeal the Texas Proviso by imposing penalties on employers of illegal immigrants, and to grant amnesty to some of the illegal immigrants already in the United States. Congress, however, was hesitant and decided that all aspects of the nation's immigration system should be studied before any specific actions were taken. Thus, in 1978, the Select Commission on Immigration and Refugee Policy (SCIRP) was formed, composed of sixteen members and chaired by the Reverend Theodore Hesburgh, at that time president of Notre Dame University.[32] Seeking to avoid the criticisms of the work of the Dillingham Commission at the beginning of the century, SCIRP conducted public hearings across the country, initiated some research studies, and solicited the extensive input of scholars, experts, and community leaders to ascertain the state of existing knowledge.

The Refugee Act of 1980

While the commission was in the midst of its work, the refugee crisis associated with events in Southeast Asia deteriorated so rapidly that Congress could not wait for it to complete its task. Thus, in March 1980 the Refugee Act of 1980—relying extensively on the preparatory work provided by SCIRP—was passed and signed into law by President Carter. It removed refugees from the 1965 law (i.e., it eliminated the refugee category and reduced the number of remaining visas to 270,000 a year) and created an essentially new admission system for refugees.[33] Under this legislation, the number of refugees to be admitted, starting in 1982, was to be determined by the president in advance of each fiscal year after a consultation with Congress (see Table 6.4). Further, the number was to be distributed geographically so that no one country or region could dominate the admissions.

Refugees were defined as anyone who had a "well-founded fear of per-

Table 6.4. Refugee Authorizations, Approvals, and Admissions to the United States, 1980–2000

Year	Authorized Admissions	Approvals[c]	Admissions[c]
1980[a]	273,700	206,912	n/a
1981[a]	217,000	155,291	n/a
1982	140,000	61,527	93,252
1983	90,000	73,645	57,064
1984	72,000	77,932	67,750
1985	70,000	59,436	62,477
1986	67,000	52,081	58,329
1987	70,000	61,529	66,803
1988	87,500	80,282	80,382
1989	104,500	95,505	101,072
1990	110,000	99,687	110,197
1991[b]	116,000	107,962	100,229
1992[b]	123,500	115,330	123,010
1993[b]	116,000	106,026	113,152
1994	117,500	105,137	114,471
1995	111,000	78,936	98,520
1996	90,000	74,491	77,600
1997	78,000	77,600	69,276
1998	88,000	n/a	n/a
1999	78,000	n/a	n/a
2000	90,000	n/a	n/a

Source: U.S. Immigration and Naturalization Service.

[a]Not including approximately 123,000 Cubans and 6,000 Haitians of the "Mariel Boatlift" era, who were later given the opportunity to apply for amnesty under the Immigration Reform and Control Act of 1986.

[b]Not including Amerasians (i.e., persons born in Vietnam between 1 January 1962 and 1 January 1976 if fathered by a U.S. citizen) who were allowed to enter the United States as legal immigrants during these years.

[c]Admissions in a given year may be higher than approvals because they include arrivals of persons approved in previous years.

secution on account of race, religion, nationality, membership in a particular group, or political opinion." They were people in a country outside their own, presently where they can be properly screened for eligibility before actually being admitted to the United States. Some persons still "within their country" could be designated as refugees by the president under certain circumstances, but individuals could not "self-proclaim" themselves as refugees, for that, it was believed, could lead to endless numbers of persons seeking such status. While the new system was being set up (1980–82), as many 50,000 refugees could be admitted each year, a number viewed as "the normal flow." It was the specific intention of Congress that this new system would finally terminate the practices of presidents of using the parole authority to admit large numbers of refugees without numerical restriction.

The Refugee Act of 1980 also created an asylum policy for the United States for the first time.[34] It authorized the attorney general to grant asylum to any alien already in the United States who sought protection because of the fear of persecution in his or her homeland. To be eligible, the individual also had to meet the law's definitions of "refugee."

Asylum policy was the least thought-through provision of the Refugee Act of 1980. It was intended to apply to individual cases; no one foresaw that the United States would become a nation of "first instance" for massive numbers of persons who, once ashore, would all seek political asylum. But that exact situation confronted the country within five weeks of adopting its new asylum policy.

Once more, unrest in Cuba led Fidel Castro to announce unilaterally that anyone dissatisfied with life in Cuba could go to the port city of Mariel and be picked up for transport to the United States. Hundreds of pleasure boats again took off from South Florida and began to transport Cubans directly to the United States, where, upon arrival, they requested political asylum. Initially, President Carter welcomed their arrival, but as their numbers quickly soared, he tried to stop the flow by impounding the vessels as they arrived. Nevertheless, between late April and early September 1980 more than 123,000 Cubans landed in Florida. The situation became even more chaotic and controversial when, amid the Cuban influx, overcrowded boats from Haiti brought an additional 6,000 persons who also sought political asylum upon disembarking. President Carter refused to grant a blanket amnesty to either group; he wanted each case be heard separately to determine whether the individual was actually fleeing political persecution (thereby qualifying as a refugee) or was seeking economic betterment (thereby being identified as an illegal alien). Ultimately, however, virtually all 129,000 of these persons were given a blanket amnesty in 1986 and allowed to remain in the country.

Thus, the prospect that the newly adopted refugee system would bring order out the previous chaos was thwarted from its onset. Worse yet, refugee policy still continues to function as an uncontrolled element of immigration policy, and the parole authority is still used regularly to admit persons outside the intentions of the law.[35]

The Immigration Reform and Control Act of 1986

Meanwhile, the Hesburgh Commission issued its final report on 1 April 1981. Its major conclusion was a statement of the obvious, that U.S. immigration policy was "out of control," and it presented a comprehensive set of proposals to remedy the situation. Warning that special interest groups were seeking to dominate the determination of U.S. immigration policy, the report stated that "the Commission has rejected the arguments of many economists, ethnic groups, and religious leaders for a great expansion in number of immigrants and refugees," because "this is not the time for a large-scale expansion in legal immigration"; "a cautious approach" was what conditions required.[36]

By this time, however, the Carter administration had been voted out of office, and the new administration of President Ronald Reagan had not made immigration reform a part of its agenda. When confronted with the report of the Select Commission, therefore, it elected to study the issue before responding. (At the time, it was more concerned with the enactment of a domestic agenda that embraced cutting taxes and social programs while building up national defense.)

When the Reagan administration finally did respond in the late summer of 1981, its proposals showed little grasp of the issue.[37] As a consequence, the initiative for reform was taken up by a bipartisan congressional movement led by Senator Alan Simpson (R-Wyoming) and Representative Romano Mazzoli (D-Kentucky). Together, they drafted a bill based on the recommendations of the Hesburgh Commission (of which Simpson had been a member). But comprehensive reform subsequently proved too politically difficult: twice, in 1982 and 1984, Congress was unable to find agreement between Senate and House versions of reform bills.[38]

By 1986, with the national perception that the problems of the nation's immigration system were worsening, a different tack was taken by proponents of reform: piecemeal changes. The first issue they chose to address was the greatest obstacle to effective immigration policy: illegal immigration. After protracted efforts in which special interest groups did all they could do to hamper its passage, the Immigration Reform and Control Act of 1986 (IRCA) was finally passed on the last day of the congressional session and was signed into law on 6 November 1986 by President Reagan.[39]

IRCA repealed the Texas Proviso and established a system of sanctions on employers who hire illegal immigrants: an escalating series of civil fines and, for persistent violators, the possibility of imprisonment. Unfortunately, this legislation too contained an enormous loophole: it failed to make employers responsible for the authenticity of the documents presented to them to establish employment eligibility. Subsequently, a cottage industry in the production of counterfeit documents made effective worksite enforcement costly and inefficient.

IRCA also contained several amnesty programs that, collectively, enabled almost 3 million illegal immigrants to come out of the shadow labor force and become permanent resident aliens or, if they desired, naturalized citizens. There was a general amnesty for most illegal immigrants who had been in the country since 1 January 1982 (the approximate date that discussions to pass this particular legislation began) and also a special adjustment program for those who had worked in perishable agriculture for at least ninety days prior to 1 May 1986. The rationale for the amnesty provisions was that the country had previously given mixed signals as to its seriousness about keeping illegal immigrants out of its labor market. But with employer sanctions in place, the message was now clear: illegal immigrant workers are not wanted. But because there were so many already in the country, it was unlikely that they would voluntarily leave. A one-time-only amnesty, therefore, made sense.

The Immigration Act of 1990

The next target in the piecemeal strategy to reform immigration policy was the legal immigration system. It was approached on the premise—which later proved to be a false assumption—that since IRCA had closed the back door to the nation's labor market, it might be possible to open the front door "a little more." In this case, however, unlike illegal immigration, there was no clear agreement among policymakers about what should be done. Should family reunification continue to be the primary focus? Should more attention be given to human resource considerations, based on the needs of employers, and to the human capital attributes of the would-be immigrant? Should anything be done about the fact that the existing system had greatly reduced the entry of immigrants from Europe and Africa whom Senator Edward Kennedy (D-Massachusetts) described at the time as being the "'old seed' sources of our heritage?"[40]

Separate bills were passed in the Senate and the House in 1990. Because of their vast differences, there appeared to be little chance of a compromise.[41] With the attention of the nation and the media focused for the moment on a fierce budget battle between Congress and President George Bush, however, a behind-the-scenes agreement was made by the respective supporters of the two bills during the last few weeks of the extended session. Their compromise bill dropped controversial sections (especially those designed to make IRCA more effective in stopping illegal immigration) and added entirely new sections that had never been debated but halved the remaining differences. It was doubtful that any member of Congress read the final version. Brought to the floor on the last day of the congressional session (along with the final federal budget agreement, which served as its smoke screen), the Immigration Act of 1990 was passed and then signed into law on 29 November 1990 by President Bush.

In its lasting impact on American society, the Act ranks as one of the most significant legislative actions of the decade of the 1990s.[42] It not only raised the high level of annual immigration already in existence by 35 percent (to about 700,000 legal immigrants a year) but cemented this high level into place for as long as the legislation remains in effect. Family reunification was retained as the primary admissions category (allocated 75 percent of the available visas), but a new diversity admissions category created an annual lottery for 55,000 visas; applicants were to come only from countries from which low numbers of immigrants had been admitted over a preceding five-year period. Like those in the family categories, the diversity immigrants would not be chosen on the basis of any human resource attributes. Rather, the diversity category reintroduced both geography and ethnicity into the admission process—considerations that previous immigration reformers had fought so long to purge from the selection process back in 1965.

By that time the Immigration Act of 1990 went into effect, on 1 October 1991, the U.S. economy was in the midst of a worsening recession. The unemployment rate for the year was 6.8 percent, and by the end of 1991 there were a million fewer employed workers in the country than when the year began. Yet 1.8 million immigrants were admitted that year, or had their status adjusted (per the earlier amnesty programs provided by IRCA). It was the largest number in any one year in the history of the country. In 1992 the national unemployment rate rose even higher—to 7.5 percent.

The Commission on Immigration Reform

In recognition of the uncertain effects of the Immigration Act of 1990, Congress included in the legislation a requirement for the formation of the Commission on Immigration Reform (CIR). Composed of nine members chosen from the public, it was empowered to study the implementation of this significant legislation for six years and to recommend any needed changes. The commission was chaired for most of its life by Barbara Jordan, until her death in early 1996.[43] She was a professor of public policy at the University of Texas at that time but had previously been a distinguished member of Congress from Texas.

Over the course of its work, CIR issued a series of interim findings preceding its final report, which was issued on 30 September 1997. CIR identified illegal immigration as having the "most immediate need" of policy attention. It called for a significant expansion of the U.S. Border Patrol, the construction of new physical barriers where practical, a verification system to validate the authenticity of Social Security cards used to establish eligibility for employment, and steps to reduce access to "breeder documents" (e.g., counterfeit birth certificates) used to obtain other documents (e.g., Social Security cards and driver's licenses) used unlawfully to gain jobs. Dismissing the self- serving protests of special interest groups "who would label efforts to control immigration as being anti-immigrant," the Jordan Commission stated unequivocally that "unlawful immigration is unacceptable."[44]

With regard to the tougher issues of legal immigration, the Jordan Commission stated emphatically that "our current immigration system must undergo major reform" and "a significant redefinition of priorities."[45] Specifically, it recommended a 35 percent reduction of legal admissions, back to the pre-1990 level; the elimination of the extended-family preferences for admission; the elimination of the employment-based provision that permitted unskilled workers to be admitted; the elimination of the diversity category; and a return to the policy of including refugees within the total number of admissions each year.

The Findings of the National Research Council

To assist in its ongoing study of immigration, the Commission on Immigration Reform requested in 1995 that the National Research Council (NRC) of the National Academy of Sciences convene a panel of experts which would independently assess the demographic, economic, and fiscal consequences of immigration. The NRC agreed and released its report in 1997. With regard to demographic findings, its "intermediate projection" was that immigration would account for two-thirds of the population growth occuring in the United States by the year 2050.[46]

As for economic findings, the report catalogued the steady decline of the educational attainment levels of post-1965 immigrants, and the consequence that foreign-born workers earn, on average, less than native-born workers—a gap that has widened over the years. Those from Latin America (including Mexico), who at present account for over half of the entire foreign-born population of the nation, earn the lowest wages. The NRC found no evidence of discriminatory wage rates for immigrants; rather, it found that immigrant workers are paid less than native-born workers because they are in fact less skilled and less educated. The relative declines in both skills and wages of the foreign-born population was attributed to the fact that most immigrants are coming from the poorer nations of the world, where the average education, income, and skill levels are far below those in the United States. As a direct consequence, post-1965 immigrants are disproportionately increasing the segment of the nation's labor supply which has the lowest human capital endowments. In the process, they are lowering the wages of all workers in the lowest skill sector of the labor market.[47]

More specifically, the study documented the fact that almost half the decline in real wages for native-born high school dropouts from 1980 to 1994 could be attributed to the adverse competitive impact of unskilled foreign workers. The chief beneficiaries of immigration are the immigrant workers themselves, because even at the low end, their wages are usually considerably higher than if they had stayed in their homelands.[48]

The NRC did find a net benefit of immigration to the nation's economy each year of from $1 to $10 billion.[49] But it is a benefit that only an economist could appreciate. It results largely from the suppression of the wages of workers who compete with the immigrant inflow that causes lower prices of goods and services for the economy. These suppressed wages are mostly those of low-skilled workers with low incomes, but they are also the wages of workers at the other end of the skills spectrum— those in some professional and technical occupations that have also had a disproportionate increase in immigrant and nonimmigrant "temporary" workers. It is unlikely that either group considers artificial manipulation of the size of their labor supply to be a benefit.

Where there are economic benefits, of course, there are likewise economic costs. In this case, the NRC calculated the net fiscal costs of public services to immigrants (in education, medical care, welfare, public housing, and incarceration), beyond the taxes that the immigrants themselves pay, to range from $14.8 to $20.2 billion a year.[50] Obviously, these fiscal costs are disproportionately distributed among taxpayers, depending on the size of the foreign-born population in their respective communities and states.

The Illegal Immigration Reform and Immigrant Responsibility Act of 1996

In response to CIR's interim reports and in anticipation of its final report in 1997, Congress made a preemptive move in 1996: it once more took up immigration reform. But with a host of special interest groups fighting every proposed change, opponents of reform were able to kill all proposals pertaining to legal immigration and refugee limitations. The watered-down Illegal Immigration Reform and Immigrant Responsibility Act that passed in 1996 did increase funding for deterrence measures against illegal immigration, but it failed to create the most important means needed to curb the abuse: the creation of a viable verification system of work eligibility for persons who seek to be employed in the United States.[51] Subsequently, when the CIR, after six years of intense work, issued its comprehensive final report in September 1997 (supported by the comprehensive NRC study of the fiscal, demographic, and economic impact of immigration),[52] it was met with nonconcern by the media and the policymakers. By this time, the proimmigration lobby had won the day, and the pursuit of the national interest had once again been thwarted.

In assessing this political debacle, political scientists James Gimpel and James Edwards wrote in 1998, "The voice of the people has had little impact on the tone or direction of the immigration debate in Washington."[53] They pointed out that the extensive research findings showing the need for significant legislative changes, and opinion polls consistently showing that the public wants these changes to take place, make no difference to the professional politicians. Immigration policy has been captured by an unholy alliance that links religious organizations, ethnic groups, libertarian economists, and the powerful American Immigration Lawyers' Association—all of whom have self-interests and financial interests in maintaining the status quo—with corporate America (ranging from agribusiness to the garment industry to the health care industry to the computer industry), which has vested interests in perpetuating cheap labor policies. Unfortunately, the labor movement—hitherto the presumptive custodian of the interests of American workers—chose to stay on the sidelines throughout this critical period. In doing so, it allowed legal immigration reform to go down the drain and made no effort to strengthen barriers to illegal immigration.

Unionism

As noted earlier, the labor movement was strongly entrenched as an important institution of American life in 1965. The unionized 30.1 percent of the labor force, the proportion had remained almost constant since 1947, was virtually as high as it has ever been. Since then, the number of union members has drastically fallen: there were 1.7 million fewer union members in 1999 than in 1965, despite the fact that the labor force had almost doubled. By 1999, only 13.9 percent of the labor force was

Table 6.5. Union Membership of Nonagricultural Employed Labor Force (1965–1983) or Waged and Salaried Employees Unionized, 1983–1999

Year	Union Membership (in thousands)	Percentage Unionized of Nonagricultural Labor Force	Percentage Unionized of Waged and Salaried Employees[a]
1965	18,269	30.1	—
1966	18,922	29.6	—
1967	19,668	29.9	—
1968	20,017	28.5	—
1969	20,185	28.7	—
1970	20,990	29.6	—
1971	20,711	29.1	—
1972	21,205	28.8	—
1973	21,881	28.5	—
1974	22,165	28.3	—
1975	22,207	28.9	—
1976	22,153	27.9	—
1977	21,632	26.2	—
1978	21,756	25.1	—
1979	22,025	24.5	—
1980	20,968	23.2	—
1981	20,647	22.6	—
1982	19,571	21.9	—
1983	18,634 (17,717)*	20.7	20.1
1984	17,340*	—	18.8
1985	16,996*	—	18.0
1986	16,975*	—	17.5
1987	16,913*	—	17.0
1988	17,002*	—	16.8
1989	16,960*	—	16.4
1990	16,740*	—	16.1
1991	16,568*	—	16.1
1992	16,390*	—	15.8
1993	16,598*	—	15.8
1994	16,748*	—	15.5
1995	16,360*	—	14.9
1996	16,269*	—	14.5
1997	16,110*	—	14.1
1998	16,211*	—	13.9
1999	16,500*	—	13.9

Sources: 1965–1983: Leo Troy and Neil Sheflin, *U.S. Union Sourcebook* (West Orange, N.J.: Industrial Relations Data and Information Services, 1985), A-2; 1983–1999: U.S. Bureau of Labor Statistics, *Employment and Earnings* (January volumes for 1984–1999). Data from this series are indicated by an asterisk (*).
[a]The data series and definitions for union membership changed slightly in 1983. See Paul O. Flaim, "New Data on Union Members," *Employment and Earnings* (January 1985): 13–14.

unionized (see Table 6.5).The legislative defeat in 1965 involving the failure of Congress to repeal section 14(b) of the Taft-Hartley Act was a harbinger of the ill times that lay ahead.

The union movement, in 1965, did not perceive the transformation of the labor market by globalization and technological change that was under way, nor did it believe that its historic nemesis, mass immigration, was about to be revived. Like most other societal institutions in that decade, the labor movement's attention was diverted by the immediate societal turmoil of the 1960s. There were also several internal distractions. The union with the most members in the 1960s was the Teamsters. But it had been expelled from the AFL-CIO in 1958, along with the bakers' union and the laundry workers' union, on charges of leadership corruption and domination by racketeers. The AFL-CIO quickly set up rival unions to recapture the bakery and laundry workers, but no such attempt was made to challenge the powerful Teamsters. Functioning as an independent entity, the Teamsters launched an aggressive campaign to organize workers regardless of their industry or occupation, or whether they belonged to another union. Not until 1987 did the Teamsters rejoined the federation.

For different reasons, the influential United Automobile Workers (UAW) also withdrew in 1968 from the AFL-CIO in a dispute over the emphasis (or lack thereof) on organizing. The UAW, led by Walter Reuther, favored a more aggressive effort to organize the nonunionized sectors of the economy. It was also the case that there were serious personality clashes between Reuther (reflecting the socially conscious and politically active roots of the union's CIO heritage) and George Meany (reflecting the more staid AFL's craft union heritage), who was still the president of the AFL-CIO. As an independent union, Reuther and the UAW also commenced efforts to organize workers irrespective of their particular industry or craft, and it did not rejoin the federation until 1981.

The AFL-CIO was also confronted during the late 1960s with charges that some of its most prominent unions—especially the older craft unions in the construction, printing, and machinist trades—overtly discriminated against minorities and women. These crafts relied heavily on formal apprenticeship training as the favored entry route into their crafts. Civil rights groups at first denounced the apprenticeship system itself as one more manifestation of the institutional racism that was under attack at the time. But others held firm in their belief that apprenticeship—with its combination of classroom training and on-the-job experience—was the ideal method of preparing workers for the skilled trades. In fact, the problem was not with apprenticeship training itself but with the practices that denied minorities and women access to it. As the result of careful research of the issue, a national apprenticeship outreach program was designed to overcome the information and preparation barriers and to assure that previously excluded groups could have equal access to apprenticeship programs.[54] With the financial support of the Department of Labor and the full endorsement of the AFL-CIO leadership, the outreach program was able to maintain the integrity of the apprenticeship training system while adding recruitment methods that allowed minorities and women to compete fairly for openings.[55] For most unions, discrimination was never an issue; to the contrary, the assurance of equal treatment on the job was one of the primary reasons that many workers sought to join. But where discrimination had been systematically practiced, the apprenticeship outreach program helped to remove this blemish on the history of American trade unionism.

By the 1970s the labor movement recognized that external challenges posed the greatest threat to its long-run survivability. One was that its organizing efforts had historically been least successful in the South. But the South was by this time in the process of freeing itself from the shackles of centuries of slavery and racial segregation that it had imposed upon itself since the founding of the republic. The region was rapidly developing and its economy was diversifying, away from its traditional dependence on agriculture. In the South, however, the labor movement was confronted by a conservative political structure avowedly opposed to the presence of unions. Indeed, many southern states linked their formal economic development strategies to the fact that unions were weak in the region, and weak was the way they intended for them to remain. All of the southern states had right-to-work laws that symbolized the political weakness of the union movement within their boundaries, and local authorities were often hostile to union organizers. Still, relying on federal labor law for protection and support, organized labor renewed its efforts to organize the largest manufacturing industry in the South: textiles.

In response, the industry employed tactics that demonstrated how labor law itself could be used to forestall rather that to advance union organizing. Although the J.P. Stevens Company was not the only one, the breadth and scope of its tactics revealed the fundamental weakness of existing labor law when it confronted recalcitrant opposition.[56] The company perfected a strategy designed to postpone for years the results of votes conducted by the NLRB to certify union elections. Not only were union supporters fired for union activity (in open violation of federal labor law), but every NLRB decision was made the subject of lengthy legal proceedings and subsequent appeals all the way to the U.S. Supreme Court—delays that were extremely costly for unions. Moreover, even when the unions finally won the appeals for certification recognition (which they usually did), Stevens found it more profitable simply to pay the fines than to recognize the duly authorized bargaining agent. Such actions would of course lead to yet another round of court proceedings with all the attendant costs and delays. Thus, both the protracted time it took for the NLRB to render an enforceable final decision and the weakness of available legal remedies for violation of the law were used to forestall union organization efforts.

The Carter administration proposed in 1977 a reform of the existing laws to counter this brazen perversion of the law. Among its terms were requirements for speedier certification of election proceedings; procedural changes to expedite unfair labor practice charges (e.g., the firing of workers for union activity); and new remedies for violators of the law. Among proposed remedies, the bill provided that any employer found guilty of willfully violating existing laws by coercing workers or discriminating against them for union activity should be barred from obtaining any federal contracts for three years. A worker who was illegally fired for union activity would be awarded double back pay when the NLRB ordered that he or she be rehired (regardless of wages earned from other sources during the time of the challenge). When an employer refused to bargain for a first contract with a duly certified bargaining agent, the NLRB would be empowered to order compensation for all the employees for the entire period of the delay.

The Carter proposals easily passed the U.S. House of Representatives in 1977 by a 58 percent margin. But by the time the bill came before the Senate, business groups and their supporters had initiated a major lobbying effort. The opposition launched a filibuster, and despite the fact that fifty-eight senators favored the bill, the sixty votes necessary to break the filibuster could not be mustered. Hence, the bill had to be abandoned in mid-1978 so that other necessary legislation could be considered. The AFL-CIO pledged to renew its effort to adopt these reforms but, in all the years since then, labor law reform has never again been seriously proposed by any subsequent administration or reached the floor of either house of Congress. Thus, the nation's labor laws remain vulnerable to easy circumvention by companies who are so disposed.

Against this backdrop of public defeat, the leadership of the AFL-CIO changed hands. George Meany, a man of strong views and forceful expression who had been bred in the era of confrontational labor-management relations, retired in late 1979 (and died the next year). He was followed into office by his handpicked successor, Lane Kirkland. Originally from the Masters, Mates and Pilots union in the maritime industry, Kirkland was a career labor bureaucrat who for thirty-three years had worked his way up within the federation to the position of secretary-treasurer before being selected president. More soft-spoken and less inclined to seek public attention than Meany, his strength lay in his executive skills. He was not, however, inclined to use forceful leadership or promote major reforms to meet changing conditions.

It was also in 1979 that the United States economy slipped into another era of deep recession, which lasted until 1983—the worst economic downturn that the nation had experienced since the 1930s. In 1982 the unemployment rate peaked at 9.7 percent. In addition to bad economic times, the labor movement was also confronted with the Reagan administration that had assumed office in January 1981 and quickly earned labor's wrath. In August 1981, members of the Professional Air Traffic Controllers Organization (PATCO), a member union of the AFL-CIO, went on strike, in defiance of an order by the U.S. Department of Transportation that as federal government employees they remain at work. The Reagan administration responded by firing all of the 11,438 members who did not immediately return to work, replacing them with controllers who did not strike plus military air controllers while a crash program was initiated to find permanent replacements. The government then proceeded to have the union decertified as the exclusive bargaining agent. By June 1982 PATCO was bankrupt and eight union leaders were sent to prison.[57] It was a stinging public rebuke to organized labor—even though by 1987 a new union of controllers had been certified, led by one of the earlier PATCO leaders who had been jailed.

The recession of 1979 to 1983 significantly weakened the bargaining position of organized labor. Emboldened by the force of the action of the federal government in confronting PATCO as well as the persistence of high national unemployment rates, a number of unionized employers took strong bargaining postures. A period of "concession bargaining" commenced in such key unionized industries as steel, trucking, meatpacking, and construction as well as in some public sector contract talks across the country.[58] Typically, the union concessions involved a relaxation of existing work rules, but in some instances wages were reduced; for example, some firms imposed a two-tiered wage system whereby newly hired employees were paid less than those already on the payroll. When existing contracts expired and concession agreements could not be reached, some firms chose to replace strikers and to continue to operate. Among them were the Phelps-Dodge Corporation in the copper industry, the Greyhound Bus Company and Continental Airlines—which added a new wrinkle by declaring bankruptcy, only to reopen under the supervision of the courts with a reduced wage structure and many replacement workers.

Clearly, the labor movement was in retreat. Economist Michael Piore proclaimed that "union power appears for the first time to be in real jeopardy in industries that have been its traditional bastions of strength."

Until this time, Piore argued, leaders in many key industries had, since the 1930s, "recognized the right, even the desirability, of union organizations and collective bargaining," but these attitudes were changing. It was not just the short-run effects of the recession that the economy was experiencing; long-term changes were also coming into play. Technological developments were rapidly altering the workplace, affecting not only unionized firms but also the nonunion companies against whom they competed. Foreign competitors were gaining greater access to the U.S. marketplace. Employers were increasingly seeking flexibility and, in the process, attempting to avoid "the restraints that unions impose upon their ability to organize production efficiently."[59]

In the 1970s and 1980s the labor movement did not give a high priority to organizing newly emerging private sectors, and when they did try, they often encountered stiff resistance from employers.[60] Increasingly, businesses responded to union organizing by hiring so-called management consultants, persons who specialized in developing antiunion personnel practices designed to contribute to union loss of certification elections. Some used openly unfair labor practices to forestall union organizing campaigns.[61] Thus, there were declines in union victories in certification elections as well as increased union losses in decertification elections (i.e., votes to terminate existing union representation) conducted by the NLRB.[62] Union membership was also affected by the mounting number of illegal immigrants who were becoming available to employers as strikebreakers or as alternative labor supplies.[63] As a consequence of all this, the percentage of the private sector labor force who were union members—which had been declining since 1978—was only 9.4 percent in 1999.[64] Private sector unionization was highest in 1999 in transportation, communications, and public utilities (25.5 percent); in construction (19.1 percent); and in manufacturing (15.6 percent). It was the lowest in the finance and real estate industry (2.1 percent).

Yet all has not been bleak for union organizing. Union membership in the public sectors has grown significantly since the mid-1960s; by 1999, 37.3 percent of all public employees were members of unions (with state government workers having the highest proportion, 42.9 percent).[65] The growth was in part a function of the rapid expansion of government employment over this same time span (see Table 6.2). The greatest increase has occurred at the local government level, given the expansion of the demand for such public services as education, fire, police, road maintenance, and sanitation.

But because public sector unionism has grown more rapidly than has public sector employment since the 1960s, other explanatory factors have also been involved.[66] Prior to the 1960s, public sector wages and benefits tended to lag behind those in the private sector, which aroused the interest of public employees in unions. Public sector employers, in general, have been less opposed to unions than have been their private sector counterparts, especially at the federal government level. Furthermore, collective bargaining in the public sector has been stimulated on occasion by the use of militant action to overcome roadblocks to recognition or impasses to agreements that relied upon lobbying. And, of course, government unionization at all levels has been greatly encouraged by the organizing actions the AFL-CIO designed to recruit members in new territories in order to offset the declines it was sustaining in its traditional strongholds. In response to the AFL-CIO initiatives, some professional organizations—such as the National Education Association—abandoned their longtime opposition to collective bargaining techniques, including strikes, and began to emulate these tactics.

Nonetheless, by the 1990s it was clear to those both inside and outside the labor movement that its future was in jeopardy. As a result of these fears and the staggering political defeat of Democratic candidates sympathetic to labor's domestic agenda in the congressional elections of 1994 (when the Republicans captured control of the House of Representatives for the first time in forty-two years and of the Senate as well), John Sweeney of the Service Employees International Union (SEIU) and several other labor leaders tried to have Lane Kirkland resign as head of the AFL-CIO in early 1995. He refused at first, but by August, with his opposition mounting, he did resign. His replacement, chosen by vote of the executive council, was the secretary-treasurer of the AFL-CIO, Thomas Donahue—who, as fate would have it, was also originally from the SEIU. Like Kirkland, however, he had been an AFL-CIO official for many years preceding his elevation, and he aspired to remain as president. But at the October 1995 convention of the AFL-CIO, which has the ultimate authority over such matters, John Sweeney won the first contested election for the office of president in fifty years.

Sweeney's ascendancy to leadership was seen as the manifestation of a new attitude toward the recruitment of members. His reform platform warned that unions were in danger of becoming irrelevant to American workers unless they adopted a culture of organizing among all members, and he pledged to make organizing the top priority of the AFL-CIO.

As part of the change in attitude, Sweeney has also sought to broaden labor's political ties, as labor historian Nelson Lichtenstein has observed:

Led by John Sweeney, the new AFL-CIO leadership has taken a series of steps, still largely symbolic, which have begun to tear down the iron curtain which for so many decades divided labor's official leadership from

America's leftist intellectuals: ethnic, gender, and racial diversity finally
made an impact on the AFL-CIO executive council, which in turn emphasized the urgent need for organizing and constructing alliances with
other progressive groups.

At a "teach-in with the labor movement" held at Columbia University in
October 1996, Lichtenstein continued, an event attended by leading liberal intellectuals, Sweeney proclaimed that "we need your help." It is reported that he received an enthusiastic response.[67] Labor's leadership was
seeking to become part of the rainbow coalition.

A more tangible sign of change occurred in 1999 when the SEIU won
an election to represent 75,000 home care workers in Los Angeles County,
thus opening union membership to a new category of workers, many of
whom were minorities and immigrants. The organizing campaign had
been a costly eleven-year effort. Moreover, it succeeded as the nation was
in the midst of the most prolonged period of economic prosperity it has
ever experienced, when labor was becoming scarce. Nonetheless, it was a
crucial victory and a struggle that labor could not afford to lose.

By the end of 1999, total union membership in the nation had grown
by 279,000 members since the year before, but the gains had still not kept
up proportionately with the growth of the labor force. Hence, the percentage of the labor force unionized in 1999 remained the same as it had
been in 1998: 13.9 percent (see Table 6.5).

As the labor movement approached the end of the twentieth century, it
found itself in a position eerily reminiscent of where it had been at its beginning of the century, when unions were fighting for their survival as an
American institution. And again, this struggle is taking place against a
backdrop of mass immigration that is swelling the size of the labor force—
especially in the lower-skilled occupations.

Consequences

As indicated, the AFL-CIO was a strong supporter of the passage
of the Immigration Act of 1965, specifically endorsing the pending reform legislation at its biannual convention before the law's passage. It
passed a resolution stating that "an intelligent and balanced immigration
policy ought to rest on practical considerations of desired skills."[68] As with
all other supporters of the new law, the labor movement did not anticipate that it would launch another era of sustained mass immigration—especially of unskilled workers. In 1965, having attained its two immediate

immigration reforms—termination of the *bracero* program and of the national origins admission system—and with the percentage of the foreign-born population (which had been declining for fifty years) at its historic low, organized labor felt free to turn its attention elsewhere.

But by the late 1970s, when the unexpected consequences of the 1965 law had led to the creation of the Hesburgh Commission and for it to propose extensive reforms, the labor movement found itself in a quandary. The percentage of the labor force belonging to unions was steadily falling (see Table 6.5), and immigration levels were rising, but it was not clear whether the surge was an aberration or the sign of a new long-term trend. Labor had not made a direct link between its state of decline and the revival of mass immigration.

The most troubling issue seemed to be illegal immigration, which the Carter administration had identified as needing immediate attention and about which state AFL-CIO organizations in the Southwest had been protesting for years.[69] Moreover, Cesar Chavez's prolonged struggle in the late 1960s and throughout the 1970s to organize farm workers in California and Texas had focused national attention on the threat that illegal immigrants posed to his efforts. Chavez repeatedly charged that employers were using illegal immigrants as strikebreakers, and because of the inability of the union and the INS to keep illegal immigrants out of the fields, he had to resort to nationwide product boycotts as the only effective way to exert pressure on employers for bargaining recognition.[70]

And so the AFL-CIO chose to focus only on illegal immigration. When the comprehensive reform bills proposed by Senator Simpson and Representative Mazzoli surfaced in 1982 and 1984, labor supported efforts to curtail illegal immigration but showed little interest in their legal immigration and refugee reforms; in fact, there was no apparent sorrow among labor leaders when these bills died in Congress in 1982 and 1984. The AFL-CIO did endorse efforts to pass the modified legislation intended to reduce illegal immigration that successfully culminated in 1986 in the Immigration Reform and Control Act (IRCA).[71] Its 1985 convention policy resolution had called for a system of employer sanctions to include "an eligibility verification system that is secure and nonforgeable"; an amnesty program for illegals already in the United States; no " new 'guestworker' or 'bracero' program"; and very careful restriction of the so-called H-1 and H-2 programs to admit foreign temporary workers, to "those situations where U.S. workers cannot reasonably be found." The resolution strongly criticized the ease by which employers were able to obtain such temporary foreign workers (those on H-1 and H-2 visas) without fully verifying whether citizen workers were available, or to allow foreign visitors (those on B-1 visas) to work in the United States in violation of the explicit terms of their visas. It went on to state that "thousands of workers in the entertainment industry, building trades, maritime, and others are suffering job losses as the result of the unlawful issuance of these visas."[72]

After IRCA was enacted, the AFL-CIO adopted a resolution in 1987 that called it "the most important and far reaching immigration legislation in 30 years," noting in particular that "the AFL-CIO applauds the inclusion in that law of employer sanctions and of a far-reaching legalization [i.e., amnesty] program."[73]

When Congress turned its attention in the late 1980s to the reform of the legal immigration system, the AFL-CIO did not take a prominent role in the political posturing preceding the passage of the Immigration Act of 1990. It did not even clearly articulate what it favored—but it did specify what it was against. In 1989 it passed a resolution "opposing any reduction in the number of family-based visas or any erosion in the definition of the family." Furthermore, it opposed increasing the number of employment-based immigrants because they represented "a brain drain" on other nations; the AFL-CIO preferred expanded domestic policies "to increase our investment in education and job training in this country."[74] The only specific provision the AFL-CIO sought to influence was a section of nonimmigrant labor policy governing the temporary admission of professional performing talent and their accompanying technical workers (i.e., foreign film crews).[75]

As it turned out, the Immigration Act of 1990 raised legal immigration levels to 700,000 visas a year for 1991 through 1994 and thereafter to 675,000. It did not reduce the number of family-based visas (in fact, it increased them), nor did it change the definition of what constitutes a family. But Congress did significantly increase the number of employment-based visas, from 54,000 to 140,000 a year; it added the new diversity admission category (originally with 40,000 visas a year but increasing to 55,000 beginning in 1995); and it expanded the ease whereby employers could get access to a variety of foreign workers on a temporary basis. Labor did obtain one tidbit it sought: a cap of 25,000 visas a year was placed on the annual number of newly created "P visas" for foreign workers in the entertainment industry.

The Dramatic Shift in Tactics

In 1993 the actions taken by the AFL-CIO pertaining to immigration suddenly reversed course. Instead of complaining about their impact on American workers, the convention's policy resolution praised the role that immigrants had played "in building the nation and its democratic ideas" and added this homily:

> The labor movement in particular has been enriched by the contribu-
> tions of immigrant workers. They played a fundamental role in building
> our movement and continue to make indispensable contributions to the
> strength of our unions to this day.[76]

Such language represents a sharp break from the expressions of facts and legislative agenda of many preceding years. But the resolution went even further to demonize unidentified advocates of immigration reform for launching "a new hate campaign cynically designed to exploit public anxiety by making immigrants and refugees the scapegoats for economic and social problems." It concluded that "immigrants are not the cause of our nation's problems" and stated that "the AFL-CIO reiterates its long standing commitment to . . . provide fair opportunities for legal immigra-tion and . . . due process of law for all people who enter, or attempt to enter, the United States illegally." The resolution also encouraged affili-ated unions "to develop programs to address the special needs of immi-grant members and potential members" and called for member unions to work with "immigrant advocacy groups and service organizations" to pro-tect the interests of new immigrants.[77] Clearly, a new immigration attitude was emerging within the AFL-CIO.

It was true, of course, that immigration was reemerging in the early 1990s as a national issue. In November 1994 the citizens of California had voted overwhelmingly for Proposition 187, which sought to reduce the local and state tax burden of providing social services and educational op-portunities for hundreds of thousands of illegal immigrants.[78] By this time the Commission on Immigration Reform was also releasing its interim re-ports, calling for reforms to curtail illegal immigration and considering proposals to reduce the level of legal immigration, to eliminate the ex-tended family admission preferences, and to place refugee admissions once more under the overall immigration ceiling. Immigration reform was back on the agenda of Congress.

Against this backdrop, the AFL-CIO entered the fray by opposing all the proposed changes. In 1995 it repeated its charge that immigration re-formers were making immigrants "scapegoats" and that proposals for comprehensive immigration reforms were being used "to unfairly exploit public concern over illegal immigrants." Furthermore, it asserted that the Jordan Commission's proposal to create a national computer database to assist in determining work eligibility "will create many problems and won't reduce undocumented immigration." Despite extensive research findings to the contrary, the policy resolution asserted, "The notion that immigrants are to blame for the deteriorating living standards of America's low-wage workers must be clearly rejected." Rather than immigration reform, it proposed increasing the minimum wage, adopting universal health care, and enacting labor law reform as the remedies for the widening income disparity in the nation.[79]

Thus, the AFL-CIO joined with other special interest groups to defeat the reforms that were introduced in Congress in 1996, even though they reflected the conclusions of the Commission on Immigration Reform after its years of investigative study. The AFL-CIO allied itself with "a formidable coalition" that "included unions, the National Association of Manufacturers, Americans for Tax Reform, the National Christian Coalition, and civil libertarians."[80] Together, they succeeded in separating legal reform measures from the pending bill and then killing them; stripping from the remaining bill the key proposals for verification of Social Security numbers as a way to reduce illegal immigration; and dropping efforts to limit refugee admissions. By joining with a coalition of some of the most antiunion organizations in the country, labor succeeded in blocking immigration reform designed primarily to protect the economic well-being of low skilled workers in the nation.

Why? James Gimbel and James Edwards, who have studied the influence of special interest groups on the immigration legislative process, state that organized labor joined the pro-immigration lobby because it was focusing its organizing efforts on the growing service industries that employ large numbers of Hispanic and Asian immigrants: "Concerned about the long-term drop in union membership, labor leaders have turned to generous immigration policy as a means for re-energizing a flagging movement."[81]

The response by labor officials is that although new organizing targets have indeed increased the encounter of some unions with large urban concentrations of immigrants, the issue is more complex. They recognize illegal immigration as a significant problem—accounting for as much as 3 percent of the total labor force and producing the most adverse economic effects of immigration. But to avoid confusing the way that the issue of immigration reform itself is formulated, they believe that discussion of this issue should be separated from considerations of the level of legal immigration and refugee accommodation issues.

Labor does believe that all workers who are in the United States ought to receive the full protection of existing labor laws, regardless of their legal status. This is seen as a social justice issue at the worksite which is a traditional union concern. But self-defense motivations are also involved; some employers use the threat (or the actual practice) of turning illegal immigrants in to the INS if they seek to vote (or do vote) in union certification elections.[82] U.S. courts have upheld the right of "all employees— including those who may be subject to termination in the future . . . to vote or whether they want to be represented by a union."[83]

To make matters worse, the INS announced in the spring of 1999 that it was essentially abandoning the worksite enforcement of employer sanctions, shifting its deterrence posture to focus on human smuggling activities, border management, and criminal deportations. Essentially this means that illegal immigrants now have little to fear about INS raids or about being apprehended unless employers report them (which is unlikely).[84] Thus, there is merit in labor's position that workers must organize the workers that employers hire, and if the INS is not going to police work sites, unions must seek to enlist the illegal immigrants as members or abandon their organizing efforts with the enterprise in question. Should unions give up such organizing, employers will have an even greater incentive to hire illegal immigrants than they already do. Thus, organizing and protecting illegal immigrants is not a matter of principle; it is a matter of necessity. But having said this, organized labor cannot seriously believe that government should not try find the illegal immigrants at the worksite or that unions should not report employers who they believe are hiring workers in violation of federal immigration law.

At its October 1999 convention in Los Angeles, the pro-immigrant element within the AFL-CIO made its move. Gaining support from unions representing janitors, garment workers, restaurant workers, and hotel housekeepers, they argued that unions must overtly embrace immigrants if the movement is to survive.[85] They buttressed their case by citing incidents of employers using immigration law to intimidate or dismiss immigrant workers who were involved in trying to form unions. In particular, these advocates sought to end the employer sanctions provision created by IRCA in 1986 (which organized labor had strongly supported at the time) and to enact yet another general amnesty for those illegal immigrants already in the country. Support for this effort was far from unanimous, and a floor fight seemed probable.

To avoid a public confrontation, AFL-CIO officials hastily began maneuvering.[86] It was agreed by the federation's leadership that the motion would be briefly debated and then referred to a committee for study; subsequently, the executive council would take up the issue at its next meeting.

When the executive council met in New Orleans in February 2000, it consummated its break from the past. It was announced that the AFL-CIO would seek to have the employer sanctions provisions of IRCA repealed and that it favored a new amnesty to cover most of the 6 million illegal

Table 6.6. The Foreign-Born Population 1965–1999

Year	Foreign-Born Population (millions)	Percentage of Total Population
1965	8,549	4.4
1970	9,619	4.7
1980	14,079	6.2
1990	19,767	7.9
1999	26,400	9.7

Sources: 1965: Jeffrey S. Passel, "30 Years of Immigration and U.S. Population Growth" (paper presented at the annual meeting of the Association for Public Policy Analysis and Management, Washington D.C., November 1995); 1970–1990: U.S. Bureau of the Census, *Historical Census Statistics on the Foreign-Born Population of the United States, 1850–1990* Working Paper no. 29 (Washington, D.C.: U.S. Department of Commerce, 1999), table 1; 1999: U.S. Bureau of the Census, "The Foreign-Born Population in the United States," in *Current Population Reports*, P20–519, 2000, 1.

immigrants believed to be in the United States. The president of the Hotel and Restaurant Employees, John Wilhelm, stated that "the labor movement is on the side of immigration in this country." Business lobbyists hailed the new policy stance. Spokesmen for the U.S. Chamber of Commerce called the proposal "a welcome embrace . . . from an employer's perspective."[87] So did members of the Congressional Hispanic Caucus. Representative Lucille Roybal-Allard (D-California), Chair of the group, said that its members "look forward to working with the AFL-CIO and the business community to reform our immigration policy" because "we believe that these immigrants have made impressive contributions to our work and to our nation."[88] In contrast, the chairman of the subcommittee on immigration in the House of Representatives, Lamar Smith (R-Texas), called it "a betrayal of American workers" and added that "apparently union bosses are so distraught about declining union membership that they will stoop to exploiting illegal workers."[89] The *New York Times*, likewise, editorialized that "the AFL-CIO's proposal should be rejected" as it would "undermine the integrity of the country's immigration laws and would depress the wages of the lowest-paid native born workers."[90]

Thus, as the twentieth century ends and a new millennium commences, organized labor finds itself once again confronting the dilemma of mass immigration. The inverse relationship between trends in union membership and the size of the foreign-born population has never been more apparent. The unionized percentage of the labor force fell from 30.1 in 1965 to 13.9 percent in 1999 (see Table 6.5). Over this same interval the foreign-born percentage of the population rose from 4.4 to 9.7 percent (see Table 6.6). Of even greater consequence is the fact that, because relatively more of the foreign-born are both male and younger than the native-born population, immigrants constitute a significantly larger percentage of the labor force—11.7 percent in 1999—than they do of the general population.[91] And that percentage is probably too low because of the statistical undercount of illegal immigrants in the country—believed to be about 6 million.

It is hard to see how organized labor can expect to gain from the continuation of mass immigration and the weakening of the enforcement of existing laws. For American workers in general and the less-skilled workers in particular, it is impossible to visualize any benefit from what prevailing policy permits and tolerates. Organized labor is at a crossroads. It can seek an expedient course and embrace mass immigration for political advantage, which it seems to be doing. But if it actually does so, it will have abandoned its traditional moral role as the advocate for the economic well-being of American workers. It cannot have it both ways.

CHAPTER SEVEN

Conclusions

With only two exceptions, membership in American unions has over time moved inversely with trends in the size of immigration inflows (see Figure 7.1). One exception was from 1897 to 1905 when both union membership and immigration increased—but it was a period when the nation's economy was rapidly industrializing and it was a time of recovery after an economic depression. The other was from 1922 to 1929 when, conversely, both union membership and immigration declined—but that was an era of all-out assault on unionism by business, government, and the courts. Other than those two periods of very special circumstances, the inverse relationship has generally prevailed and has been manifestly the case since 1932.

To be sure, there have been multiple influences on both the expansions and contractions of union membership rolls and the flow of immigrants. But after the temporal and quixotic short-run influences are examined, the one factor that remains as the consistent barometer of the state of American unionism is the prevailing trend of immigration. Immigration has the power to influence the size of the labor supply and thereby, both wage and employment conditions. One might anticipate, therefore, that the labor movement would flounder during periods of high immigration and flourish during periods of low immigration. And Figure 7.1 shows that far more often than not, this has been the case.

The impact of immigration has never been evenly distributed throughout the economy, however, but has always disproportionately affected selective segments of the labor force. Over the course of the American ex-

Figure 7.1. Comparison of the Percentage of the Labor Force Who Belong to Unions

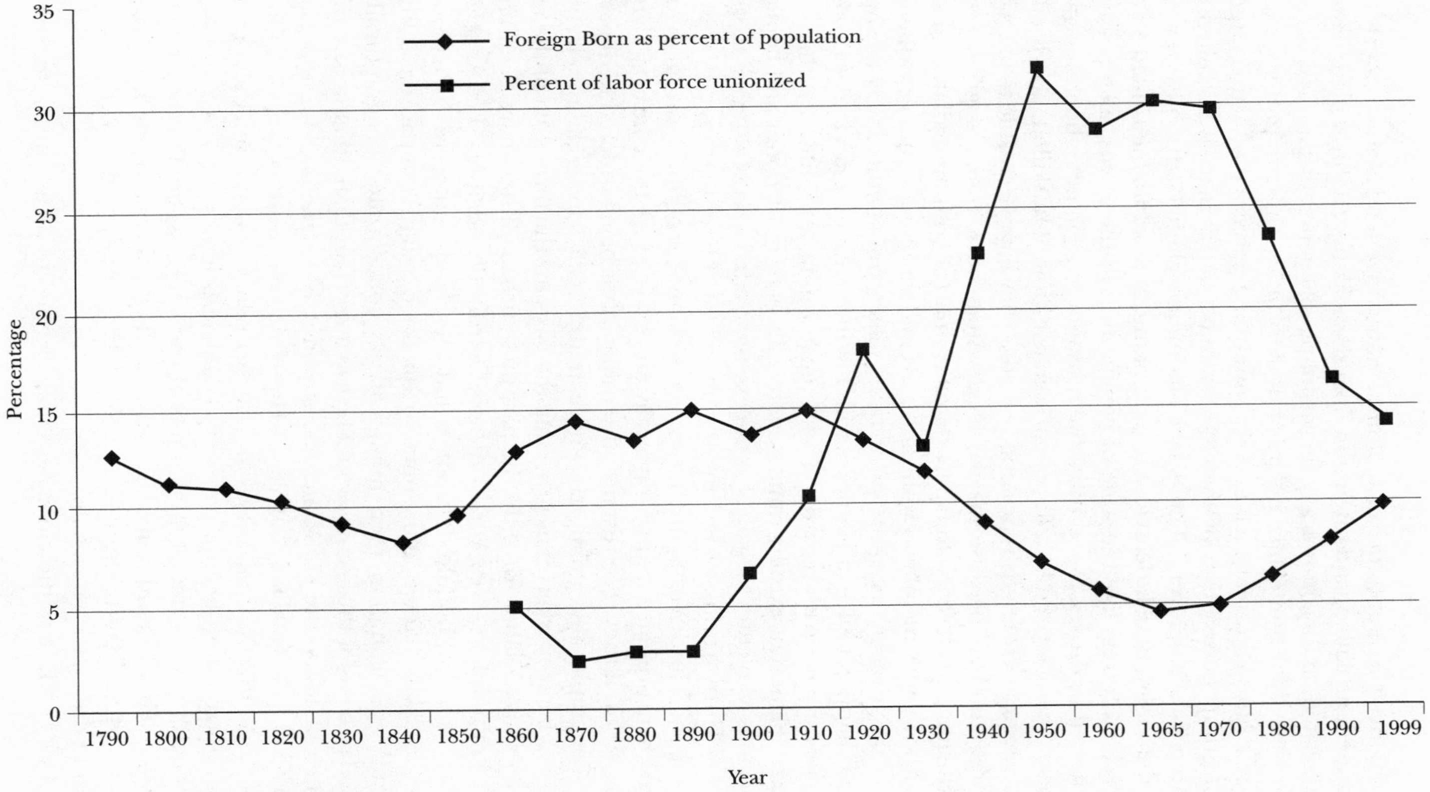

Year

Percentage

Foreign Born as percent of population

Percent of labor force unionized

Sources: See preceding chapters.

perience the preponderance of immigrants have tended to be poorly educated, unskilled, and often non-English-speaking. Highly skilled, better-educated, and economically successful people generally have less reason to leave their homelands in large numbers unless they are pushed out by some unusual threat such as a war, or are the perceived or actual targets of group persecution by their government, or are actively recruited by American employers. Those lacking human capital attributes, on the other hand, have little to lose by emigrating, and before the United States decided to regulate the scale of immigration in the 1920s, such persons entered in droves. Since 1965, the revival of mass immigration has again been characterized by a disproportionate inflow of unskilled, poorly educated and non-English-speaking persons. They have been able to enter in large numbers because (1) the legal system since 1965 has given overwhelming preference to family reunification (of both immediate and extended family members) without regard to their human capital attributes; (2) the diversity category, since 1991, selects immigrants solely because they happen to live in countries with low immigration rates to the United States and not with regard to their human capital attributes; (3) the massive violation of existing immigration ceilings by mostly poor and hapless persons who enter illegally; (4) the extensive admission of refugees mostly from Third World nations; and (5) the arrival of poor persons also mostly from the Third World, who falsely make claims for political asylum to justify their presence and who typically abscond before their hearing dates are set or, if they receive a negative ruling, after being ordered to depart.

Geographically, immigrants have traditionally clustered in selective urban labor markets thus providing the basis for the formation of the nation's urban labor force. In the past these urban clusters have been limited in number—New York, Chicago, Detroit, Philadelphia, Los Angeles, San Francisco, Buffalo, Pittsburgh and Cleveland—but were the nation's largest labor markets at the time, so that the immigrant impact was significant on the nation even though it was concentrated geographically. Today, a few of those cities would be less important than other large cities one can add to the list: Miami, San Antonio, New Orleans, Houston, Dallas, San Jose, Oakland, Las Vegas, Honolulu, and Washington, D.C. Only in the Southwest (Texas, New Mexico, Arizona, Colorado, and California) has immigration been a persistent characteristic of rural areas and—although the presence of immigrants in rural areas of the Prairie States of Iowa, Nebraska, and Kansas as well as in the rural areas of the East Coast states of Maryland, Virginia, and North Carolina also increased in number in the 1990s—it remains so.

In its early days the labor movement tended to focus on the organization of blue-collar workers in the goods-producing sector of the economy. The only heavily unionized service industry was the transportation, communication, and public utility sector. With the exception of those in mining, most unionized workers were found in large urban areas, where immigration was a constant issue for union organizers to confront. Even though many of labor's most prominent leaders were immigrants themselves (or close relatives of recent immigrants), the union movement was always in the forefront of efforts to control, to regulate, and to reduce immigration, for unions conscientiously made the interest of American workers their first priority—whether native-born or foreign-born. Union leaders did not cater to immigrant workers on the basis of their nonnativity or their perceived diversity but acted in the self-interest of their members: that is, to gain a semblance of control over the supply of labor. Their persistent advocacy of immigration controls and ceilings were perfectly consistent with the main reason for unions to exist: to improve wages, hours, and working conditions for workers already in the country. The goal of union organizing did not include the promotion of immigrants' causes or interests except as those might be derivatives of their status as workers. Once the newcomers were organized, unions did assist in their assimilation process into American life. But this collateral role was a far cry from being involved in any efforts to praise immigrants for being immigrants or from encouraging more to come.[1]

Throughout most of the history of American labor, unions were fighting merely to exist or to maintain any toeholds they could establish, and in concert with strong employer opposition, ongoing mass immigration, was the most persistent threat to union organizing efforts. It provided employers with a source of strikebreakers and alternative supplies of workers. If its scale was high, the very presence of immigrants assured that local wages would barely exceed subsistence levels, that hours of work would be long, and that working conditions would be dire. Mass immigration was a threat to the creation of a viable labor movement and an obstacle to the quest of existing unions to improve the standard of living for workers. There were, of course, additional impediments, but mass immigration reinforced all the other retarding influences.

Only after a century of mass immigration ended during the 1914–1924 era was the labor movement able to take root. From the early 1930s to the mid-1960s, unionism flourished. Freed of the external pressure of mass immigration, labor could finally internalize its power and devote its full attention to the pursuit of workers' welfare. The same was true for the pioneering governmental policies, enacted over these same years, which sought to protect and to enhance the well-being of workers and to ensure equal employment opportunity in the labor market. In every instance, organized labor was instrumental in their passage of such laws. With immigration sharply curtailed, the protection and well-being of the labor force became national priorities for government, and unions benefited.

As a consequence, there was an unprecedented movement toward greater equality of both opportunity and income in the nation during these years of low immigration. From 1947 (the first year the Census Bureau began annually to track income distribution trends in the nation) until 1968 there was a 7.4 percent decline in family income inequality. The greatest gains were made by the bottom 20 percent of American families. After 1968, with the resumption of mass immigration, income inequality among families dramatically increased. By 1982, income inequality was back to the same level as it was in 1947 and, by 1994, family income inequality in the nation had increased by 22.4 percent over the distribution that existed in 1968.[2] (Recall that 1968 was the year that the Immigration Act of 1965 went into full effect.) Since 1995 there have been signs that income inequality tendencies have stabilized: inequality has not worsened, but neither has it improved, despite the fact that the nation has been in the midst of the most protracted period of prosperity in its history.[3] Income disparity has been the Achilles heel of these economic boom times.

The Council of Economic Advisers to the President (CEA) identified the post-1965 experience of mass immigration as one of the contributing factors for the worsening income distribution. In 1994 the CEA reported that "immigration has increased the relative supply of less educated labor and appears to have contributed to the increasing inequality of income."[4] Although the CEA report claimed that the aggregate effect on the overall distribution of income of the nation was "small," immigration was identified as a major factor in the deterioration of wages and incomes at the lower end of the distribution. A 1995 study by the Bureau of Labor Statistics, for example, found that "immigration accounted for approximately 20 to 25 percent of the increase in the wage gap between low and high skilled workers during the 1980s in the 50 largest metropolitan areas of the United States." The same study revealed that half of the decline in real wages for native-born high school dropouts over that time span can be attributed to the impact of unskilled foreign workers.[5] Thus, the critical issue that is so often overlooked is not only that a disproportionate number of the immigrants themselves are unskilled and poor but that, by their presence, they also impoverish similarly situated native-born workers and their families in the same local labor markets.

Mass immigration's impact on wages, employment, and labor mobility adversely and disproportionately affects the income patterns of workers at the bottom of the economic ladder. Given the geographic concentration of the foreign-born population, it is the urban labor force with its large minority populations that is most adversely affected.[6] Therefore, even if the effects of immigration are dissipated when measured at the aggregate national level, that does not mean they are less significant. Indeed, in many of the nation's major urban markets, immigration and its effects are dominating factors in interpreting wage, employment, and income trends.

In 1995 the CEA also cited the decline in unionism since the early 1970s as a significant explanatory factor for the widening income disparity within the nation: "Empirical evidence suggests that unions tend to raise wages for workers who would otherwise be in the bottom half of the wage distribution."[7] Noting that union membership had plunged since the early 1970s (when income disparity was beginning to widen), the CEA added that the decline in union membership had been greatest in the private sector where foreign-born workers are disproportionately employed (in 1999 only 9.4 percent of private-sector workers belonged to unions). The CEA indicated that perhaps as much as 20 percent of the increase in wage inequality since the early 1970s—"especially of men"—could be attributed to this decline in union membership.[8]

Hence, it takes no great leap of faith to conclude that if the rapid increase in immigration and the decline of unionism are both causal explanations for widening income disparity, the revival of mass immigration is likely to be a contributing factor to the decline in unionism. Indeed, there are ample specific case studies to document the fact. One in southern California carefully documented the situation whereby black janitorial workers, who in the 1970s had successfully built a strong union that provided high wages and good working conditions, were almost totally displaced and the union broken in the 1980s by nonunion Hispanic immigrants who were willing to work for far lower pay and fewer benefits.[9] In another case, management in the hotel industry in Los Angeles in the 1980s, was able to lower its wage rates and benefits by switching from a Teamsters' local union made up mostly of black workers to a Seafarers' local whose members were mostly recent immigrants.[10] In a 1982 strike at a Los Angeles tortilla factory, native-born American workers were replaced by illegal immigrants whom management recruited to break the strike, and wages were cut by 40 percent for those workers who returned.[11] Likewise, in the High Plains and Midwest the meatpacking industry successfully shifted the cutting and packaging of meat from unionized butchers in stores to lower-cost packing houses by using nonunion Asian refugees and Mexican immigrants (legal and illegal) as the replacement workers.[12] Similar examples of the substitution of nonunion immigrants for unionized native-born workers have occurred in the furniture-making and melon-growing industries as employers shifted the work from one region of California to another.[13]

In Los Angeles the much publicized "Justice for Janitors" campaign led by the Service Employees International Union (SEIU) did win an organizational victory in 1990 after witnessing a dramatic membership collapse in the 1980s.[14] After employers tapped in to the surge of Hispanic immigrants during that decade to replace higher-paid, unionized, native-born black and white workers, the "Justice for Janitors" campaign sought to recapture the jobs that had been lost and to organize the new jobs created in the rapidly expanding building service industry in southern California. It took a strike and a highly publicized encounter with the Los Angeles police, who broke up a union protest march along a public highway, for a settlement to be reached. Union recognition was achieved, and fringe benefits were won but the negotiated wage rates were still half of what they had been in 1982. Subsequent contracts were successfully renegotiated over the decade, but in April 2000, after a three-week strike, the SEIU was unable to win the dollar-an-hour increase for each of the following three years that it had sought.[15] Essentially, that strike was settled on the terms offered by the employers.

In 1990 the International Association of Machinists (IAM) won a recognition victory for eight hundred manufacturing workers at American Racing Equipment in Los Angeles after six months of negotiations, following a three-day wildcat strike. Most of the newly unionized production workers there, however, were long-settled Mexican immigrants with legal status, not recent arrivals or illegal immigrants. Also, prior to the union election the company had been bought by a Canadian company, which did not contest the voting results.[16] But a coalition effort by nine unions in 1995 to organize other manufacturers in Los Angeles, and to establish a union presence in Latino immigrant communities, failed and was abandoned in 1998.[17] Efforts to organize garment workers, who were overwhelmingly immigrants, in Los Angeles in the mid-1990s were also unsuccessful.[18]

In 1992 a five-month strike by immigrant Mexican construction workers in southern California ultimately did succeed in reestablishing a union presence for drywallers in the residential construction sector of the industry and in restoring the high membership levels that had existed in the 1970s.[19] The negotiated wages, however, were still well below the levels that had prevailed before native-born workers were replaced by Latino immigrants in the late 1970s and throughout the 1980s.

The AFL-CIO's Policy Reversal

On its face, the policy turnabout taken by the AFL-CIO in February 2000 looks like an act of desperation. Confronted since 1965 with declining membership and the adverse labor supply consequences of mass immigration, the federation appears to be groping to find a survival strategy.

To the degree that there is logic to its new policy stance, it would seem to be as follows. In the rapidly changing labor market environment of the late 1990s and early 2000s—involving globalization, technological change, and mass immigration pressures—the one sector of the economy that might be receptive to concentrated union organization is the low-skilled labor market, which is infused with a growing supply of immigrant workers. Because the preponderance of the present immigrant inflow is coming from less economically developed nations, these workers are frequently from impoverished backgrounds.[20] Many lack skills, are poorly educated, and are non-English speaking, and this lack of human capital restricts them to the low-skilled labor market. But the low wages and poor working conditions associated with jobs in this sector—as judged by American standards—are not so perceived by many of the immigrants themselves and are regarded, rather, as being considerably better than those they previously experienced in their homelands. Hence, they are more than willing to fill these jobs. And given the extensive ethnic networking that is often associated with their growing communities, many employers have discovered that hiring immigrants means they no longer need to worry about recruiting workers for many of their low-skilled occupations; hence, immigrant workers are often preferred workers.[21] And illegal immigrants in particular are seen as more docile and more dependent on employers—especially if they are obligated to smugglers or labor contractors for the cost of their transit to the United States.[22]

Accordingly, the AFL-CIO position seems to be that this expanding segment of the labor force sector is amenable to organization if unions endear themselves to immigrant causes. Given the difficulties the labor movement has experienced in recent years in organizing and retaining members in industries where it was strong in the past, the low-skilled, perhaps the immigrant-dominated sector of the labor market is the key to future union growth.

But such a strategy comes with a heavy cost. First, successes in organizing immigrants will not translate into any real ability to increase workers' wages or benefits significantly. As long as the labor market continues to be flooded with low-skilled immigrant job seekers, unions will not be able to defy the market forces that suppress upward wage pressures. For example, the aforementioned Justice for Janitors campaign to raise wages for janitors in Los Angeles took place in the context of an effort by the Los Angeles Living Wage Coalition to raise janitors wages by law. Reflecting the surplus of unskilled labor in the city and the resulting prevalence of low wages in many occupations, the coalition successfully obtained passage of a local ordinance that required private companies doing business with the city to pay "a livable wage" ($8.76 an hour at the time). This was considerably higher than the federal minimum wage ($5.15 an hour at the time), which would otherwise have been the wage floor. But if the company becomes unionized, an "opt-out" clause in the ordinance permits a *lower wage* if it is the result of collective bargaining negotiations.[23]

The rationale for this unusual provision was that the ordinance could be repealed in the future (in fact, the Los Angeles ordinance was enacted over the veto of Mayor Richard Riordan by the city council) whereas the union, it was believed, would be there indefinitely. It should be noted that from 1993 (when the California economy began to recover from the deep recession of the prior three years) until 1998, Los Angeles County added 300,000 new jobs. But the vast majority of these jobs paid less than $25,000 a year. Almost none paid what the *Los Angeles Times* called "solid middle class salaries" of between $40,000 to $60,000.[24] Thus, the wage suppression effects of mass immigration on the overall labor market will not be alleviated even if immigrants prove receptive to a specific appeal to their political causes to join unions.

Second, a focus on the advancement of the interests of low-skilled immigrants can only cause the alienation of low-skilled native-born workers who must compete for the same jobs, because they too lack the human capital to qualify for higher-paid work. How long can it be until they recognize that their ambitions for higher wages and better living standards cannot be achieved as long as mass immigration is allowed to function without regard for its economic consequences?

The fundamental issue for labor has never been whether unions should organize immigrants; of course they must, as they have always tried to do. Rather, it is whether labor should seek to organize workers specifically *because* they are immigrants and, in the process, become an advocate for immigrant causes. Or should unions do as they have done in the past: try to organize all workers purely on the grounds of the pursuit of their employment well-being? If labor seeks to organize immigrants on the same basis as native-born workers, making no distinction between them, there is no reason to embrace the broad range of immigrant policy issues. Indeed, the hard reality of the lessons of labor history is that the more generous the immigration policy, the worse it is for all workers in their efforts to raise wages, to improve working conditions, and to secure employment opportunities.

In the AFL-CIO's policy resolution for the year 2000, there is the innocuous statement "Regulated immigration is better then unregulated illegal immigration." But no mention is made of the need for any serious reforms in legal immigration or in refugee and political policies. There is the usual statement of opposition to "guestworker" (i.e., temporary foreign worker) programs because they "depress wages and distort labor markets." (But this general charge can legitimately apply to all forms of immigrant entry into the labor force.) If there have to be guestworker programs, the AFL-CIO contends, there should be "more rigorous labor market tests and the involvement of unions in the labor certification process."[25] Yet the major thrust of the federation's policy statement pertains to the accommodation of illegal immigrants by abolishing employer sanctions and the granting of a new amnesty for many of those already in the labor force.

Peter Kwong, like most other scholars who have seriously studied the issue, has concluded that "illegal immigrants are the most difficult workers to organize" because their precarious status renders it difficult for them to complain about wages, hours, and working conditions.[26] Not only are they less informed about available legal protections or what unions are all about, but they fear deportation and the possible return to lives of poverty and despair back home. Yet rather than hold firm to its historic positions that call for stronger measures to reduce the magnitude of illegal immigration, the AFL-CIO executive council has announced a surrender. If the employers will not abide by the law and if the INS will no longer enforce the law at the worksite, the labor movement has chosen to give up. Its new position aligns the AFL-CIO with the special interests that put their own selfish goals ahead of the national interest in an enforceable immigration policy. What is needed for American workers is immigration reform like that recommended by both the Hesburgh and Jordan Commissions—not immigration capitulation.

The presence of illegal immigrants in the labor market affects *all workers* with whom they compete. Theoretically, underdocumented workers are potential union members, but experience clearly shows that unions are unlikely to organize more than a small fraction of them. If illegal immigrants remain a significant proportion of workers in low-skilled occupations (agriculture, hotels, restaurants, residential construction, landscaping, home health care, warehousing, retail sales), other workers need protection from competition with them over the terms of employment. Unions have traditionally put the interest of workers first and immigrants second, if at all. The proposal to strip away the few safeguards that immigration policy currently has to protect American workers from the adverse consequences of illegal immigration represents a major reversal of attitude, putting the interest of illegal immigrant workers ahead of the larger interest of American workers in general. The new policy itself is analogous to taking a shortcut through quicksand. American workers—especially those in low-skilled occupations, who far outnumber the stock of illegal immigrants currently in the country—could only regard it as a betrayal of their welfare.

Employer sanctions are the only protection that citizens (and permanent resident aliens) in the workforce have from the unfair competition of job seekers who have no right to be in the country or in its workplace. Employer sanctions set the moral tone for the issue for the nation. Just as the Civil Rights Act of 1964 stated explicitly that employment discrimination would not be tolerated in the workplace, the employer sanctions provisions of IRCA perform the same function for immigration law. Title 7 of the Civil Rights Act (the equal employment opportunity provisions) did not end labor market discrimination but did make an emphatic declaration about what is right and what is wrong. Similarly, IRCA's employment sanctions provisions make it adamantly clear that the workplace of the United States is reserved for native-born citizens, naturalized citizens, permanent resident aliens, and foreign nationals who have been granted special temporary work visas.

There is nothing more important for most workers in the United States than the opportunity to seek employment and to be fairly compensated for their efforts without having to confront the corrosive effects of people who have no right to be competitive for jobs or to influence labor market conditions. As Kwong has so aptly stated, "There is no doubt that the continual influx of cheap and exploitable illegal labor degrades the position of American workers."[27] Yet the AFL-CIO executive council seems to believe that abolishing employer sanctions and granting a new amnesty to those already here would so ingratiate it to these immigrants that they will then flock to unions. The assumption is dubious given the state of American labor law, but even if it should prove true, what is the implication for other low-skilled workers who are not unionized? And what of the future? Without employer sanctions in place and enforced, one can certainly expect that the entire amnesty process will have to be repeated again several years down the road. The end of sanctions and the granting of a new amnesty could only be seen as a green light for more illegals to come.

The historical experience catalogued in this book—and bolstered by the accumulating research—shows that it is the low-skilled workers in the United States who are the most adversely effected by the massive violation of the existing immigration system. The chronic need is to strengthen this system of deterrence, not to undermine its intentions. Without employer sanctions, the only deterrence left in the law would be more effective border management—which *is* desperately needed. But better border management is only part of the problem of stopping illegal entry. Many immigrants who enter with legal documents become illegal by overstaying their entry visas or seek work in violation of their visitor visas' terms. Others have learned to use the vagaries of the nation's political asylum system by entering, making a phony claim, and then simply disappearing. As one frustrated immigration official said of the political asylum policy: "It is so easy to defeat the system that a 10 year old kid could do it."[28] It is a common practice for would-be illegal immigrants simply to walk up to U.S. border checkpoints or to arrive at international airports and ask for political asylum so that they can enter the country without having to pay a smuggler. Once in, they are typically assigned a hearing date, but never show up. The only way to stop the visa abusers and phony asylum seekers is stringent worksite enforcement of employer sanctions. Take away the sanctions, and there is nothing.

The amnesty proposal is likewise counterproductive. The only reason to have granted the amnesties under IRCA in 1986 was that the United States had previously given such mixed signals about illegal immigrants. But once employer sanctions were enacted, the era of uncertainty ended. A new amnesty for the 6 million illegal immigrants in the country in the year 2000 would do two things—both detrimental to American workers. First, it would give approval to the actions of those who have willfully violated the nation's laws. Second, it would add dramatically to the size of the nation's low-skilled labor pool in a variety of industries, since instead of being limited to work in specific immigrant enclaves where their presence is least obvious, these formerly illegal immigrants could spread like an epidemic throughout the low-skilled labor market. That may happen anyway, because of the self-imposed impotence of the Immigration and Naturalization Service. But for organized labor to sanction such an infusion on an ongoing basis can only be considered the act of a Judas. Organized labor might thereby become the friend of the self-serving immigrant advocacy groups, but it could no longer be considered a champion of American workers. The proposal is a betrayal of the legacy of the past in which unions always placed the interests of workers, whether native- or foreign-born, ahead of any subsidiary consideration. Why imperil this honored legacy?

What Needs to Be Done?

To the degree that the causes of the income disparity in the United States emanate from the labor market, the policy remedies required to increase the rewards for low-skilled and semiskilled workers are surprisingly consistent with the remedies needed to revive the nation's labor movement.

Immigration Reform

Of all of the policies, those dealing with immigration reforms are the most necessary, and they should be the easiest to put in place and the quickest to bring positive rewards. Immigration policy is a discretionary act of the federal government. The needed reforms can, if adopted, reduce the size of the low-wage worker pool. If immigration policy were made accountable for its economic consequences, immigration flows could become congruent with prevailing labor market trends and not, as is presently the case, be a counterproductive influence.

With respect to the legal immigration system, the 1997 recommendations of the Commission on Immigration Reform (the Jordan Commission) discussed in Chapter 6 are an excellent starting point. Immigration should be reduced to the levels in place prior to the passage of the Immigration Act of 1990. The assumptions on which that legislation was enacted were false. Illegal immigration had not been halted or even significantly reduced. The reliance on family reunification as the primary admission criterion needs to be modified by eliminating all *extended* family admission categories. As the eminent immigration authority, John Higham wrote in 1991,

> This [i.e., family preferences] will be difficult to change as were the earlier anomalies and deficiencies in American immigration policy [i.e., the national origins admission system]. Like the earlier deficiencies, the family preference scheme will have a stubborn consistency in the ethnic groups that believe they benefit from it. Just as the national origin quotas suppressed variety in the alleged interests of the older American population, so the current law does the same in the supposed interest of the groups that have dominated the incoming stream.[29]

Likewise, the diversity category should be eliminated. Within the employment-based categories, the admission of unskilled workers (those without a high school diploma) should be prohibited. There should be

no guestworker program for unskilled workers except in a national emergency duly certified by the president, and any such program should cease
when the emergency ends. The number of refugees to be admitted each
year should be included within the overall number of immigrants admitted in that year (as was the case from 1965 to 1980). Exceptions could be
granted by Congress should a special international circumstance arise but
the use of the open-ended parole authority to admit groups of individuals
as refugees should be explicitly barred (as Congress implicitly sought to
do on two occasions).

All these changes could reduce the flow of poorly skilled, uneducated,
non-English-speaking workers pouring into the low-skilled labor market.
The wisdom of Melvin Reder, a pioneer in the analysis of immigration's
impact on the labor market, should always be kept in mind: "Our immigration policy inevitably reflects a kind of national selfishness of which
the major beneficiaries are the least fortunate among us. We could not
completely abandon the policy, even if we so desired."[30]

With regard to illegal immigration, employer sanctions must be retained
and strengthened. It is mandatory to establish a system whereby the eligibility of a job applicant to work in the United States can be easily verified.
The Jordan Commission recommended, as a minimum, a telephone call-
in system for verifying the validity of Social Security numbers offered by
job applicants. This is essential, but it would be preferable to take the issue
of identification to the next stage: namely, a way to validate that the name
given is actually that of the person applying for the job, who is the actual
person to whom the proffered Social Security card applies. Methods of
doing this would not be much different from the way credit card companies authorize purchases for those who use their cards: they would probably entail the reissuance of Social Security cards with photographs and
magnetic tape codes containing identification information.[31]

The utility of such cards would far exceed simply the enforcement of
the right to work in the United States. They could be used to reduce iden-
tity theft, welfare fraud (similar cards are already used in some states for
this purpose), and entitlement program abuse where criminals make multiple applications for coverage or steal other people's identities. Such
cards would *not* be national identification cards to be carried by citizens
and permanent resident aliens; they would have to be produced only on
those few occasions over one's lifetime when one is hired for a new job—
and then only *after* the hiring decision has been made. Once the authenticity of the card was verified, the employers (who would receive a confirmation number) would not be responsible for any subsequent finding
that the user of the card had somehow obtained it illegally.

In the electronic age it is no longer possible to use hiring practices of the past. A job is the most important thing that the U.S. economy provides for its citizens and permanent resident aliens. Protecting access to its labor market is as important as safeguarding eligibility for public entitlements (food stamps, welfare, unemployment compensation); access to the public records (driver's license, tax and Social Security records); and the security of private-sector finances (bank accounts, pensions, education credentials, medical histories). Accordingly, the fears of those who resist the use of a better system of identification for work eligibility should take heed of the words of the Reverend Theodore Hesburgh (chair of the Select Commission on Immigration and Refugee Policy and, before that, of the U.S. Civil Rights Commission), who has said, "Raising the specter of 'Big Brotherdom,' calling a worker identification system totalitarian or labeling it 'the computer taboo' does not further the debate on U.S. immigration policy; it only poisons it."[32]

Closing the identification loophole would put muscle back in the employer sanctions system. But strengthening that system makes sense only if the INS withdraws its ill-conceived policy, announced in 1999, of essentially abandoning worksite inspections (see Chapter 6). Better border controls are necessary but by no means sufficient conditions for reducing illegal entry; regular but unannounced worksite inspections must be part of an overall strategy to purge the labor market of illegal immigrants. As long as a substantial proportion (possibly as high as 40 percent) of the actual illegal immigration population originally entered with valid documents, it is absurd to regard border control as the only actual line of defense. Without worksite inspections, it is understandable that unions are upset with the employer sanctions system. Unions must seek to organize whatever workers employers hire. If the INS does its interior enforcement job, there will not be illegal immigrants whom employers can manipulate or intimidate to prevent them (albeit illegally) from voting in union certification elections.

Interior enforcement, then, must be raised to the same level of concern as border management, or the entire effort to reduce illegal immigration by the federal government must be regarded as a cruel hoax for American workers. Likewise, the concession won by agricultural employers (as a condition for passage by Congress of IRCA in 1986) to end open-field raids must be repealed.[33] Before 1986 it was legal for the INS to go into open fields on private property without first securing a search warrant, on the grounds of probable cause that illegal immigrants were at work there. The legal position at the time was that as open space, fields were different from buildings and homes where privacy protections justifiably require the issuance of a warrant before they can be entered. Congress, in response to pressures from agribusiness interests, inserted in IRCA a requirement for such warrants. But in rural areas that are distant from courts, it is simply not feasible for INS inspectors to identify prospective violators in an open field, return to a city and obtain a warrant, and then come back to the field and expect the illegal farm workers to still be there. Open-field raids prior to 1986 were a successful tactic for apprehending large numbers of illegal immigrant workers. Since IRCA ended the practice, it is not surprising that researchers have concluded in the 1990s that the law had failed "to convert the agricultural labor market into a legal market."[34]

Finally, although the issue is far more complex than this discussion can fully address, the mass abuse of the nation's generous political asylum policy as a pretext for illegal immigration must be stopped. The only way to do so is to require the detention of most asylum applicants until their cases are heard and resolved. This will be costly, but so is the entry of illegal immigrants and the adverse human toll they exact on the well-being of low-skilled American workers. When asylum applicants are released on their own recognizance to await a hearing, many just disappear. As a consequence, not only is the integrity of the asylum system being undermined but the system itself is being manipulated by organized human smuggling rings (especially in China) who send thousands of illegal immigrants into the U.S. labor market to work under terms of human bondage: they must work for decades under often subhuman conditions to pay back the costs charged by the smugglers.[35] With numerous military bases across the country being decommissioned for budgetary reasons, why not convert some of them to humane detention centers where asylum applicants—those whose cases are not obvious—could be held until final decisions can be rendered?

Enhanced Enforcement of Labor Standards

It is a cynical indictment of the state of public policy in the United States that the lack of enforcement of existing employment protection laws is a recurrent issue. Passing laws to assure fair and humane treatment for working people is a meaningless gesture unless there is ongoing enforcement of their terms; their effects are purely illusory unless they are supported by commensurate funds and personnel. The issue extends far beyond the nonenforcement of employer sanctions. It pertains to the whole range of issues involving child labor, minimum wages, maximum hours, health and safety conditions, and equal employment opportunity requirements. The issue is much larger than the treatment of illegal immigrants as exploitable commodities. It involves the well-being of citizen workers in low-skilled occupations who often have to compete with illegal immigrants as to who will work the hardest, for the lowest pay, for the longest hours, and under the worst working conditions.

There are, of course, abuses of worker protection laws that do not directly involve illegal immigrants, but the two concerns sometimes overlap. Immigrants, especially those illegally working or seeking work in the nation's labor market, can all too easily be exploited and, by their very presence, they can lead to the exploitation of citizens who try to compete with them.

In fact, the most serious violations of labor protection laws do usually involve the employment of illegal immigrants: because of their precarious legal status, they are the most vulnerable to exploitive elements in the U.S. society.[36] Exploitation, in this case, usually means being paid less than the federal minimum wage or working under conditions that are in violation of the existing standards and practices prescribed by law. Hence, all studies that seek to address the issue of illegal immigration usually contain homilies about the need to enforce existing labor protection laws. Some studies, in fact, essentially conclude that such enforcement should be the centerpiece of any strategy to address the issue.[37] Indeed, the February 2000 statement of the AFL-CIO executive council, states that the workplace enforcement of labor standards, coupled with making it a criminal offense for employers to use a worker's illegal status as a means to prevent workplace enforcement, should be sufficient to deter future illegal immigration.[38]

With the possible exception of economic libertarians, who oppose most government regulation as a matter of principle, few would be willing to argue against the need for more extensive enforcement of prevailing labor protection laws for all workers—citizens or not. But this is a weak reed upon which to place much weight for any serious assault on the prevalence of illegal immigration. To begin with, the few studies that have focused specifically on the issue have found that most illegal workers do receive the federal minimum wage.[39] Documenting compliance with occupational health and safety laws is another matter, as "sweatshop" conditions and child labor violators can be found in most of the local labor markets where immigrant enclaves are found. Greater enforcement efforts—more inspections and more inspectors—could reduce human abuse in these areas, and such efforts certainly should be made. But it is doubtful that better enforcement of standards will do much to reduce the employment of illegal immigration. Although it is true that some enforcement activities are initiated by government agencies, most violations are discovered by investigating individual employee complaints. The United States is not a police state in which enforcement officials are ever present; those officials rely heavily upon noncompliance reports by those who have been taken advantage of—and illegal immigrants are least likely to know how to make such complaints or, even if they do, to initiate them. Hence, labor standard enforcement—though vitally important—is unlikely to be an effective measure to rid the worksite of illegal immigrants. That is why employer sanctions against hiring them must remain a mandatory component of public policy measures to protect workers.

Labor Law Reform

Although the significance of labor law reform extends beyond the scope of the subject matter at hand, the state of the nation's laws that supposedly protect its collective bargaining system is in fact appalling. Since 1935, federal law (the National Labor Relations Act and its subsequent amendments) has stated that workers should have the unimpeded right to come together to form organizations of their own choosing in order to bargain collectively with employers over the terms of employment. Supposedly, employers may not interfere with those efforts. Both labor and management are expected to put forth "good faith" efforts to reach agreements. Given the only alternatives—unilateral determination by management or government—collective bargaining has been recognized as the most consistent means of settling disputes over the terms of employment according to American principles of self-government.

But these high ideals—as discussed briefly in Chapter 6—have been made a mockery of by inadequate penalties for the gross violation of the laws on the part of employers who seemingly will do anything to remain nonunionized. There are many factors involved in the decline of membership in American unions since the 1960s, and immigration policy has contributed to the ease by which these laws can be violated. But at the core of the decline in unionism is the clear fact that the system of collective bargaining—especially for low-wage workers—can be so easily circumvented by any employer wishing to do so. It is cynical for policymakers to praise the evolution of the nation's collective bargaining system as a means of peaceably resolving inevitable differences of opinion that arise from the employment relationship yet at the same time, turn a blind eye to ways the system can be easily undermined. There should be severe penalties for employers who dismiss workers for seeking to exercise their legal right to organize, and the National Labor Relations Board should give procedural priority to hearing charges of unfair labor practices involving such firing. There should also be expedited certification procedures for the conduct of union representation elections, and companies that violate these procedures should be barred from receiving federal contracts. The NLRB should be empowered to order back pay for all employees when an employer refuses to bargain a first contract after a duly certified bargaining agent has been designated. Finally, the provisions that allow state laws to supersede federal law with respect to the ability of unions to bargain for union security clauses in contracts should be repealed.

A significant portion of the history of American workers has been their struggle to form unions to represent them in negotiations with employers. Many lives have been lost and much blood shed in the pursuit of that ideal. The union movement should not be crippled by laws that praise collective bargaining as a symbol of America's support for a participatory worksite but at the same time permit the easy neutering of the system by the willful misconduct of employers whose workers attempt to put it into action.

Labor law reform does not have anything directly to do with immigration but immigration has much to do with labor law reform, since most immigrants will enter the labor force immediately or eventually. Over the long run, many immigrants have as much at stake as do citizens or permanent resident aliens in an effective and vibrant labor movement. Labor law reform is essential to the achievement of that reality.

Notes

Introduction

1. Stanley M. Elkins, *Slavery* (New York: Grosset & Dunlap, 1959), 38.
2. "Immigration," *AFL-CIO Executive Council Actions*, New Orleans, La. (February 16, 2000), 1–4.
3. See *Ekiu v. United States*, 142 U.S. 651 (1892); *Henderson v. Mayor of the City of N.Y.*, 92 U.S. 259 (1876); and *Lung v. Freeman*, 92 U.S. 276 (1876).
4. Vernon M. Briggs Jr., *Mass Immigration and the National Interest*, 2d ed. (Armonk, N.Y.: M. E. Sharpe, 1996).
5. Charles C. Killingsworth, "Epilogue: Organized Labor in a Free Enterprise Economy," in *The Structure of American Industry*, 3d ed., ed. by Walter Adams (New York: Macmillan, 1961), 569.

1. The Base Line

1. Arthur M. Schlesinger Jr., *The Age of Jackson* (New York: New American Library, 1945), 5.
2. Philip Taft, *Organized Labor in American History* (New York: Harper & Row, 1964), 299.
3. Stanley Lebergott, *Manpower in Economic Growth: The American Record since 1800* (New York: McGraw-Hill, 1964), 139.
4. Alvin M. Josephy Jr., *The Indian Heritage of America* (New York: Bantam Books, 1968).
5. Henry Pelling, *American Labor* (Chicago: University of Chicago Press, 1960), 5.
6. Select Commission on Immigration and Refugee Policy, *U.S. Immigration Policy and the National Interest: Staff Report* (Washington, D.C.: U.S. Government Printing Office, 1981), 169. See also David Montgomery, "The Working Classes of the Pre-Industrial American City," *Labor History*, Winter 1968, 9.

7. Elizabeth W. Gilboy and Edgar M. Hoover, "Population and Immigration," in *American Economic History*, ed. Seymour E. Harris (New York: McGraw-Hill, 1961), 267, table 6.

8. Taft, *Organized Labor*, 299.

9. Lebergott, *Manpower*, 23.

10. The 13 percent figure for the foreign born living in the South in 1860 probably does not include foreign-born slaves. By 1860, the preponderance of the slave population in the South was native born. But, as discussed, the importation of slaves continued until the eve of the Civil War even though the practice was illegal since 1808. Because of the illegality, it is unlikely that slaves were reported as foreign born as late as 1860 even if they were.

11. Lebergott, *Manpower*, 20.

2. Mass Immigration Begins

1. Carey McWilliams, *North from Mexico* (New York: Greenwood Press, 1968), 103.

2. Ibid., 51.

3. Stanley Lebergott, *Manpower in Economic Growth: The American Record since 1800* (New York: McGraw-Hill, 1964), 102.

4. Ibid., 125–27.

5. Ibid., 19.

6. Ibid., 139.

7. David Montgomery, "The Working Classes of the Pre-Industrial American City," *Labor History*, Winter 1968, 9.

8. Lebergott, *Manpower*, 128.

9. Ibid.

10. Rodman W. Paul, "The Origins of the Chinese Issue in California," *Mississippi Valley Historical Review*, September 1938, 181–96.

11. Edward Pessen, "The Working Men's Party Revisited," *Labor History*, Fall 1963, 203–26.

12. Foster Rhea Dulles, *Labor in America* (New York: Thomas Y. Crowell, 1955), Chapter 5.

13. Lloyd Ulman, *The Rise of the National Trade Union* (Cambridge: Harvard University Press, 1955).

14. Philip Taft, *Organized Labor in American History* (New York: Harper & Row, 1964), 42–43.

15. Dulles, *Labor in America*, 75.

16. Barbara M. Tucker, *Samuel Slater and the Origins of the American Textile Industry* (Ithaca: Cornell University Press, 1984), 198, 187.

17. Dulles, *Labor in America*, 78.

18. Hugh Davis Graham and Ted Robert Gurr, *The History of Violence in America* (New York: Bantam Books, 1968), 53–54. (This was a report submitted to the National Commission on the Causes and Prevention of Violence.)

19. Ibid.; Dulles, *Labor in America*, 79.

20. Vernon M. Briggs Jr., *Immigration Policy and the American Labor Force* (Baltimore: Johns Hopkins University Press, 1984), 21–22.

21. John F. Kennedy, *A Nation of Immigrants* rev. ed. (New York: Harper & Row, 1964), 70–71.

22. John R. Commons and Associates, *History of Labor in the United States* (New York: Macmillan, 1918), 1:424.

23. Maurice F. Neufeld, "The Size of the Jacksonian Labor Movement: A Cautionary Account," *Labor History*, Fall 1982, 607.

3. "Second Wave"

1. Vernon L. Parrington, *The Beginnings of Critical Realism in America* (New York: Harcourt, Brace, 1930), 7.

2. Ibid., 23–26.

3. Robert D. Patton, *The American Economy* (Chicago: Scott, Foresman, 1953), chap. 10.

4. Stanley Lebergott, *Manpower in Economic Growth: The American Record since 1800* (New York: McGraw-Hill, 1964), 28.

5. Joseph Rayback, *A History of American Labor* (New York: Free Press, 1959), 109.

6. Charles A. Madison, *American Labor Leaders* (New York: Harper, 1950), 22.

7. Rayback, *History of American Labor*, 119–20.

8. Madison, *American Labor Leaders*, 41.

9. Mary R. Coolidge, *Chinese Immigration* (New York: Holt, 1909).

10. Rayback, *History of American Labor*, 139.

11. Ibid., 140.

12. Madison, *American Labor Leaders*, 48.

13. Peter Kwong, *Forbidden Workers: Illegal Chinese Immigrants and American Labor* (New York: New Press, 1997), 42–43.

14. T. V. Powderly, *Thirty Years of Labor* (Columbus: Excelsior, 1889, 418–19.

15. Max Thalen, "The Chinese Exclusion Act," *Social Contract*, Winter 1997–98, 113.

16. Powderly, *Thirty Years of Labor*, 420.

17. Ibid., 420–21.

18. Ibid., 421–23.

19. Quoted in ibid., 424–25.

20. Ibid., 427.

21. Ibid., 430.

22. Ibid., 433–34.

23. *U.S. Statutes at Large* 23 (1885): 332.

24. Samuel P. Orth, "The Alien Contract Law and Labor Law," *Political Science Quarterly*, March 1907, 49–60.

25. Ruth Alice Allen, *Chapters in the History of Organized Labor in Texas* (Austin: University of Texas Press, 1941), 45–88.

26. *U.S. Statutes at Large* 24 (1887): 414.

27. *U.S. Statutes at Large* 25 (1888): 566

28. Norman J. Ware, *The Labor Movement in the United States: 1860–1895* (New York: Vintage Books, 1929), 49, 51.

29. Quoted in Philip Taft, *Organized Labor in American History* (New York: Harper & Row, 1964), 303.

30. Madison, *American Labor Leaders*, 74.

31. Taft, *Organized Labor*, 304.

32. Robert Asher, "Union Nativism and the Immigrant Response," *Labor History*, Summer 1982, 325–48.

33. Lebergott, *Manpower*, 162–63.

34. Ibid., 163.

35. Timothy J. Hatton and Jeffrey G. Williamson, *The Impact of Immigration on American Labor Markets prior to Quotas*, Working Paper no. 5185 (Cambridge, Mass.: National Bureau of Economic Research, 1995), 30.

36. Asher, "Union Nativism," 327.

37. Kwong, *Forbidden Workers*, 141; Taft, *Organized Labor*, 302.

38. Kwong, *Forbidden Workers*, 143.

39. Ibid., 45.

4. The "Third Wave"

1. Robert D. Patton, *The American Economy* (Chicago: Scott, Foresman 1953), 238.

2. *U.S. Statutes at Large* 26 (1890): 209.

3. Harry A. Millis and Royal E. Montgomery, *Labor's Progress and Some Basic Labor Problems* (New York: McGraw-Hill, 1938), 239.

4. Ibid., 244.

5. E.g., see the descriptions of urban living conditions in this era in Jacob Riis, *How the Other Half Lives* (1890; reprint New York: Hill & Wang, 1957).

6. Leon Wolff, *Lockout: The Story of the Homestead Strike of 1892* (New York: Harper & Row, 1965), 4.

7. William T. Moye, "The End of the 12 Hour Day in the Steel Industry," *Monthly Labor Review*, September 1977, 22–27.

8. Upton Sinclair, *The Jungle* (1906; reprint New York: Viking Press, 1950).

9. John Turnbull, C. Arthur Williams, and Earl R. Cheit, *Economic and Social Security* (New York: Ronald Press, 1957), 250.

10. Peter Roberts, *The New Immigration* (New York: Macmillan, 1913), 61.

11. Oscar Handlin, *The Uprooted: The Epic Story of the Great Migration That Made the American People* (New York: Grosset & Dunlap, 1951), 5.

12. Booker T. Washington, "The Atlanta Exposition Address," in *Three Negro Classics* (New York: Avon Books, 1965), 147–48.

13. Roberts, *New Immigration*, 363–64. U.S. Immigration Commission, *Abstracts of the Reports of the U.S. Immigration Commission* (Washington, D.C.: U.S. Government Printing Office, 1911), 1:58–59.

14. U.S. Immigration Commission, *Abstracts*, 1:60.

15. Carey McWilliams, *North from Mexico* (New York: Greenwood Press, 1968), 52.

16. *U.S. Statutes at Large* 26 (1891): 1084.

17. *Ekiu v. United States*, 142 U.S. 951 (1892).

18. Senate Committee on the Judiciary, *History of the Immigration and Naturalization Service* 96th Cong. 2d sess. (Washington, D.C.: U.S. Government Printing Office, 1980), 13.

19. Charles A. Madison, *American Labor Leaders* (New York: Harper, 1959), 68. For the endemic corruption on Ellis Island, see Henry Guzda, "Ellis Island: A Welcome Site? Only After Years of Reform," *Monthly Labor Review*, July, 1986, 30–36.

20. Thorstein Veblen, *The Theory of the Leisure Class* (1899; reprint New York: Mentor Books, 1959).

21. See Wolff, *Lockout*; also see Jeremy Brecher, *Strike!* (San Francisco: Straight Arrow Books, 1972).

22. Samuel Gompers, *Seventy Years of Life and Labor* (New York: Dutton, 1925), 2:155.

23. Almont Lindsey, *The Pullman Strike* (Chicago: University of Chicago Press, 1942). See also Brecher, *Strike!* 78–96.

24. Nick Salvatore, *Eugene V. Debs: Citizen and Socialist* (Urbana: University of Illinois Press, 1982).

25. Melvyn Dubofsky, *We Shall Be All: A History of the Industrial Workers of the World* (Chicago: Quadrangle Books, 1969), 24.

26. Vernon H. Jensen, *Heritage of Conflict: Labor Relations in the Nonferrous Metals Industry up to 1930* (Ithaca: New York School of Industrial and Labor Relations, Cornell University, 1950), chaps. 2–5.

27. Dubofsky, *We Shall Be All.* See also Paul F. Brissenden, *The IWW: A Study of American Syndicalism* (1919; reprint New York: Russell & Russell, 1957).

28. Joyce L. Kornbluh, *Rebel Voices: An IWW Anthology* (Ann Arbor: University of Michigan Press, 1964), chap. 6.

29. Brissenden, *IWW,* App. 4, table D.

30. Philip Taft, *Organized Labor in American History* (New York: Harper & Row, 1964), 247–48.

31. Gompers, *Seventy Years,* 2:171.

32. *Hitchman Coal and Coke v. Mitchell,* 245 U.S. 229 (1917); and *Duplex Printing v. Deering,* 224 U.S. 443 (1921).

33. David Brody, *Labor in Crisis: The Steel Strike of 1919* (Philadelphia: Lippincott, 1965), 75.

34. Ibid., 135–45, 157–59.

35. Robert Asher, "Union Nativism and the Immigrant Response," *Labor History,* Summer 1982, 347–48, quoting remarks made by Foster before a commission of the Interchurch World Movement in 1919.

36. Brody, 145.

37. Gompers, *Seventy Years,* 2:154, 157.

38. Quoted in Taft, *Organized Labor,* 306.

39. Gompers, *Seventy Years,* 2:159.

40. Quoted in Alexander Saxton, *The Indispensable Enemy: Labor and the Anti-Chinese Movement in California* (Berkeley: University of California Press, 1971), 276–77.

41. Gompers, *Seventy Years,* 2:153.

42. Ibid., 158.

43. A.T. Lane, "American Trade Unions, Mass Immigration, and the Literacy Test, 1900–1917," *Labor History,* Winter 1984, 13.

44. Thomas A. Bailey, *Theodore Roosevelt and the Japanese-American Crisis* (Palo Alto, Calif.: Stanford University Press, 1934), 4.

45. Gompers, *Seventy Years.*

46. Bailey, *Theodore Roosevelt,* Chap. 2.

47. Fred Greenbaum, "The Social Ideas of Samuel Gompers," *Labor History,* Winter 1966, 43–44.

48. 34 *U.S. Statutes at Large* 34 (1907): 898; also see Bailey, *Theodore Roosevelt,* 114–49. The law allowed the president to deny entry to persons with foreign passports if he believes their presence would be detrimental to labor conditions in this country. It does not say that it is directed at Japanese workers seeking to move from Hawaii to the mainland, but it was understood to mean precisely that, and that is how the administration applied it.

49. Paul H. Clyde, *The Far East: A History of the Impact of the West on Eastern Asia* (Englewood, N.J.: Prentice-Hall, 1958), 492–96.

50. Lane, "American Trade Unions," 6.

51. Vernon M. Briggs Jr., *Immigration Policy and the American Labor Force* (Baltimore: Johns Hopkins University Press, 1984), 35–36.

52. Gompers, *Seventy Years*, 2:167.

53. Oscar Handlin, *Race and Nationality in American Life* (Garden City, N.Y.: Doubleday, 1957), 80–84.

54. David North and Allen LeBel, *Manpower and Immigration Policies in the United States* (Washington, D.C.: National Commission for Manpower Policy, 1978), 26.

55. U.S. Immigration Commission, *Abstracts*, 1:297–313, 151.

56. Timothy J. Hatton and Jeffrey G. Williamson, *The Impact of Immigration on American Labor Markets prior to Quotas*, Working Paper no. 5185 (Cambridge, Mass.: National Bureau of Economic Research, 1995), 30 (original emphasis). See also Stanley Lebergott, *Manpower in Economic Growth* (New York: McGraw-Hill, 1964), 162, for similar conclusions.

57. Millis and Montgomery, *Labor's Progress*, 31.

58. Gompers, *Seventy Years*, 2:171.

59. Taft, *Organized Labor*, 308.

60. Gompers, *Seventy Years*, 2:172.

61. Ibid., 172–73.

62. *U.S. Statutes at Large* 39 (1917): 874.

63. The only exceptions were made for the Philippines, because they were a U.S. colony, and Japan, because immigration was already restricted under the terms of the Gentlemen's Agreement.

64. *U.S. Statutes at Large* 42 (1921): 5.

5. Mass Immigration Ceases

1. See Irving Bernstein, *A Caring Society: The New Deal, the Worker, and the Depression* (Boston: Houghton Mifflin, 1985); Garth Mangum, *The Emergence of Manpower Policy* (New York: Holt, Rinehart & Winston, 1969); and Sar A. Levitan, *The Great Society's Poor Law: A New Approach to Poverty* (Baltimore: Johns Hopkins University Press, 1969).

2. Richard D. Alba, "The Twilight of Ethnicity among Americans of European Ancestry: The Case of the Italians," in *Ethnicity and Race in the USA: Toward the 21st Century*, ed. Alba (London: Routledge & Kegan Paul, 1985), 168.

3. Stanley Lebergott, *Manpower in Economic Growth* (New York: McGraw-Hill, 1964), 163.

4. Arthur S. Link, *American Epoch* (New York: Knopf, 1956), 297.

5. See Vernon M. Briggs Jr. *Immigration Policy and the American Labor Force* (Baltimore: Johns Hopkins University Press, 1984), 51–52.

6. Harry A. Millis and Royal E. Montgomery, *Labor's Progress and Some Basic Labor Problems*, (New York: McGraw-Hill, 1938), 222–27.

7. Robert D. Patton, *The American Economy* (Chicago: Scott, Foresman, 1953), 292–94.

8. Theodore G. Joslin, *Hoover off the Record* (New York: Doubleday, Doran, 1934), 252; Broadus Mitchell, *Depression Decade* (New York: Rinehart, 1947), 4.

9. Harris G. Warren, *Herbert Hoover and the Great Depression* (New York: Oxford University Press, 1959), 162.

10. John Kenneth Galbraith, *The Great Crash* (Cambridge, Mass.: Riverside Press, 1955), 191, 187–88.

11. Irving Bernstein, "Unemployment in the Great Depression," in *The Social Welfare Forum* (New York: Columbia University Press, 1959), 40.

12. Lebergott, *Manpower*, 512, table A-3.

13. Bernstein, "Unemployment," 41.

14. David Shannon, *The Great Depression* (Englewood Cliffs, N.J.: Prentice-Hall, 1960).

15. Bernstein, "Unemployment," 48.

16. Joseph G. Rayback, *A History of American Labor* (New York: Free Press, 1966), 375.

17. Philip Taft, *Organized Labor in American History* (New York: Harper & Row, 1964), 567.

18. Mangum, *Emergence*, 20–21.

19. U.S. Bureau of the Census, *A Brief Look at Postwar U.S. Income Inequality* (Washington, D.C.: U.S. Government Printing Office, 1994), 120.

20. Senate Special Committee on Unemployment Problems, 86th Congress, 2d Sess., *Report* (Washington, D.C.: U.S. Government Printing Office, 1960).

21. Walter Heller, "The Administration's Fiscal Policy," and Otto Eckstein, "Aggregate Demand and the Current Unemployment," both in *Unemployment and the American Economy*, ed. Arthur Ross (New York: Wiley, 1964), 93–115, 116–34. Cf. Charles C. Killingsworth "Automation, Jobs, and Manpower: The Case for Structural Unemployment," in *The Manpower Revolution,* ed. Garth L. Magnum (Garden City, N.Y.: Doubleday Books, 1965), 97–117.

22. Walter Buckingham, *Automation: Its Impact on Business* (New York: Mentor Books, 1961), 17–18.

23. Patton, *American Economy*, 330.

24. Ray Marshall, *The Negro and Organized Labor* (New York: Wiley, 1965), chap. 2.

25. For elaboration, see Vernon M. Briggs Jr., *Mass Immigration and the National Interest,* 2d ed. (Armonk, N.Y.: M. E. Sharpe, 1996), 84–85.

26. Killingsworth, "Automation."

27. Sar A. Levitan, *Federal Aid to Depressed Areas* (Baltimore: Johns Hopkins University Press, 1964).

28. *U.S. Statutes at Large* 43 (1924): 153.

29. W. S. Bernard, "America's Immigration Policy: Its Evolution and Sociology," *International Migration* 2, no. 4 (1965): 235.

30. The language of the legislation forbade the immigration of persons who were ineligible for citizenship. In 1922, the Supreme Court had ruled that persons of Japanese ancestry were "ineligible for citizenship" through naturalization: *Ozawa v. United States,* (1922), 260, U.S. 178.

31. Paul Clyde, *The Far East: A History of the Impact of the West on Eastern Asia,* 3d ed. (Englewood Cliffs, N.J.: Prentice-Hall, 1958), 499–500.

32. Senate Committee on the Judiciary, *History of the Immigration and Naturalization Service,* 96th Cong., 2d sess. (Washington, D.C.: U.S. Government Printing Office, 1980), 36.

33. Lebergott, *Manpower,* 163–64.

34. Abraham Hoffman, "Mexican Repatriation during the Great Depression: A Reappraisal," in *Immigration and Immigrants: Perspectives on Mexican Labor Migration to the*

United States, ed. Arthur F. Corwin (Westport, Conn.: Greenwood Press, 1978), 226. For a more complete discussion, see Briggs, *Immigration Policy*, 54–56.

35. Maurice Davie and Samuel Kolnig, "Adjustment of Refugees to American Life," *Annals of the American Academy of Political and Social Sciences*, March 1949, 159–65.

36. Ibid., 160.

37. See detailed discussion in Briggs, *Mass Immigration*, 89–92.

38. Senate Committee on the Judiciary, *The Immigration and Naturalization System of the United States* (Washington, D.C.: U.S. Government Printing Office, 1950), 455.

39. *U.S. Statutes-at-Large* 66 (1952): 163.

40. House Doc. 520, 82nd Cong., 2d sess. (25 June 1952), 5–6.

41. For elaboration, see Briggs, *Mass Immigration*, 94–95, 105.

42. Robert F. Kennedy introduction to John F. Kennedy, *A Nation of Immigrants*, rev. ed., (New York: Harper & Row, 1964), ix.

43. Kennedy, *Nation of Immigrants*, 102–3, 80.

44. "Statement by Secretary of State Dean Rusk before the Subcommittee on Immigration of the U.S. Senate Committee on the Judiciary," as reprinted in the *Department of State Bulletin*, 24 August 1965, 276.

45. U.S. Congress, Senate, *Congressional Record*, 89th Congress, (September 17, 1965), p. S24,225; Statement of Senator Edward Kennedy before Subcommittee on Immigration and Nationality of the Senate Committee on the Judiciary, 89th Congress, 1st sess., 10 February 1965, in *Hearings on S. 500* (Washington D.C.: U.S. Government Printing Office, 1965), 1–3.

46. Technically speaking, the Immigration Act of 1965 provided that the Western Hemisphere ceiling would take effect on 1 July 1968 unless other legislation was enacted prior to that date to change it. A special commission—the Select Commission on Western Hemisphere Immigration—was appointed to study the issue but was unable to agree on a firm recommendation to Congress. As a result, the ceiling went into effect on the specified date.

47. Testimony of Robert F. Kennedy, U.S. Attorney General, before Subcommittee No. 1 of the House Committee on the Judiciary, 88th Cong., 2d sess., *Hearings on H.R. 7700 and 55 Identical Bills to Amend the Immigration and Nationality Act and For Other Purposes* (Washington D.C.: U.S. Government Printing Office, 1964), 418.

48. For more detailed discussion of the evolution of the family reunification system, see Briggs, *Mass Immigration*, 109–14.

49. *U.S. Statutes at Large* 79 (1965): 911.

50. Elizabeth J. Harper, *Immigration Laws of the United States* (Indianapolis: Bobbs-Merrill, 1975), 38.

51. Senate Committee on the Judiciary, *History of the Immigration and Naturalization Service*, 41.

52. Vernon M. Briggs Jr., "The Administration of U.S. Immigration Policy," *Social Contract*, Spring 1994, 192–97.

53. U.S. Department of Labor, *The Anvil and the Plow: A History of the United States Department of Labor, 1913–1963* (Washington, D.C.: U.S. Government Printing Office, 1963), 121.

54. For a thorough discussion of this transfer and its consequences, see Briggs, *Mass Immigration*, 86–89.

55. Frances Perkins, *The Roosevelt I Knew* (New York: Viking Press, 1946), 361.

56. Irving Bernstein, *The Lean Years: A History of the American Worker, 1920–1933* (Baltimore, Md.: Penguin Books, 1960).

57. *Duplex v. Deering* 224 U.S. 431 (1921).

58. Felix Frankfurter and Nathan Greene, *The Labor Injunction* (New York: Macmillan, 1930).

59. For a review of these activities, see Bernstein, *The Lean Years;* see also Jerold Auerbach, *Labor and Liberty* (Indianapolis: Bobbs-Merrill, 1966).

60. George Barnett, "American Trade Unionism and Social Insurance," *American Economic Review,* March 1933, 1.

61. Bernstein, *The Lean Years,* chap. 11.

62. *NLRB v. Jones and Laughlin Steel,* 301 *U.S.* 1 (1937).

63. *Lauf v. E. G. Shinner & Company,* 303 U.S. 323 (1938).

64. Donald G. Sofchalk, "The Chicago Memorial Day Incident: An Episode of Mass Action," *Labor History,* Winter 1965, 3–43.

65. Lloyd Ulman, "The Development of Trades and Labor Unions," in *American Economic History,* ed. Seymour E. Harris (New York: McGraw-Hill, 1961), 413.

66. Taft, *Organized Labor,* 305; Louis S. Reed, *The Labor Philosophy of Samuel Gompers* (New York: Columbia University Press, 1930), 178.

67. Taft, *Organized Labor,* 308.

68. A. Philip Randolph, "Immigration and Japan" *The Messenger,* August 1924, 247, quoted in Daryl Scott, "Immigrant Indigestion: A. Philip Randolph, Radical and Restrictionist," in *Backgrounder* (Washington, D.C.: Center for Immigration Studies, 1999), 3.

69. Rayback, *History of American Labor,* 278; Millis and Montgomery, *Labor's Progress,* 211; Lebergott, *Manpower,* 164.

70. *Report of the Proceedings of the Sixty-Fifth Convention of the American Federation of Labor* (Washington, D.C.: AFL, 1946), 520–21.

71. *Constitutional Convention Proceedings of the AFL-CIO, 1955* (New York: AFL-CIO, 1955) 104–5.

72. *Second Constitutional Convention Proceedings of the AFL-CIO, 1957* (Atlantic City, N.J.: AFL-CIO, 1957), 1:252–53, 244–45. For elaboration of the labor issues associated with the *bracero* program, see Briggs, *Mass Immigration,* 89–91.

73. *Third Constitutional Convention Proceedings of the AFL-CIO 1959* (San Francisco: AFL-CIO 1959), 1:323. For elaboration of the labor issues concerning border commuters, see Briggs, *Immigration Policy,* 231–36. See also John D. Privett, "Agricultural Unionism among Chicanos in Texas" (M.B.A. report, University of Texas at Austin, 1971), 162–63.

74. *Fifth Constitutional Convention Proceedings of the AFL-CIO, 1963* (New York: AFL-CIO, 1963), 232, 353.

6. Mass Immigration Returns

1. "Transcript of Presidential Message to Congress on the State of the Union," *New York Times,* 5 January 1965, A-17.

2. *AFL-CIO News,* 30 January 1965, 12.

3. "Senate Denied Vote on 14(b) as Filibuster Blocks Action," *AFL-CIO News,* 16 October 1965, 7.

4. "Labor Backs LBJ on Immigration Bill," *AFL-CIO News*, 12 June 1965, 12.

5. Quoted in "New Immigration Bill Favors Easy Entry for Skilled Immigrants," *AFL-CIO News*, 20 February 1965, 1.

6. National Advisory Commission on Civil Disorders, *Report* (New York: New York Times Company, 1968).

7. Vernon M. Briggs Jr., *Black Employment in the South, vol. 1, The Houston Labor Market* (Washington, D.C.: U.S. Department of Labor, 1971), 95.

8. *Economic Report of the President, 1999* (Washington, D.C.: U.S. Government Printing Office, 1999), p. 444, table B-103.

9. Steven Camarota, "Immigration: Trade by Other Means?" *Immigration Review*, Spring 1998, 9–10.

10. See, e.g., Jay Mazur, "Labor's New Internationalism," *Foreign Affairs*, January–February 2000, 79–90.

11. Nathan Rosenberg, *Inside the Blackbox: Technology and Economics* (Cambridge: Cambridge University Press, 1982), chaps. 8–9.

12. Norbert Wiener, *The Use of Human Beings: Cybernetics and Society* (1950; reprint New York: Avon Books, 1967), 200.

13. Richard M. Cyert and David C. Mowry, *Technology and Employment* (Washington, D.C.: National Academy Press, 1987), chap. 4; Edward A. Feigenbaum and Pamela McCorduck, *The Fifth Generation: Artificial Intelligence and Japan's Computer Challenge to the World* (Reading, Mass: Addison-Wesley, 1983), chap. 2–3.

14. Douglas Braddock, "Occupational Employment Projections to 2008," *Monthly Labor Review*, November 1999, 51–77.

15. Ibid., 75–77. See also John Bound and George Johnson, "Changes in the Structure of Wages in the 1980s: An Evaluation of Alternate Explanations," *American Economic Review*, Fall 1992, 371–92.

16. Charles Killingsworth, "Automation, Jobs, and Manpower: The Case for Structural Unemployment," in *The Manpower Revolution*, ed. Garth L. Mangum (Garden City, N.Y.: Doubleday, 1965), 97–116.

17. Hudson Institute, *Workforce 2000: Work and Workers for the Twenty-First Century* (Indianapolis: Hudson Institute, 1987).

18. Commission on Workforce Quality and Labor Market Efficiency, *Investing in People* (Washington, D.C.: U.S. Department of Labor, 1989).

19. Commission on the Skills of the American Workplace, *America's Choice: High Skills or Low Wages* (Rochester, N.Y.: National Center on Education and the Economy, 1990).

20. *Daily Labor Report* (Washington, D.C.: Bureau of National Affairs), 10 January 1997, E13–E17.

21. Robert Reich, "The Revolt of the Anxious Class" (speech before the Democratic Leadership Conference, Washington, D.C., 22 November 1994), 3.

22. Alison Thomson, "Industry Output and Employment Projections to 2008," *Monthly Labor Review*, November 1999, 33–50.

23. For details concerning the provisions of the Immigration Act of 1965, see Vernon M. Briggs Jr., *Mass Immigration and the National Interest*, 2d ed. (Armonk, N.Y.: M. E. Sharpe, 1996), 109–14.

24. Ibid., 120–22.

25. *Silva v. Levi*, N.D. Ill., No. 76-C4268, (1 April 1978).

26. Philip L. Martin, *Promises to Keep: Collective Bargaining in California Agriculture* (Ames: Iowa State University Press, 1996), 66–71; Ernesto Galarza, *Merchants of Labor: The Mexican Bracero Story* (Charlotte, N.C.: MacNally & Loftin, 1964).

27. J. Edward Taylor, Philip L. Martin, and Michael Fix, *Poverty amid Affluence: Immigration and the Changing Face of Rural California* (Washington, D.C: Urban Institute, 1997), 82; see also Martin, *Promises*, 86–100.

28. Vernon M. Briggs Jr., Walter Fogel, and Fred H. Schmidt, *The Chicano Worker* (Austin: University of Texas Press, 1977), 81–82.

29. Briggs, *Mass Immigration*, 114–15.

30. Dianne Schmidley and Herman A. Alvarado, "The Foreign-Born Population in the United States: March 1997 (update)," *Current Population Reports*, P20–507, March 1998, 1.

31. For elaboration of this theme, see Briggs, *Mass Immigration*.

32. The Select Commission comprised four senators, four congressmen, four members of the president's cabinet, and four persons from the public. The initial chairman was Reubin Askew, former governor of Florida, but he soon resigned to take another presidential appointment and was replaced by Rev. Hesburgh.

33. For elaboration, see Vernon M. Briggs Jr., *Immigration Policy and the American Labor Force* (Baltimore: Johns Hopkins University Press, 1984), 199–203.

34. Ibid., 203–4.

35. For elaboration and examples involving Salvadorians, Guatemalans, Nicaraguans, Soviet emigrés, Chinese students, and another round of Cubans and Haitian entrants, see Briggs, *Mass Immigration*, 132–54.

36. Select Commission on Immigration and Refugee Policy, *U.S. Immigration Policy and the National Interest* (Washington, D.C.: U.S. Government Printing Office, 1981), 5, 7, 8.

37. Nicholas Laham, *Ronald Reagan and the Politics of Immigration Reform*, (Westport, Conn.: Praeger, 2000).

38. For details of the legislative effort, see Briggs, *Immigration Policy*, 87–92, and Briggs, *Mass Immigration*, 159–60.

39. For details of the legislative struggle, see Briggs, *Mass Immigration*, 160–63.

40. Congressional Research Service, "Immigration: Numerical Limits and the Preference System," *Issue Brief*, 28 March 1998, CRS-3.

41. Briggs, *Mass Immigration*, 170–75.

42. For a complete discussion of the multiple provisions of this significant legislation, see ibid., 229–40.

43. The original chair was Cardinal Bernard Law of Boston, who was appointed by President Bush in 1992. When President Clinton took office, he used his prerogative to replace the chair with Barbara Jordan. After her death in January 1996, Clinton appointed Shirley Hufstedler, a lawyer from Los Angeles who had been Secretary of Education during the Carter administration.

44. U.S. Commission on Immigration Reform, *U.S. Immigration Policy: Restoring Credibility* (Washington, D.C.: U.S. Commission on Immigration Reform, 1994), 1–2.

45. U.S. Commission on Immigration Reform, *Legal Immigration: Setting Priorities* (Washington, D.C.: U.S. Commission on Immigration Reform, 1996), i, letter of transmittal.

46. National Research Council, *The New Americans: Economic, Demographic, and Fiscal Effects of Immigration*, ed. James P. Smith and Barry Edmonton (Washington, D.C.: National Academy Press, 1997), 95.

47. Ibid., 181–85, 235–36.

48. Ibid., 236, 181. See also David A. Jaeger, *Skill Differences and the Effect of Immigrants on the Wages of Natives*, Working Paper no. 173 (Washington, D.C.: Bureau of Labor Statistics, 1995).

49. National Research Council, *New Americans*, 153.

50. Ibid., 293.

51. *U.S. Statutes at Large* 110 (1996): 3009.

52. U.S. Commission on Immigration Reform, *Becoming an American: Immigration and Immigrant Policy* (Washington, D.C.: Commission on Immigration Reform, 1997).

53. James G. Gimpel and James R. Edwards, "The Silent Majority," *Journal of Commerce*, 23 June 1998, 8A.

54. Ray Marshall and Vernon M. Briggs Jr., *The Negro and Apprenticeship* (Baltimore: Johns Hopkins University Press, 1967), chap. 3–12.

55. Ibid., chap. 13. See also Roslyn D. Kane and Jill Miller, "Research Findings on Programs to Achieve Increased Participation of Women in Apprenticeship: Some Preliminary Results," in *Apprenticeship Research: Emerging Findings and Future Trends*, ed. Vernon M. Briggs Jr. and Felician F. Foltman (Ithaca: State School of Industrial and Labor Relations, Cornell University, 1981).

56. J. Gary DiNunno, "J. P. Stevens: Anatomy of an Outlaw," *AFL-CIO American Federationist*, April 1976, 1–8.

57. Herbert R. Northrup, "The Rise and Fall of PATCO," *Industrial and Labor Relations Review*, January 1984, 167–84.

58. Everett M. Kassalow, "Will Union Concessions Expand Areas of Bargaining?" *Monthly Labor Review*, March 1983, 32–33; David Lewin, "Implications of Concession Bargaining: Lessons from the Public Sector," *Monthly Labor Review*, March 1983, 33–35.

59. Michael J. Piore, "American Labor and the Industrial Crisis," *Challenge*, March–April 1982, 5, 8.

60. Richard Freeman and James L. Medoff, *What Do Unions Do?* (New York: Basic Books, 1984), 228–38.

61. Thomas A. Kochan, "Accepting Labor as a Legitimate Partner," *New York Times*, 26 July 1987, B-2.

62. William T. Dickens and Jonathan Leonard, "Accounting for the Decline in Union Membership, 1950–1980," *Industrial and Labor Relations Review*, April 1985, 323–34.

63. E.g., see Martin, *Promises*, 100, 295–302; Peter Kwong, *Forbidden Workers: Illegal Chinese Immigrants and American Labor* (New York: New Press, 1997), 161–83, 207–33; Charles Craypo, "Meatpacking: Industry Restructuring and Union Decline," in *Contemporary Collective Bargaining*, ed. Paula Voos (Madison, Wis.: Industrial Relations Research Association, 1994), 63–96; and Eliot S. Orton, "Changes in Skill Differentials: Union Wages in Construction, 1907–1972," *Industrial and Labor Relations Review*, October 1976, 16–24.

64. U.S. Department of Labor, "Labor Force Statistics from the Current Population Survey: Union Member Summary, 1999" news release, 9 January 2000).

65. Ibid.

66. For general discussions of the growth of public-sector unionism, see in *Public Sector Employment*, ed. Dale Belman et al. (Madison, Wis.: Industrial Relations Research Association, 1996): Dale Belman, Morley Gunderson, and Douglas Hyatt, "Public Sector in Transition, " 1–20; John Lund and Cheryl Maranto, "Public Sector Law: An Update," 21–58; and Richard Freeman, "Through Public Sector Eyes: Employee Attitudes toward Public Sector Labor Relations in the U.S.," 59–84.

67. Nelson Lichtenstein, "America's Left-Wing Intellectuals and the Trade Union Movement," in *Proceedings of the 50th Annual Meeting of the Industrial Relations Research As-*

sociation (Madison, Wis.: Industrial Relations Research Association, 1998), 2: 1163–64.

68. "Resolution 172 Immigration Reform," in *Fifth Constitutional Convention Proceedings of the AFL-CIO* (New York: AFL-CIO, 1963), 1:353.

69. See discussion throughout John D. Privett, "Agricultural Unionism among Chicanos in Texas" (M.B.A. report, University of Texas at Austin, 1971).

70. Richard Severo, "The Flight of the Wetbacks," *New York Times Magazine*, 10 March 1974, 81. See also Martin, *Promises*, 100; and Winthrop Griffith, "Is Chavez Beaten?" *New York Times*, 15 September 1974, 24.

71. *Proceedings of the Sixteenth Convention of the AFL-CIO* (Washington, D.C.: AFL-CIO, 1985), 173–75.

72. "Immigration Reform," in *AFL-CIO Policy Resolutions Adopted October 1985 by the Sixteenth Constitutional Convention* (Washington, D.C.: AFL-CIO, 1986), 45–46.

73. "Immigration Reform," in *AFL-CIO Policy Resolutions Adopted October 1987* (Washington, D.C.: AFL-CIO, 1988), 47–48.

74. "Immigration Reform," in *AFL-CIO Policy Resolutions Adopted November 1989* (Washington, D.C.: AFL-CIO, 1990), 46.

75. "Immigration Reform" (1987), 49.

76. "Immigrants and the Labor Movement," *Policy Resolutions Adopted October 1993 by the AFL-CIO Convention* (Washington, D.C.: AFL-CIO, 1994), 13.

77. Ibid., 14.

78. Philip Martin, "Proposition 187 in California," *International Migration Review*, Spring 1995, 255–63. The key provisions of the proposition, after a three-year legal delay by the federal courts, were struck down at the district level. When the newly elected governor of California, Gray Davis, refused in 1999 to appeal the decision, the citizen initiative was killed.

79. "Immigration Reform," *Policy Resolutions Adopted October 1995 by the AFL-CIO Convention* (Washington, D.C.: AFL-CIO, 1996), 68. Cf. Vernon M. Briggs Jr., "Income Disparity and Unionism: The Workplace Influences of Post-1965 Immigration Policy," in *The Inequality Paradox: Growth of Income Disparity*, ed. James A. Auerbach and Richard S. Belous (Washington, D.C.: National Policy Association, 1998), 112–32.

80. See commentary by Muzaffar Chisti, director of the Immigration Project, Union of Needletrades, Industrial and Textile Employees (UNITE), "Immigration and Ethnicity," in *Summary* (Annandale-on-Hudson, N.Y.: Jerome Levy Economics Institute of Bard College, 1996), 17.

81. Gimpel and Edwards, "Silent Majority."

82. E.g., see Kimberly Hayes Taylor, "Hotel Housekeepers Released from INS Custody," *Minneapolis Star-Tribune*, 20 October 1999, 1.

83. *National Labor Relations Board v. Kolkka*, 9th Cir., No. 97-71132 (17 March 1999).

84. "Meissner Announces New INS Strategy to Combat Smuggling of Illegal Workers," *Daily Labor Report*, 31 March 1999, no. 61, A-9; "Ex-Panel Member Blasts INS Decision to De-Emphasize Worksite Enforcement," *Daily Labor Report*, 2 July 1999, No. 127, A-3.

85. Nancy Cleeland, "Union Questioning Sanctions against Employers over Hiring," *Los Angeles Times*, 12 October 1999, 1.

86. Ibid.

87. Franks Swoboda, "Unions Reverse On Illegal Aliens," *Washington Post*, 17 February 2000, A-1.

88. Quoted in Art Pine, "Union's Immigration Stance Leaves GOP Congress Cold," *Los Angeles Times*, 18 February 2000.

89. Swoboda, "Unions Reverse."

90. "Hasty Call for Amnesty," *New York Times*, 22 February 2000, A-22.

91. U.S. Bureau of the Census, "The Foreign Born Population in the United States," *Current Population Reports*, P20–519, 2000, Table 1.6.

7. Conclusions

1. Robert Asher, "Union Nativism and the Immigrant Response," *Labor History*, Summer 1982, 348.

2. See Daniel H. Weinberg, "A Brief Look at Postwar U.S. Income Inequality," *Current Population Reports*, P60–191, 1996, 1.

3. Council of Economic Advisers, *Economic Report of the President: 1999* (Washington D.C.: U.S. Government Printing Office, 1999), 41–42.

4. Council of Economic Advisers, *Economic Report of the President, 1994* (Washington, D.C.: U.S. Government Printing Office, 1994), 120.

5. David A. Jaeger, *Skill Differences and the Effect of Immigrants on the Wages of Natives*, Working Paper no. 273 (Washington, D.C.: U.S. Department of Labor, Bureau of Labor Statistics, 1995), 21.

6. Randall W. Eberts, *Urban Labor Markets*, Staff Working Paper no. 95–32 (Kalamazoo, Mich.: W. E. Upjohn Institute for Employment Research, 1995).

7. Council of Economic Advisers, *Economic Report of the President, 1995* (Washington, D.C.: U.S. Government Printing Office, 1995), 182. For supporting findings, see Francine D. Blau and Lawrence M. Kahn, *Wage Inequality* (Washington, D.C.: American Enterprise Institute, 1996), 8–9.

8. Council of Economic Advisers, *Economic Report, 1994*, 120.

9. Richard Mines and Jeffrey Avina, "Immigrants and Labor Standards: The Case of California Janitors," in *U.S.-Mexico Relations: Labor Market Interdependence*, ed. Jorge Bustamante, et al. (Stanford, Calif.: Stanford University Press, 1992), 429–48.

10. Richard Mines and David Runsten, "Immigrants' Networks and California Industrial Sectors" Berkeley, Calif. (manuscript, 1985), cited in U.S. Department of Justice and U.S. Department of Labor, *The Triennial Comprehensive Report on Immigration* (Washington, D.C.: U.S. Department of Justice 1999), 113.

11. Richard Mines, "Tortillas: A Bi-National Industry" Berkeley, Calif., (manuscript, 1985), cited in *Triennial Comprehensive Report*, 113.

12. Louise Lamphere, Alex Stepick, and Guillermo Grenier, eds., *Newcomers in the Workplace: Immigrants and the Restructuring of the U.S. Economy* (Philadelphia: Temple University Press, 1994); and Mark A. Grey, "Pork, Poultry, and Newcomers in Storm Lake, Iowa," in *Any Way You Cut It: Meat Processing and Small Town America*, ed. Donald Stull, David Griffith, and Michael Broadway (Manhattan: University of Kansas Press, 1995), 109–27.

13. Mines and Runsten, "Immigrants' Networks"; see also David Runsten and Sandra Archibald, "Technology and Labor Intensive Agriculture: Competition between the United States and Mexico," in Bustamante et al., *U.S-Mexico Relations*, 449–76.

14. Catherine L. Fisk, Daniel J. B. Mitchell, and Christopher L. Erickson, "Union Representation of Immigrant Janitors in Southern California: Economic and Legal

Challenges," in *Organizing Immigrants: The Challenge for Unions in Contemporary California*, ed. Ruth Milkman (Ithaca: ILR-Cornell University Press, 2000), 169–98.

15. "Los Angeles Janitors End Three-Week Strike, Approve New Contract," *Daily Labor Report*, 25 April 2000, 1.

16. Carol Zabin, "Organizing Latino Workers in the Los Angeles Manufacturing Sector: The Case of American Racing Equipment," in Milkman, *Organizing Immigrants*, 225–38.

17. Hector L. Delgado, "The Los Angeles Manufacturing Action Project: An Opportunity Squandered?" in Milkman, *Organizing Immigrants*, 169–98.

18. Edna Bonacich, "Interim Challenges, Tentative Possibilities: Organizing Immigrant Garment Workers in Los Angeles," in Milkman, *Organizing Immigrants*, 130–49.

19. Ruth Milkman and Kent Wong, "Organizing the Wicked City: The 1992 Southern California Drywall Strike," in Milkman, *Organizing Immigrants*, 169–98.

20. National Research Council, *The New Americans: Economic, Demographic, and Fiscal Effects of Immigration* (Washington, D.C.: National Academy Press, 1997), 235–36.

21. Philip L. Martin, "Network Recruitment and Labor Displacement, in *Immigration Policy in the 1980s*, ed. David Simcox (Boulder, Colo.: Westview Press, 1988), 67–91. See also Donatella Lorch, "Ethnic Niches Creating Jobs That Fuel Immigrant Growth," *New York Times*, 12 January 1992, A-1, A-20.

22. See, e.g., Ted Conover, *Coyotes: A Journey through the Secret World of America's Illegal Aliens* (New York: Vintage Books, 1987), 27–28, 106, 136–37.

23. Louise Uchitelle, "Minimum Wages, City by City," *New York Times*, 19 November 1999, C-1, C-19.

24. Don Lee, "L.A. County Jobs Surge since '93 but Not Wages," *Los Angeles Times*, 26 July 1999, A-1.

25. AFL-CIO, "Immigration," in *Executive Council Actions* (New Orleans, La.: AFL-CIO, 2000), 1.

26. Peter Kwong, *Forbidden Workers: Illegal Chinese Immigrants and American Labor*, (New York: New Press, 1997) 208–9.

27. Ibid., 14.

28. Tim Weiner, "Pleas for Asylum Inundate System for Immigration," *New York Times*, 25 April 1993, A-1.

29. John Higham, "The Purpose of Legal Immigration in the 1990s and Beyond," *Social Contract*, Winter 1990–91, 64.

30. Melvin W. Reder, "The Economic Consequences of Increased Immigration," *Review of Economics and Statistics*, August 1963, 31.

31. E.g., see David Simcox, "Inalienable Identification Key to Halting Illegal Employment," in *Backgrounder* (Washington, D.C.: Center for Immigration Studies, 2000).

32. Theodore Hesburgh, "Nothing Totalitarian about a Worker's ID Card," *New York Times*, 24 September 1982, A 26.

33. For elaboration, see Vernon M. Briggs Jr., *Mass Immigration and the National Interest*, 2d ed. (Armonk, N.Y.: M. E. Sharpe, 1996), 165–66.

34. Gary D. Thompson and Philip L. Martin, "Immigration Reform and the Agricultural Labor Force," *Labor Law Journal*, August 1991, 532.

35. E.g., see Kwong, *Forbidden Workers*, 32–33, 49–50, 63–64, 164–65.

36. For a sampling of the voluminous literature documenting the employment abuses of illegal immigrants, see ibid.; Connor, *Coyotes*; Chaya Piotrkowski and Joanne Carriba, "Child Labor and Exploitation," in *Young Workers: Varieties of Experiences*, ed. Ju-

lian Barling and Kevin Kelloway (Washington, D.C.: American Psychological Association, 1999), 129–58; and Ko-Lin Chin "Safe Home or Hell House? Experiences of Newly Arrived Undocumented Chinese," in *Human Smuggling: Chinese Migrant Trafficking and the Challenge to America's Immigrant Tradition,* ed. Paul J. Smith (Washington, D.C.: Center for Strategic and International Studies, 1997), 160–65.

37. Michael J. Piore, "Undocumented Workers and U.S. Immigration Policy," in House Select Committee on Population, *Hearings: Immigration to the United States* (Washington, D.C., U.S. Government Printing Office, 1978), 491.

38. AFL-CIO, "Immigration," 2.

39. Neither of the two principal studies that were actually able to collect reliable data on the subject found noncompliance with wage laws to be widely prevalent; most illegal immigrants received the minimum wage. See David North and Marion Houston, *The Characteristics and Role of Illegal Aliens in the U.S. Labor Market: An Exploratory Study* (Washington, D.C.: Linton, 1976); and Maurice VanArsdol et al., *Non- Apprehended and Apprehended Undocumented Residents in the Los Angeles Labor Market* (Washington, D.C.: U.S. Government Printing Office, 1979).

Index

About the Author

Vernon M. Briggs Jr. is Professor of Labor Economics at the New York State School of Labor and Industrial Relations at Cornell University in Ithaca, New York. He received his B.S. degree in economics from the University of Maryland and his M.A. and Ph.D. degrees in economics from Michigan State University. Before coming to Cornell in 1978, he taught at the University of Texas at Austin for fourteen years.

Professor Briggs specializes in the area of human resource economics and public policy. The effects of immigration policy on American workers has been a frequent subject of his research and of numerous articles. He is the author of the following related books: *Chicanos and Rural Poverty* (1973); *The Chicano Worker* (1977); *Immigration Policy and the American Labor Force* (1984); *Immigration and the U.S. Labor Market: Public Policy Gone Awry* (1993); *Still an Open Door? U.S. Immigration Policy and the American Economy* (1994); and *Mass Immigration and the National Interest* (1992 and 1996).

Briggs was a member of the National Council on Employment Policy from 1977 to 1987 and chairman from 1985 to 1987. He has also served on the board of directors of the Corporation for Public and Private Ventures and of the Center for Immigration Studies, and the editorial boards of the *Journal of Human Resources*, the *Industrial and Labor Relations Review*, the *Texas Business Review*, and the *Journal of Economic Issues*.